437 EDIBLE WILD PLANTS

OF THE

ROCKY MOUNTAIN WEST

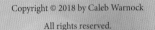

Published by Familius LLC, www.familius.com

Familius books are available at special discounts for bulk purchases, whether for sales promotions or for family or corporate use. For more information, contact Familius Sales at 559-876-2170 or email orders@familius.com.

Inherent dangers exist when ingesting wild plants. The material in this book is presented for general information purposes only. The publisher and author accept no liability of any kind. Any application of the information in this book is at the sole discretion and responsibility of the user.

Library of Congress Cataloging-in-Publication Data

2018937303
Print ISBN 9781945547836
Ebook ISBN 9781641700962

Printed in China

Edited by Leah Welker
Cover design by David Miles
Book design by inlinebooks
and David Miles

10 9 8 7 6 5 4 3 2

First Edition

CALEB WARNOCK

437 EDIBLE WILD PLANTS
OF THE
ROCKY MOUNTAIN WEST

Berries, Roots,
Nuts, Greens,
Flowers, and Seeds

FAMILIUS

CONTENTS

Welcome to the World of Wild Foods 1

PART ONE: THE PLANTS

46 *Balsamorhiza incana* (hoary balsamroot)

47 *Balsamorhiza sagittata* (arrowleaf balsamroot)

48 *Barbarea orthoceras* (American yellowrocket)

49 *Barbarea verna* (land cress)

50 *Barbarea vulgaris* (garden yellowrocket)

51 *Berberis fendleri* (Colorado barberry)

52 *Brassica juncea* (brown mustard)

53 *Brassica napus* (rape mustard)

54 *Brassica nigra* (black mustard)

55 *Brassica rapa* (field mustard)

56 *Bromus breviaristatus* (mountain brome)

57 *Bromus carinatus* (California brome)

58 *Bromus diandrus* (ripgut brome)

59 *Bromus japonicus* (Japanese brome, field brome)

60 *Bromus marginatus* (mountain brome)

61 *Bromus secalinus* (cheat, rye brome)

62 *Bromus tectorum* (downy brome, cheat grass)

63 *Calandrinia ciliata* (redmaids)

64 *Callirhoe involucrata* (buffalo rose, winecup poppy mallow)

65 *Calochortus ambiguus* (doubting mariposa lily)

66 *Calochortus apiculatus* (pointedtip mariposa lily)

67 *Calochortus aureus* (golden mariposa lily)

68 *Calochortus bruneaunis* (Bruneau mariposa lily)

69 *Calochortus elegans* (elegant mariposa lily)

70 *Calochortus eurycarpus* (white mariposa lily)

71 *Calochortus flexuosus* (winding mariposa lily)

72 *Calochortus gunnisonii* (Gunnison's mariposa lily)

73 *Calochortus invenustus* (plain mariposa lily)

74 *Calochortus kennedyi* (desert mariposa lily)

75 *Calochortus leichtlinii* (smokey mariposa lily)

76 *Calochortus macrocarpus* (sagebrush mariposa lily)

77 *Calochortus nitidus* (broadfruit mariposa lily)

78 *Calochortus nuttallii* (sego lily)

79 *Calochortus panamintensis* (Panamint Mountain mariposa lily)

80 *Calochortus striatus* (alkali mariposa lily)

81 *Calypso bulbosa* (fairy slipper)

82 *Calystegia sepium* (hedge bindweed)

83 *Camelina microcarpa* (lesser gold of pleasure)

84 *Camelina sativa* (gold of pleasure)

85 *Campanula rapunculoides* (creeping bellflower)

86 *Capsella bursa-pastoris* (shepherd's purse)

87 *Cardamine hirsuta* (hairy bittercress)

88 *Cardamine oligosperma* (spring cress)

89 *Cardamine pensylvanica* (Pennsylvania bittercress)

90 *Cardaria draba* (whitetop, hoary cress)

91 *Carduus nutans* (musk thistle)

92 *Carum carvi* (common caraway)

93 *Castilleja angustifolia* (northwestern Indian paintbrush)

94 *Castilleja applegatei Fernald* (wavyleaf Indian paintbrush)

95 *Castilleja aquariensis* (Indian paintbrush)

96 *Castilleja hispida* (harsh Indian paintbrush)

97 *Castilleja linariifolia* (Wyoming Indian paintbrush)

98 *Castilleja miniata* (giant red Indian paintbrush)

99 *Castilleja sessiliflora* (downy paintedcup)

100 *Celtis laevigata* (southern hackberry, sugarberry)

101 *Celtis occidentalis* (common hackberry)

102 *Celtis reticulata* (netleaf hackberry)

103 *Cenchrus longispinus* (longspine sandbur)

104 *Centaurea cyanus* (garden cornflower)

105 *Centaurea jacea* (brown knapweed)

106 *Chamerion angustifolium* (fireweed)

107 *Chamerion latifolium* (dwarf fireweed)

108 *Chenopodium album* (lambsquarters, wild spinach)

109 *Chenopodium berlandieri* (goosefoot, netseed lambsquarters)

110 *Chenopodium murale* (nettleleaf goosefoot)

111 *Chorispora tenella* (blue mustard)

112 *Chrysothamnus nauseosus* (rubber rabbitbrush)

113 *Chrysothamnus viscidiflorus* (douglas rabbitbrush, green rabbitbrush)

114 *Cichorium intybus* (chicory)

115 *Cirsium arvense* (Canada thistle)

116 *Cirsium ochrocentrum* (yellowspine thistle)

117 *Cirsium vulgare* (common thistle, bull thistle)

118 *Claytonia perfoliata* (miner's lettuce, winter purslane)

119 *Cleome serrulata* (Rocky Mountain bee plant)

120 *Convolvulus arvensis* (field bindweed)

121 *Conyza canadensis* (horseweed)

122 *Cornus canadensis* (creeping dogwood)

123 *Cornus sericea* (western dogwood)

124 *Cornus unalaschkensis* (bunchberry)

125 *Corylus cornuta* (beaked hazelnut)

126 *Crataegus chrysocarpa* (red haw tree, fireberry hawthorn)

127 *Crataegus douglasii* (black hawthorn)

128 *Crataegus erythropoda* (cerro hawthorn)

129 *Crataegus monogyna* (common hawthorn, English hawthorn, one-seed hawthorn)

130 *Crataegus rivularis* (river hawthorn)

131 *Crataegus saligna* (willow hawthorn)

132 *Crataegus succulenta* (fleshy hawthorn) fruit

133 *Crepis acuminata* (tapertip hawksbeard)

134 *Crepis atribarba* (slender hawksbeard)

135 *Crepis capillaris* (smooth hawksbeard)

136 *Crepis intermedia* (limestone hawksbeard)

137 *Crepis modocensis* (Modoc hawksbeard)

138 *Crepis occidentalis* (largeflower hawksbeard)

139 *Crepis runcinata* (fiddleleaf hawksbeard)

140 *Cucurbita foetidissima* (buffalo gourd)

141 *Cycloloma atriplicifolium* (winged pigweed)

142 *Cymopterus globosus* (globe springparsley)

143 *Cymopterus montanus* (mountain springparsley)

144 *Cymopterus purpurascens* (gamote)

145 *Cymopterus purpureus* (purple springparsley)

146 *Cynoglossum officinale* (houndstongue, gypsyflower)

147 *Cyperus erythrorhizos* (redroot flatsedge)

148 *Cyperus esculentus* (yellow nutsedge)

149 *Cyperus fendlerianus* (Fendler's flatsedge)

150 *Cyperus odoratus* (fragrant flatsedge)

151 *Cyperus rotundus* (nut grass)

152 *Cyperus schweinitzii* (Schweinitz's flatsedge)

153 *Cyperus squarrosus* (bearded flatsedge)

154 *Daucus carota* (wild carrot)

155 *Descurainia incana* (mountain tansy mustard)

156 *Descurainia obtusa* (blunt tansy mustard)

157 *Descurainia pinnata* (western tansy mustard)

158 *Descurainia sophia* (flixweed, herb sophia)

159 *Digitaria sanguinalis* (hairy crabgrass)

160 *Diospyros virginiana* (American persimmon)

161 *Elaeagnus angustifolia* (Russian olive)

162 *Elaeagnus commutata* (silverberry)

163 *Eleusine indica* (goosegrass)

164 *Elymus repens* (quackgrass)

165 *Equisetum arvense* (horsetail grass)

166 *Equisetum hyemale* (scouringrush horsetail)

167 *Equisetum laevigatum* (smooth horsetail)

168 *Equisetum pratense* (meadow horsetail)

169 *Equisetum scirpoides* (dwarf scouringrush)

170 *Equisetum telmateia* (giant horsetail)

171 *Equisetum variegatum* (variegated scouringrush)

172 *Eriogonum alatum* (winged buckwheat)

173 *Eriogonum baileyi* (Bailey's buckwheat)

174 *Eriogonum cernuum* (nodding buckwheat)

175 *Eriogonum corymbosum* (crispleaf buckwheat)

176 *Eriogonum davidsonii* (Davidson's buckwheat)

177 *Eriogonum fasciculatum* (California buckwheat)

178 *Eriogonum flavum* (alpine golden buckwheat)

179 *Eriogonum hookeri* (Hooker's buckwheat)

180 *Eriogonum inflatum* (desert trumpet)

181 *Eriogonum longifolium* (longleaf buckwheat)

182 *Eriogonum microthecum* (slender buckwheat)

183 *Eriogonum nudum* (naked buckwheat)

184 *Eriogonum plumatella* (yucca buckwheat)

185 *Eriogonum pusillum* (yellowturbans)

186 *Eriogonum racemosum* (redroot buckwheat)

187 *Eriogonum rotundifolium* (roundleaf buckwheat)

188 *Eriogonum umbellatum* (sulphur-flower buckwheat)

189 *Erodium cicutarium* (redstem filaree, stork's bill)

190 *Fragaria vesca* (woodland, alpine, or wild strawberry)

191 *Fragaria virginiana* (Virginia strawberry)

192 *Gaillardia Aristata* (Indian blanket)

193 *Gaillardia pinnatifida* (red dome blanketflower)

194 *Galega officinalis* (goatsrue)

195 *Galium aparine* (cleavers, goosegrass)

196 *Gaultheria hispidula* (creeping snowberry)

197 *Gaultheria ovatifolia* (western teaberry)

198 *Geranium bicknellii* (Bicknell's cranesbill)

199 *Geranium caespitosum* (pineywoods geranium)

200 *Geranium richardsonii* (Richardson's geranium, Rocky Mountain geranium)

201 *Geranium viscosissimum* (sticky purple geranium)

202 *Hedysarum alpinum* (alpine sweetvetch)

203 *Hedysarum boreale* (Utah sweetvetch)

204 *Helianthus annuus* (common sunflower)

205 *Helianthus anomalus* (western sunflower)

206 *Helianthus arizonensis* (Arizona sunflower)

207 *Helianthus ciliaris* (Texas blueweed)

208 *Helianthus cusickii* (Cusick's sunflower)

209 *Helianthus maximiliani* (Maximilian sunflower)

210 *Helianthus niveus* (showy sunflower)

211 *Helianthus nuttallii* (Nuttall's sunflower)

212 *Helianthus pauciflorus* (stiff sunflower)

213 *Helianthus petiolaris* (prairie sunflower)

214 *Helianthus pumilus* (little sunflower)

215 *Helianthus tuberosus* (sunchokes, Jerusalem artichoke)

216 *Heracleum sphondylium montanum* (cow parsnip)

217 *Hibiscus trionum* (venice mallow)

218 *Hordeum jubatum* (foxtail barley, squirrel-tail grass)

219 *Iliamna rivularis* (mountain hollyhock)

220 *Juglans major* (Arizona walnut)

221 *Juglans microcarpa* (little walnut)

222 *Juglans nigra* (black walnut)

223 *Juglans regia* (English walnut)

224 *Juniperus osteosperma* (juniper tree)

225 *Kochia scoparia* (kochia)

226 *Lactuca pulchella* (blue lettuce)

227 *Lamium amplexicaule* (henbit)

228 *Lamium purpureum* (purple dead nettle)

229 *Lathyrus latifolius* (everlasting peavine, wild sweet pea)

230 *Lepidium latifolium* (perennial pepperweed)

231 *Lepidium perfoliatum* (clasping pepperweed)

232 *Lolium perenne* (Italian ryegrass)

233 *Lomatium ambiguum* (Wyeth biscuitroot)

234 *Lomatium canbyi* (Canby's biscuitroot)

235 *Lomatium cous* (cous biscuitroot)

236 *Lomatium dissectum* (giant biscuitroot, fernleaf biscuitroot)

237 *Lomatium foeniculaceum* (desert parsley, desert biscuitroot)

238 *Lomatium gormanii* (Gorman's biscuitroot)

239 *Lomatium grayi* (Gray's biscuitroot)

240 *Lomatium macrocarpum* (bigseed biscuitroot)

241 *Lomatium nudicaule* (pestle parsnip, barestem biscuitroot)

242 *Lomatium triternatum* (nineleaf biscuitroot)

243 *Lonicera involucrata* (twinberry honeysuckle)

244 *Lonicera utahensis* (Utah honeysuckle)

245 *Lycium barbarum* (gojiberry, wolfberry)

246 *Lythrum salicaria* (purple loosestrife, purple lythrum)

247 *Mahonia aquifolium* (Oregon grape)

248 *Mahonia fremontii* (Fremont's mahonia, desert holly, desert Oregon grape)

249 *Mahonia repens* (creeping Oregon grape)

250 *Malus coronaria* (sweet crab apple)

251 *Malus pumila* (paradise apple)

252 *Malus sylvestris* (European crab apple)

253 *Malva neglecta* (common mallow)

254 *Matricaria discoidea* (pineapple weed)

255 *Medicago lupulina* (black medic)

256 *Medicago polymorpha* (California burclover)

257 *Medicago sativa* (alfalfa)

258 *Melilotus albus* (white sweetclover)

259 *Melilotus indicas* (Indian sweetclover, sour sweetclover, annual yellow sweetclover)

260 *Melilotus officinalis* (yellow sweetclover)

261 *Morus alba* (white mulberry)

262 *Nasturtium officinale* (watercress)

263 *Nuphar polysepala* (spatterdock, Rocky Mountain pond lily)

264 *Opuntia polyacantha* (plains prickly pear cactus)

265 *Orogenia linearifolia* (Indian potato)

266 *Oxalis corniculata* (creeping woodsorrel)

267 *Oxalis stricta* (yellow woodsorrel)

268 *Panicum capillare* (witchgrass)

269 *Panicum dichotomiflorum* (fall panicum)

270 *Panicum miliaceum* (wild proso millet, broom corn millet)

271 *Parthenocissus quinquefolia* (Virginia creeper)

272 *Pediomelum esculentum* (large Indian breadroot)

273 *Perideridia gairdneri* (Gardner's yampah)

274 *Perideridia lemmonii* (Lemmon's yampah)

275 *Perideridia parishii* (Parish's yampah)

276 *Phlox austromontana* (southern mountain phlox)

277 *Phlox diffusa* (spreading phlox)

278 *Phlox hoodii* (spiny phlox)

279 *Phlox longifolia* (longleaf phlox)

280 *Phlox multiflora* (Rocky Mountain phlox)

281 *Phlox paniculata* (common phlox)

282 *Phlox stansburyi* (cold desert phlox)

283 *Phlox variabilis* (variegated phlox)

284 *Phragmites australis* (common reed)

285 *Physalis acutifolia* (sharpleaf groundcherry)

286 *Physalis angulata* (cutleaf groundcherry)

287 *Physalis cinerascens* (smallflower groundcherry)

288 *Physalis crassifolia* (yellow nightshade groundcherry)

289 *Physalis hederifolia* (ivyleaf groundcherry)

290 *Physalis heterophylla* (clammy groundcherry)

291 *Physalis latiphysa* (broadleaf groundcherry)

292 *Physalis longifolia* (longleaf groundcherry)

293 *Physalis philadelphica* (Mexican groundcherry)

294 *Physalis virginiana* (Virginia groundcherry)

295 *Pinus contorta* (lodgepole pine)

296 *Pinus edulis* (two-needle pinyon pine)

297 *Pinus flexilis* (limber pine)

298 *Pinus lambertiana* (sugar pine)

299 *Pinus monophylla* (single-leaf pinyon pine)

300 *Pinus monticola* (western white pine)

301 *Pinus ponderosa* (ponderosa pine)

302 *Plantago lanceolata* (narrowleaf plantain)

303 *Plantago major* (broadleaf plantain)

304 *Polygonum amphibium* (willow grass, water knotweed)

305 *Polygonum arenastrum* (small-leafed knotweed, oval-leaf knotweed)

306 *Polygonum bistortoides* (American bistort)

307 *Polygonum cuspidatum* (Japanese knotweed)

308 *Polygonum douglasii* (Douglas's knotweed)

309 *Polygonum lapathifolium* (curlytop knotweed)

310 *Polygonum persicaria* (spotted ladysthumb)

311 *Polypogon monspeliensis* (rabbitfoot polypogon)

312 *Portulaca oleracea* (common purslane)

313 *Prosopis glandulosa* (western honey mesquite)

314 *Prunus americana* (American wild plum)

315 *Prunus andersonii* (desert peach)

316 *Prunus angustifolia* (Chickasaw plum)

317 *Prunus armeniaca* (apricot)

318 *Prunus avium* (sweet cherry)

319 *Prunus besseyi* (western sandcherry)

320 *Prunus cerasifera* (cherry plum)

321 *Prunus cerasus* (sour cherry)

322 *Prunus domestica* (European plum)

323 *Prunus dulcis* (sweet almond) seed

324 *Prunus emarginata* (bitter cherry)

325 *Prunus fasciculata* (desert almond)

326 *Prunus mahaleb* (mahaleb cherry)

327 *Prunus pensylvanica* (pin cherry)

328 *Prunus persica* (common peach)

329 *Prunus pumila* (sandcherry)

330 *Prunus rivularis* (creek plum)

331 *Prunus serotina* (black cherry)

332 *Prunus spinosa* (blackthorn)

333 *Prunus tomentosa* (Nanking cherry)

334 *Prunus virginiana* (western chokecherry, black chokecherry)

335 *Pyrus communis* (common pear)

336 *Quercus gambelii* (Gambel oak)

337 *Raphanus raphanistrum* (wild radish)

338 *Raphanus sativus* (garden radish)

339 *Rheum rhabarbarum* (garden rhubarb)

340 *Rhus glabra* (smooth sumac)

341 *Rhus trilobata* (three-leaf sumac)

342 *Rhus typhina* (staghorn sumac)

343 *Ribes aureum* (golden currant)

344 *Ribes cereum* (wax currant)

345 *Ribes hudsonianum* (western black currant)

346 *Ribes inerme* (whitestem gooseberry)

347 *Ribes lacustre* (prickly black currant)

348 *Ribes laxiflorum* (trailing black currant)

349 *Ribes leptanthum* (trumpet gooseberry)

350 *Ribes montigenum* (gooseberry currant, mountain currant)

351 *Ribes niveum* (snow currant)

352 *Ribes oxyacanthoides* (Canadian gooseberry)

353 *Ribes velutinum* (desert gooseberry)

354 *Ribes viscosissimum* (sticky currant)

355 *Ribes wolfii* (wolf's currant)

356 *Rosa × harisonii* (Harison's yellow)

357 *Rosa canina* (dog rose)

358 *Rosa manca* (Mancos rose)

359 *Rosa nutkana* (Nootka rose)

360 *Rosa rubiginosa* (sweetbriar rose)

361 *Rosa woodsii* (Woods' rose, western wild rose)

362 *Rubus arcticus* (Arctic raspberry)

363 *Rubus armeniacus* (Himalayan blackberry)

364 *Rubus deliciosus* (delicious raspberry)

365 *Rubus idaeus* (wild raspberries)

366 *Rubus laciniatus* (cutleaf blackberry)

367 *Rubus leucodermis* (whitebark raspberry)

368 *Rubus neomexicanus* (New Mexico raspberry)

369 *Rubus nivalis* (snow raspberry)

370 *Rubus occidentalis* (black raspberry)

371 *Rubus parviflorus* (thimbleberry)

372 *Rubus pedatus* (strawberryleaf raspberry)

373 *Rubus pubescens* (dwarf red blackberry)

374 *Rubus spectabilis* (salmonberry)

375 *Rubus ulmifolius* (elmleaf blackberry)

376 *Rubus ursinus* (California blackberry)

377 *Rumex acetosella* (sheep sorrel)

378 *Rumex crispus* (curly dock, yellow dock)

379 *Rumex obtusifolius* (broadleaf dock)

380 *Rumex occidentalis* (western dock)

381 *Sagittaria cuneata* (wapato, arumleaf arrowhead)

382 *Salsola tragus* (Russian thistle)

383 *Sambucus nigra* (blue elderberry)

384 *Sambucus racemosa* (red elderberry)

385 *Sambucus racemosa* var. *melanocarpa* (black elderberry)

386 *Sarcocornia utahensis* (Utah pickleweed)

387 *Secale cereale* (cereal rye)

388 *Setaria pumila* (yellow foxtail)

389 *Shepherdia argentea* (silver buffaloberry)

390 *Shepherdia canadensis* (russet buffaloberry)

391 *Sisymbrium irio* (London rocket)

392 *Sonchus arvensis* (sowthistle)

393 *Sonchus asper* (spiny sowthistle)

394 *Sonchus oleraceus* (common sowthistle)

395 *Sorghum bicolor* (wild grain sorghum)

396 *Sorghum halepense* (Johnsongrass)

397 *Sporobolus flexuosus* (mesa dropseed)

398 *Stellaria media* (chickweed)

399 *Streptopus amplexifolius* (wild cucumber, claspleaf twistedstalk)

400 *Streptopus streptopoides* (small twistedstalk)

401 *Symphoricarpos albus* (snowberry, waxberry)

PART TWO: POISONS, USEFUL LISTS, AND Q&A

INTRODUCTION: WELCOME TO THE WORLD OF WILD FOODS!

I wrote this book because it's the book I wish had existed when I started my journey into the world of wild foods. If you want to learn only a handful of edibles, there are shelves of books about that. But when you want to go beyond dandelions, resources are few. Globally, roughly 10 percent of all plants are considered edible. Archeology and written history has proven repeatedly that most if not all of this 10 percent was widely eaten at some point. Since the advent of industrialization, the number of species we eat has fallen dramatically. Knowledge of what is edible, knowledge our ancestors three generations ago held deeply, has slipped away with astonishing speed.

I knew from the beginning that I wanted this book to be different in many ways.

1. I wanted a book with as many full-color photos as could be stuffed onto the pages, including the pictures of flowers that are crucial to correct identification, leaves when it is important, berries, and other photos to help you, the reader, make identification more practical. It was not possible to get every photo we desired, but we have worked hard to include as many photos as possible.
2. I wanted this book to be in the running for the most comprehensive book on wild edibles ever printed—a book that could be used for generations.
3. Most books on wild edibles focus on greens. I am well-known for telling my homesteading students that greens are great but roots, grains, seeds, and nuts are sustenance. Not many people can live happily on a steady diet of salad, but when most people think of wild edibles, they think of greens. I want this book to change that.
4. I spent years futilely searching for a list of the best wild edible berries of the West to no avail. I am proud to say this book includes dozens.
5. Wild grains are rarely mentioned in other sources, but they are perhaps the most important wild food because grains are the foundation of nutrition. This book lists wild grains in depth.
6. Roots such as onions, potatoes, and carrots are the most widely used part of the garden, but finding any truly useful information on wild roots is hard. This book solves that problem.
7. Wild nuts were widely collected by the American Indians for centuries, but today, collecting nuts from the wild has fallen out of favor. I hope this book will begin to change that.
8. This book will give you information on the flavor of wild edibles from a person with firsthand experience. I quickly discovered that the same old misinformation gets passed widely around the internet by people without actual firsthand experience looking to put up a quick blog post. The internet has created the most dangerous illusions of reality in the history of the world, and it has led to many people misidentifying dangerous plants as edible and vice versa.
9. This book also notes some uses of these plants beyond food. On these pages, you will find plants useful for making rennet, rope, medicine, and more.
10. I've included a beginner's list of plants to avoid (see "Poisons" on page 474). It was never my intention to include a list of poisonous wild plants in this book until one day

my grandson and I had an experience that quickly and completely changed my mind. More about that in a moment.

11. Finally, wild edibles are more than just the fast food of Mother Nature. I have noticed over the years that the more I eat them, the more my immune system seems to hum.

Recently, our family took a trip to Spain. (Indeed, as I write this introduction, I am at the Alhambra in Granada, Spain, which may have the most beautiful gardens in the world.) Because I would be gone for two weeks, and the July heat was regularly hitting triple digits at the foot of the Rocky Mountains, I spent the last hours before leaving for the airport giving my gardens a deep drink. When I finally dashed into the house to grab my luggage and head for the car, I found our son-in-law groaning, flat on the couch, complaining that he could not have chosen a worse time to catch a bug.

I immediately knew that it would be elderberry to the rescue—a berry bush that grows everywhere in the local mountains. I gave him elderberry every four hours. By the time we had landed in Spain, my son-in-law had begun to feel better. Because I had no interest in getting his bug, for the next several days, I gave him, me, my wife, and the rest of the family elderberry twice a day. Halfway through the trip, he remarked casually that he was surprised to be feeling so much better. As the words came out of his mouth, I saw the realization dawn on him. "I guess that stuff you're giving me is working," he said, grudgingly.

A full discussion of how and when and what herbs to use as natural medicine is beyond the scope of this book, but I do highlight on these pages some of the most important and popular medicinal herbs, berries, and roots that I use regularly.

I eat wild edibles almost every day of the year, wherever I go—locally, across the country, and across the globe. I have eaten wild purslane in Portugal, happy to see its cheerful yellow flowers. I have eaten wild German chamomile at the German border. I eat extensively out of my backyard and my farm fields, in the deep desert, and in the yards of students, clients, and friends.

To make sure I have a supply of clean, organic wild foods available when I want them, I grow wild edibles in my garden spring, summer, and fall and in my geothermal greenhouses in winter—and not just for eating, because as you will see in these pages, they have other valuable uses too.

As a permaculture expert, I do property consultations, visiting people's homes to help them design the best gardens and landscapes for their specific needs. I eat "weeds" at almost every home I visit. I want to show my clients what great food Mother Nature has provided at our fingertips. I eat from their yards to help give people a sense that it is normal, it is OK and acceptable and wonderful, to eat wild. For most people, this simple matter of having permission from someone is key. Recently, a client—a woman and her children—walked me through their garden, abandoned to weeds. I asked about her goals. One goal, she said, was backyard greens for smoothies.

"I was hoping you would say that," I said, picking a handful of purslane. The flavor, I explained as I munched, is like crunchy romaine lettuce with a built-in lemon vinaigrette. I also picked wild spinach (lambsquarters), flixweed, clover, and others. She and the kids followed my lead, picking and eating.

"Do you eat like this a lot?" she asked, smiling at the lemony sensation. "You are going to outlive us all."

Introducing people to the vitamin-rich, nutrient-dense, flavorful organic greens which cost nothing and are already growing at their doorstep has given me a lot of pleasure over the years. On another occasion, a young family hired me to assess the yard of their new home in the desert. As we walked the property, I picked and ate roughly a dozen weed species, explaining each. The husband tasted them tentatively. Later, in a crowded class I was teaching, the man told my students, "This guy came out to my house and just started eating the weeds. I couldn't believe it—and now I eat them all the time too!" These are the moments teachers live for.

I'm also pleased when no one is impressed when I feast on wild foods. On several occasions I have begun to eat a "weed" in a client's yard, hoping for a reaction of delight and astonishment, only to be told, "Oh yeah, we eat that in our green smoothies every morning." And sometimes, clients even introduce wild edibles to me that I didn't know about.

Occasionally, my efforts backfire. Early this spring, I took a group of people into the Great Basin Desert to explore a cave. When we finished, we decided to go on a short walk to a nearby pond. Along the way, I was picking and eating wild edibles, showing off what the desert had to offer. My eleven-year-old grandson, Xander, who has been eating wild edibles with me since birth, was walking behind me, showing the greens to the kids his age.

Only half paying attention, I peripherally heard him say, "This flower is edible too." But I hadn't shown anyone an edible flower that day, nor had I seen any. I turned around just in time to see that Xander had picked a death camas lily, which is one of the most dangerous plants in the Rocky Mountain West. Some children have reportedly been killed simply by eating a flower petal. Death camas is so poisonous that I usually caution people to never even touch the plant—and especially to not let children touch the plant. And now, here was my beloved oldest grandchild, literally following in my footsteps, with a camas lily in his hand.

I knew I had to act swiftly, and carefully. I knew that I could not cause a panic, because that would not help. Quietly, I said to him and everyone with us, "Don't put that in your mouth. That is actually a death camas lily, one of the most poisonous plants in the desert." The color drained from my beloved Xander's face, and the adults walking with me stopped in their tracks. Everyone looked at me for direction. Xander instinctively dropped the lily to the ground.

"Don't touch your fingers to your eyes or face," I said quietly. "Don't touch anything with your hands. Let's walk back to the car and get one of the water bottles to wash your hands with."

And we did. As we walked, one of the adults whispered to me, "Is he going to be OK?"

Everyone was now somber. But I knew we were going to be fine, because Xander was not a tiny child, and he had not eaten the lily.

We washed his hands with soap, and I gave him a hug and told him to go play. He was fine. Had he eaten any part of the plant, or gotten its sap on his fingers, or touched his eyes with the pollen, I would have driven immediately to the nearest place with cell phone reception and called for a medical helicopter. We've never had to do that.

I learned a valuable lesson that day. Xander had seen me eat so many wild things over the years, I think he had gotten the idea in his head that we can eat anything wild. Ever since that day, I have been careful to teach him and everyone that you **never, ever put anything into your mouth unless you know with surety the identity of the plant and that it is safe to eat**.

While the focus of this book is not on poisonous plants, I have chosen to include some of the most abundant as a reminder to us all that caution is the rule of the day. A book like this is a starting point. Seeing one or two pictures of a plant does not qualify you to begin wild harvesting. A photograph of a plant records just one moment in time, but the way a plant looks changes every single day of its life cycle and depends heavily on environmental conditions such as hours of sunlight per day, available water, soil nutrients, seasons, microclimate, and more.

I teach classes in which students are taught to identify wild edibles. If you can't get to one of my classes, find someone in your local area who is an expert. The most dangerous thing you can do is rely on photos from a quick Google search before wandering outside to start picking plants. In my considerable experience, photos of wild edibles online are misidentified at least half of the time. Species-specific online searching is a learned art, and simply typing the scientific name of a plant into the search bar does not work. Most of the time, because of the way search engines work, the pictures are not of the species but the genus. Putting the species name in quote marks can give better results, but the results—especially photos—will still be filled with examples of the genus instead of the species. And almost every plant has a look-alike, and sometimes the look-alikes are deadly poisons.

However, while caution is important, being immobilized by fear is a mistake. When we go to the grocery store, we don't pause to consider whether a carrot is poisonous or not. This is because we know people who have eaten carrots and not died. We know that carrots are commonly eaten. But somewhere, in the history of the world, there was a day when people did not know whether wild carrots were food or medicine or poison. All the knowledge that we have today about what is edible or not edible comes directly from our ancestors, who experimented to find out. We owe them a debt of gratitude for passing this knowledge to us.

Some of them paid with their lives, but it is important to note that very few plants are deadly poison. Most plants that are not edible may just make your stomach upset. When you think about it, our ancestors' experience of learning the hard way what is edible is not as foreign to us as we might want it to be. Today, every day, people put pharmaceutical drugs, chemicals, and manufactured foods in their mouths, thinking they must be safe because they are in stores, only to discover later that the cumulative, long-term effect of these drugs or fake foods results in permanent damage to our bodies. Few people realize that there is no government oversight for the long-term effects of what is sold and no testing for long-term effects required. In my view, we are all probably much safer eating known wild edibles, filled with beneficial properties, than many of the so-called processed "foods" in the grocery store. Wild edibles, for example, are not going to give you type 2 diabetes—but the vast majority of the stuff on store shelves will.

If you learn just one thing from this book, please let it be this: wild food is for everyday living. Most people think of Mother Nature's buffet as "survival" food—a last resort to be used in a day of need, with fingers crossed that the day will never come. But if you pay quiet, careful attention, you will notice something startling: that day is already here. Pay attention to the number of people around you whose health is deteriorating, who are on an ever-increasing number of pharmaceutical and over-the-counter drugs. Pay attention to the number of people around you whose lives are crippled by autoimmune disorders.

Notice that almost everything in the grocery store is a product, not a simple, true food. A product is created by someone and requires advertising for attention and dollars. True food does not require advertising or fancy packaging or patents or trademarks. Notice that advertising squarely aims at our children, trying to convince them that energy drinks and garbage food and empty calories will give them their best life. But when our children are sick, those same companies that courted them with billions of dollars in advertising suddenly have nothing to say. This book is all about natural health. I've written many books on gardening and self-reliance. I've taught thousands of students on the same subjects. With this book, there should be no excuse. No one should be able to say that they can't afford organic food, or that real food is too expensive, that natural living is too hard. With all the love for you in my heart, I say, "No more excuses." With this book, you can start eating real food today. And you can have fun and fall in love with the natural outdoor world all over again while you do it.

—*Caleb Warnock, July 2017*

PART ONE:

THE PLANTS

NOTE: Though the plants in this book may be found in other states, since this book covers the plants of the Rocky Mountain West, only Rocky Mountain states will be listed in the descriptions.

Abutilon theophrasti

(VELVETLEAF)

STATES: Arizona, Colorado, Idaho, Montana, Nevada, New Mexico, Utah, Wyoming.

FLOWER: Yellow.

CHARACTERISTICS: Leaves are heart shaped and can grow as large as dinner plates in some cases. Seeds can be up to one-third oil. This plant was brought to the United States in the seventeenth century and grown for its useful fibers.

HABITAT: Sunny, dry locations.

FORM: Summer annual, growing 3–7 feet tall.

EDIBLE PARTS: Immature seeds, immature seedpod.

HARVESTABLE: Late spring.

FLAVOR: Nutty and mild, like wild sunflower seeds.

Acer glabrum

(ROCKY MOUNTAIN MAPLE)

STATES: Arizona, Colorado, Idaho, Montana, Nevada, New Mexico, Utah, Wyoming.

FLOWER: Green.

CHARACTERISTICS: This maple has low water requirements, making it an excellent choice for the arid West. This tree is also popular because in autumn, its leaves turn a blaze of yellow and sometimes orange. It is extremely hardy, happily overwintering in temperatures as low as 43 degrees below zero.

HABITAT: Slopes, mountainsides, plains.

FORM: Perennial tree, growing 30 feet tall.

EDIBLE PART: Sap of the tree, also called "maple water."

HARVESTABLE: Spring.

FLAVOR: Slightly sweet fresh from the tree; strongly sweet when the sap is boiled to make syrup.

NOTES: There are numerous online resources that can teach you how to tap maple trees for sap. Timing, however, is critical: the sap runs only early in the year—late winter or early spring. Sap is tapped by wounding the tree; it is then collected in a container and can be used raw but must not be contaminated with dirt or anything unclean.

Raw sap is believed by many to have health benefits because of its mineral content.

Sap is boiled to make syrup, but it varies in sugar content by species. Nationwide, *A. saccharum*, *A. nigrum*, and *A. rubrum* are the most sought after because their sap contains between 2 percent and 5 percent sugar and are thus easier to boil down for syrup, but all maples produce drinkable sap.

In addition to the native varieties listed here, there are many non-native varieties with edible sap that have been widely planted around the Rocky Mountain West as landscape trees.

Acer negundo

(BOX ELDER MAPLE)

STATES: Arizona, Colorado, Idaho, Montana, Nevada, New Mexico, Utah, Wyoming.

FLOWER: White or greenish or sometimes pale yellow.

CHARACTERISTICS: Host of box elder bugs, which many homeowners find to be pests. This tree species is different than most maples in two ways: the tree is either entirely male or entirely female, and it has odd-pinnate compound leaves with 3–5 toothed leaflets. Leaves turn yellow in autumn.

HABITAT: Slopes, mountainsides, plains.

FORM: Perennial tree, growing 60 feet tall.

EDIBLE PART: Sap of the tree, also called "maple water."

HARVESTABLE: Spring.

FLAVOR: Slightly sweet when raw, or strongly sweet when the sap is boiled to make syrup.

Achillea millefolium

(WESTERN YARROW)

STATES: Arizona, Colorado, Idaho, Montana, Nevada, New Mexico, Utah, Wyoming.

FLOWER: White, and sometimes shades of pink; rarely red.

CHARACTERISTICS: Once you learn to recognize this plant, you will begin to see it everywhere.

NOTES: Yarrow flower is widely used medicinally.

HABITAT: Rocky soils in a wide range of areas including fields, roadsides, meadows, plains, mountainsides. Grows in both moist and desert areas.

FORM: Perennial plant, growing 12–36 inches tall.

EDIBLE PART: Leaves.

HARVESTABLE: Spring, summer, autumn.

FLAVOR: Grasslike.

Aegilops cylindrica

(JOINTED GOATGRASS)

––––––––

STATES: Arizona, Colorado, Idaho, Montana, Nevada, New Mexico, Utah, Wyoming.

FLOWER: Green.

CHARACTERISTICS: Separating the edible grain from the chaff is difficult, which reduces the usefulness of this grain.

HABITAT: Open, sunny, and dry disturbed areas such as roadsides, field edges, and sometimes plains.

FORM: Summer annual, typically growing 18–24 inches tall.

EDIBLE PART: Grain.

HARVESTABLE: Summer.

FLAVOR: Grain.

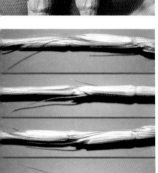

5

Agastache urticifolia

(HORSEMINT, NETTLELEAF GIANT HYSSOP)

STATES: Colorado, Idaho, Montana, Nevada, Utah, Wyoming.

FLOWER: Lavender purple.

CHARACTERISTICS: Once you begin to recognize this plant, you will find it growing everywhere along canyon slopes and mountain roads. The word *agastache* means "many ears of grain" in Greek, which likely refers to the edible seeds.

HABITAT: Mountainsides.

FORM: Perennial rhizomatous plant with summer flowers, totaling 2–3 feet tall.

EDIBLE PARTS: Leaves, seeds.

HARVESTABLE: Leaves in spring, summer, autumn; seeds in autumn.

FLAVOR: Mint.

Allium acuminatum

(TAPERTIP ONION, HOOKER'S ONION)

———

STATES: Arizona, Colorado, Idaho, Montana, Nevada, New Mexico, Utah, Wyoming.

FLOWER: Purple; rarely pink or white.

CHARACTERISTICS: Each plant typically has 1–12 bulbs with yellow or light brown skins. Flowers are campanulate (bell-shaped) with yellow pollen, and blooms can appear April through July.

EDIBLE PARTS: Bulbs, flowers, seeds.

HARVESTABLE: The flavor is best when harvested in the spring, just before flowering. However, before they flower, wild onion plants strongly resemble death camas, a plant that also has a bulb but is deadly if any part is eaten, so harvesting wild onions before they flower is not recommended. Flavor may become spicier after the plant goes to flower, and the bulb will be less tender, but that is your safer option.

HABITAT: Open, sunny, and somewhat dry slopes and plains.

FORM: Spring and summer perennial with multiple stems, growing typically 1 foot tall.

FLAVOR: Onion.

Allium bispectrum

(TWINCREST ONION, ASPEN ONION)

———

STATES: Arizona, Idaho, Nevada, New Mexico, Utah.

FLOWER: Lilac or white.

CHARACTERISTICS: Typically produces 1–7 bulbs with brown to gray skin. Onion flesh may be white or pink. Flowers are stellate (a pattern radiating outward from center like that of a star) with yellow pollen.

HABITAT: Open, sunny, and somewhat dry slopes and plains.

FORM: Spring and summer perennial with multiple stems, growing typically 1 foot tall.

EDIBLE PARTS: Bulbs, flowers, seeds.

HARVESTABLE: The flavor is best when harvested in the spring, just before flowering. However, before they flower, wild onion plants strongly resemble death camas, a plant that also has a bulb but is deadly if any part is eaten, so harvesting wild onions before they flower is not recommended. Flavor may become spicier after the plant goes to flower, and the bulb will be less tender, but that is your safer option.

FLAVOR: Onion.

Allium brevistylum

(SHORTSTYLE ONION)

STATES: Colorado, Idaho, Montana, Utah, Wyoming.

FLOWER: Pink.

CHARACTERISTICS: Produces 2–4 bulbs typically with gray or brown skin and white onion flesh. Flowers are narrowly urceolate (shaped like an urn or pitcher) with light yellow pollen.

HABITAT: Open, sunny, and somewhat dry slopes and plains.

FORM: Spring and summer perennial with multiple stems, growing typically 1 foot tall.

EDIBLE PARTS: Bulbs, flowers, seeds.

HARVESTABLE: The flavor is best when harvested in the spring, just before flowering. However, before they flower, wild onion plants strongly resemble death camas, a plant that also has a bulb but is deadly if any part is eaten, so harvesting wild onions before they flower is not recommended. Flavor may become spicier after the plant goes to flower, and the bulb will be less tender, but that is your safer option.

FLAVOR: Onion.

Allium macropetalum

(LARGEFLOWER ONION)

STATES: Arizona, Colorado, New Mexico, Utah.

FLOWER: Pink with deeper pink or reddish midveins.

CHARACTERISTICS: Each plant typically has 1-5 bulbs with brown skins. Flowers are campanulate (bell-shaped) with anthers in yellow or purple; pollen is yellow. Flowers may appear as early as March or as late as June.

HABITAT: Open, sunny, and somewhat dry slopes and plains.

FORM: Spring and summer perennial with multiple stems, growing typically 1 foot tall.

EDIBLE PARTS: Bulbs, flowers, seeds.

HARVESTABLE: The flavor is best when harvested in the spring, just before flowering. However, before they flower, wild onion plants strongly resemble death camas, a plant that also has a bulb but is deadly if any part is eaten, so harvesting wild onions before they flower is not recommended. Flavor may become spicier after the plant goes to flower, and the bulb will be less tender, but that is your safer option.

FLAVOR: Onion.

Allium textile

(TEXTILE ONION)

STATES: Colorado, Idaho, Montana, Nevada, New Mexico, Utah, Wyoming.

FLOWER: White or rarely pink, with red or reddish-brown midribs.

CHARACTERISTICS: Typical plant produces 1–3 bulbs with brown or gray skins. Flowers are urceolate (shaped like an urn or pitcher) to campanulate (bell-shaped).

HABITAT: Open, sunny, and somewhat dry slopes and plains.

FORM: Spring and summer perennial with multiple stems, growing typically 1 foot tall.

EDIBLE PARTS: Bulbs, flowers, seeds.

HARVESTABLE: The flavor is best when harvested in the spring, just before flowering. However, before they flower, wild onion plants strongly resemble death camas, a plant that also has a bulb but is deadly if any part is eaten, so harvesting wild onions before they flower is not recommended. Flavor may become spicier after the plant goes to flower, and the bulb will be less tender, but that is your safer option.

FLAVOR: Onion.

11

Amaranthus albus

(TUMBLEWEED, TUMBLE PIGWEED, PROSTRATE PIGWEED, WHITE AMARANTH)

STATES: Arizona, Colorado, Idaho, Montana, Nevada, New Mexico, Utah, Wyoming.

FLOWER: Green.

CHARACTERISTICS: One of the benefits of this plant is that the leaves stay tender even when they reach midsize or larger, so they can be harvested for many weeks.

The seeds are harvested after they have naturally dried on the plant in autumn.

HABITAT: Disturbed, sunny, open spaces and waste spaces in alkaline soil.

FORM: Annual, typically growing 2–4 feet tall.

EDIBLE PARTS: Leaves, seeds.

CHARACTERISTICS: Bushy when fully grown. When dried and dead, this is the famous tumbleweed of the West that spreads its seeds as it is tumbled by the wind.

HARVESTABLE: Leaves are harvested from May through August. Seeds are harvested in September and October.

FLAVOR: Leaves have a mild flavor that is good for salad or green smoothies or eating raw.

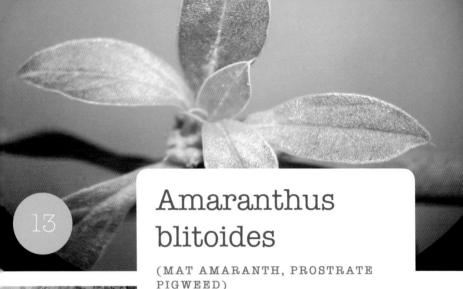

Amaranthus blitoides

(MAT AMARANTH, PROSTRATE PIGWEED)

———

STATES: Arizona, Colorado, Idaho, Montana, Nevada, New Mexico, Utah, Wyoming.

FLOWER: Green.

CHARACTERISTICS: This plant lies prostrate to the ground with many branches from the center, which is how it got its "mat" prefix.

HABITAT: Disturbed, sunny, open spaces and waste spaces in alkaline soil.

FORM: Annual, typically growing up to six inches tall but 1–4 feet broad on the ground.

EDIBLE PARTS: Leaves, seeds.

HARVESTABLE: Leaves are harvested from May through August. Seeds are harvested in September and October.

FLAVOR: Leaves have a mild flavor that is good for salad or green smoothies or eating raw.

NOTES: One of the benefits of this plant is that the leaves stay tender even when they reach midsize or larger, so they can be harvested for many weeks.

The seeds are harvested after they have naturally dried on the plant in autumn.

13

Amaranthus blitum

(PURPLE AMARANTH, SLENDER AMARANTH)

———

STATE: Utah.

FLOWER: Green.

CHARACTERISTICS: A typically spiky, upright amaranth that is a popular food the world over. There are other varieties also called purple amaranth.

HABITAT: Disturbed, sunny, open spaces and waste spaces in alkaline soil.

FORM: Annual, typically growing 2–4 feet tall.

EDIBLE PARTS: Leaves, seeds.

HARVESTABLE: Leaves are harvested from May through August. Seeds are harvested in September and October.

FLAVOR: Leaves have a mild flavor that is good for salad or green smoothies or eating raw.

NOTES: One of the benefits of this plant is that the leaves stay tender even when they reach midsize or larger, so they can be harvested for many weeks.

The seeds are harvested after they have naturally dried on the plant in autumn.

SYNONYMS: *Amaranthus lividus, Amaranthus ascendens.*

Amaranthus palmeri

(PALMER AMARANTH, CARELESS WEED)

STATES: Arizona, Colorado, Nevada, New Mexico, Utah.

FLOWER: Green.

CHARACTERISTICS: A tall, spiky plant. An invasive plant native to the Rocky Mountains that has now spread even overseas.

HABITAT: Disturbed, sunny, open spaces and waste spaces in alkaline soil.

FORM: Annual, typically growing 2–4 feet tall.

EDIBLE PARTS: Leaves, seeds.

HARVESTABLE: Leaves are harvested from May through August. Seeds are harvested in September and October.

FLAVOR: Leaves have a mild flavor that is good for salad or green smoothies or eating raw.

NOTES: One of the benefits of this plant is that the leaves stay tender even when they reach midsize or larger, so they can be harvested for many weeks.

Amaranthus retroflexus

(REDROOT PIGWEED, REDROOT AMARANTH, WILD-BEET AMARANTH, ROUGH PIGWEED, COMMON AMARANTH)

STATES: Arizona, Colorado, Idaho, Montana, Nevada, New Mexico, Utah, Wyoming.

FLOWER: Green.

CHARACTERISTICS: A tall, spiky plant with stems that are red near the base. Originally an American native, this plant has now aggressively spread almost worldwide.

HABITAT: Disturbed, sunny, open spaces and waste spaces in alkaline soil.

FORM: Annual, typically growing 2–4 feet tall.

EDIBLE PARTS: Leaves, seeds.

HARVESTABLE: Leaves are harvested from May through August. Seeds are harvested in September and October.

FLAVOR: Leaves have a mild flavor that is good for salad or green smoothies or eating raw.

NOTES: One of the benefits of this plant is that the leaves stay tender even when they reach midsize or larger, so they can be harvested for many weeks.

The seeds are harvested after they have naturally dried on the plant in autumn.

Amelanchier alnifolia

(SASKATOON SERVICEBERRY)

STATES: Colorado, Idaho, Montana, Nevada, New Mexico, Utah, Wyoming.

FLOWER: White.

CHARACTERISTICS: A tree that can be spindly and even shrubby, often found tucked between or growing out from between other trees on riverbanks or in moist shaded areas near water, but not always near water.

EDIBLE PARTS: Berries, or leaves for tea.

BERRY: Purple.

HABITAT: Moist, shady mountainsides. Commonly found in aspen or maple groves on hiking trails, in campgrounds, at meadow edges, and on creek banks. Prefers to grow in the shade of larger trees.

FORM: Shrub tree with multiple stems, growing 5–15 feet tall.

HARVESTABLE: Late July, August.

FLAVOR: Sweet.

NOTES: Serviceberries are absolutely one of my favorite wild berries. These have been called mountain blueberries, and with good reason. I actually like them better than blueberries. They are sweet and fleshy and larger than most blueberries from the grocery store. The flavor is fantastic, and for that reason these berry plants are sometimes sold in nurseries for backyard growing. However, this small tree produces well only in shady and humid conditions usually found in the high mountains in the Rocky Mountain West. If you try to grow them, the north side of a house is a good option.

The berries change color as they ripen, turning pink, then red, then purple, and finally dark purple. For peak ripeness, harvest when the berries are soft and dark purple but before the berries have begun to desiccate.

One of the great things about this plant is that the fruit does not all ripen at once, so you can hand-harvest the berries over several weeks. When these berries are in season, I drive to the local canyon weekly to pick them and eat them fresh, on the spot. They are irresistible. One downside is that these trees do not produce in prolific amounts, so I never have enough to preserve.

Amelanchier pumila

(DWARF SERVICEBERRY)

STATES: Arizona, Colorado, Idaho, Montana, New Mexico, Utah, Wyoming.

FLOWER: White.

CHARACTERISTICS: Often found in north-facing hillsides in hiking areas that are populated by shrubs and not trees. This dwarf version does not require as much moisture or shade as its taller siblings. Berries look like other serviceberries in this book.

EDIBLE PARTS: Berries, or leaves for tea.

BERRY: Purple.

HABITAT: Moist, shady mountainsides. Commonly found in aspen or maple groves on hiking trails, in campgrounds, at meadow edges, and on creek banks. Prefers to grow in the shade of larger trees.

FORM: Shrub tree with multiple stems, growing 2–5 feet tall.

HARVESTABLE: Late July, August.

FLAVOR: Sweet.

19

Amelanchier utahensis

(UTAH SERVICEBERRY, JUNEBERRY)

————

STATES: Arizona, Colorado, Idaho, Montana, Nevada, New Mexico, Utah, Wyoming.

FLOWER: White.

CHARACTERISTICS: The earliest of all the servieberry species, and one of the earliest wild berries to ripen in the Rocky Mountains, which makes it a wonderful hiker's treat. The berries stay on the plant longer than other serviceberries. Flowers often bloom in early May. Usually found between 5,000- and 9,000-foot elevations.

EDIBLE PARTS: Berries, or leaves for tea.

BERRY: Purple.

HABITAT: Moist, shady mountainsides. Commonly found in aspen or maple groves on hiking trails, in campgrounds, at meadow edges, and on creek banks. Prefers to grow in the shade of larger trees.

FORM: Shrub tree with multiple stems, growing 5–15 feet tall.

HARVESTABLE: Late July, August.

FLAVOR: Sweet.

Amsinckia tesselata

(BRISTLY FIDDLENECK)

———

STATES: Arizona, Idaho, Nevada, New Mexico, Utah.

FLOWER: Yellow.

CHARACTERISTICS: This plant is covered in hairs that can be irritating to the touch, so harvest the seed with care.

HABITAT: Sunny, disturbed soils such as roadsides and open waste areas.

FORM: Annual herb, typically growing 1–2 feet tall.

EDIBLE PART: Seeds.

HARVESTABLE: Leaves in spring, seeds in summer and autumn.

FLAVOR: Grain.

21

Anthriscus caucalis

(BUR CHERVIL)

___

STATES: Arizona, Idaho, Wyoming.

FLOWER: White.

CHARACTERISTICS: Typically found growing in shady areas or moist soil. Blooms in April, May, or June.

HARVESTABLE: Best flavor and tenderness before the plant begins to flower, but correct identification before flowering is difficult.

HABITAT: Mountainsides.

FORM: Annual, typically growing 2–4 feet tall.

EDIBLE PARTS: Leaves, roots.

FLAVOR: Aromatic. Root can be bitter after flowering.

NOTES: Caution! These plants can easily be mistaken for poisonous look-alikes such as water hemlock, especially if you are inexperienced or if the plant is in its early stages.

SYNONYMS: *A. scandicina, A. cerefolium.*

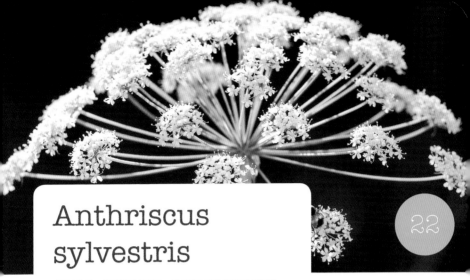

Anthriscus sylvestris

(WILD CHERVIL, COW PARSLEY)

STATE: Idaho.

FLOWER: White.

CHARACTERISTICS: The stem is often but not always purple. Prefers moist disturbed soil.

HARVESTABLE: Best flavor and tenderness before the plant begins to flower, but correct identification before flowering is difficult.

HABITAT: Mountainsides.

FORM: Annual, typically growing 2–4 feet tall.

EDIBLE PARTS: Leaves, roots.

FLAVOR: Aromatic. Root can be bitter after flowering.

NOTE: Caution! These plants can easily be mistaken for poisonous look-alikes such as water hemlock, especially if you are inexperienced or if the plant is in its early stages.

SYNONYM: *Chaerophyllum sylvestre.*

Antirrhinum majus

(SNAPDRAGON)

STATE: Utah.

FLOWER: Varies—yellow, red, purple, orange, or bicolor or tricolor.

CHARACTERISTICS: These are the same snapdragon flowers that are commonly grown in flower beds around the country. In places in Utah where it can find water, it has escaped into the wild—even my backyard—but it is found only in areas with reliable spring and early summer moisture. They reliably self-seed in the garden.

HABITAT: Moist areas, including some roadsides and mountainsides.

FORM: Herbaceous perennial, 1–3 feet tall.

EDIBLE PART: Flowers.

HARVESTABLE: June through frost.

FLAVOR: Flowers are mild and slightly sweet. These make a good garnish for salad because of the many beautiful colors.

Aquilegia coerulea

(ROCKY MOUNTAIN COLUMBINE,
COLORADO BLUE COLUMBINE)

———————

STATES: Arizona, Colorado, Idaho, Montana, Nevada, New Mexico, Utah, Wyoming.

FLOWER: White, blue, cream, or bicolor or tricolor. Rarely pink-tinged spurs.

CHARACTERISTICS: These are easily and widely found all over the mountains of the Rocky Mountain West. We grow these in our yard as landscape flowers as well, and they reliably self-seed year after year.

These make a good snack while hiking or a garnish for salad because of the beautiful colors.

HABITAT: Mountainsides, occasionally in shaded desert areas.

FORM: Herbaceous perennial, growing about 18–24 inches tall.

EDIBLE PART: Flowers.

CHARACTERISTICS: The flowers are usually taller than the rest of the plant. Often found in meadows and open areas in moist soil. Often found near hiking trails.

HARVESTABLE: May, June, July.

FLAVOR: Mild and slightly sweet.

Aquilegia formosa

(WESTERN COLUMBINE)

———

STATES: Idaho, Montana, Nevada, Utah, Wyoming.

FLOWER: Red, yellow, or bicolor or tricolor. Sometimes orange and other colors.

CHARACTERISTICS: The flowers are usually taller than the rest of the plant. Often found in meadows and open areas in moist soil. Often found near hiking trails. *Aquila* is Latin for "eagle," so named because of the spurs on the flowers. *Formosa* means "beautiful."

HABITAT: Mountainsides, occasionally in shaded desert areas.

FORM: Herbaceous perennial, growing about 18–24 inches tall, sometimes up to 3 feet.

EDIBLE PART: Flowers.

HARVESTABLE: May, June, July.

FLAVOR: Mild and slightly sweet.

NOTES: These are easily and widely found all over the mountains of the Rocky Mountain West. We grow these in our yard as landscape flowers as well, and they reliably self-seed year after year.

These make a good snack while hiking or a garnish for salad because of the beautiful colors.

Arctium lappa

(GREATER BURDOCK, GOBO)

STATES: Colorado, Idaho, Montana, Nevada, Utah, Wyoming.

FLOWER: Purple.

CHARACTERISTICS: The leaves are nearly 4 percent protein by weight. Roots are about 3 percent protein and can be dried and stored for winter use.

HABITAT: Found widely in calcareous (chalky) soils in mountains, deserts, residential areas, roadsides.

FORM: Herbaceous biennial, growing 2–3 feet tall.

EDIBLE PARTS: Root, leaves, flower stalks, leaf stems.

HARVESTABLE: Spring, summer, autumn.

FLAVOR: Stems have a flavor like celery. Root has a mild and slightly sweet flavor. Young leaves have a bitter flavor that is eliminated when cooked.

NOTES: My favorite part of this plant is the stems, which have a high water content. If I were looking for water in the desert, the stems of this plant would be one of the first places I would try.

The young stems can be eaten whole, raw, or cooked. To eat older stems, I usually only scrape out the inside of the stem because the outside is fibrous.

The root is easiest to eat when it is thinly sliced.

Arctium minus

(LESSER BURDOCK)

STATES: Arizona, Colorado, Idaho, Montana, Nevada, New Mexico, Utah, Wyoming.

FLOWER: Purple.

CHARACTERISTICS: The roasted root of both lesser and greater burdock is used historically for making root beer and as a coffee substitute. Both plants are also prized in traditional medicine as a detoxifier.

HABITAT: Found widely in calcareous (chalky) soils in mountains, deserts, residential areas, roadsides.

FORM: Herbaceous biennial, growing 2–3 feet tall.

EDIBLE PARTS: Root, leaves, flower stalks, leaf stems.

HARVESTABLE: Spring, summer, autumn.

FLAVOR: Stems have a flavor like celery. Root has a mild and slightly sweet flavor. Young leaves have a bitter flavor that is eliminated when cooked.

NOTES: My favorite part of *Arctium* species is the stems, which have a high water content. If I were looking for water in the desert, the stems of this plant would be one of the first places I would try.

The young stems can be eaten whole, raw, or cooked. To eat older stems, I usually only scrape out the inside of the stem because the outside is fibrous.

The root is easiest to eat when it is thinly sliced.

Argentina anserina

(SILVERWEED CINQUEFOIL)

STATES: Arizona, Colorado, Idaho, Montana, Nevada, New Mexico, Utah, Wyoming.

FLOWER: Yellow.

CHARACTERISTICS: Roots are generally small.

HABITAT: Mountainsides.

FORM: Herbaceous perennial, growing 6 inches tall.

EDIBLE PART: Root.

HARVESTABLE: Spring, summer, autumn.

FLAVOR: Starchy and nutty, especially in spring.

Artemisia frigida

(FRINGED SAGEBRUSH, PRAIRIE SAGEWORT)

STATES: Arizona, Colorado, Idaho, Montana, Nevada, New Mexico, Utah, Wyoming.

FLOWER: Yellow.

CHARACTERISTICS: The plant often forms a mound shape. Flowers are a quarter inch in diameter.

HABITAT: Desert, alkaline soils.

FORM: Shrub, typically 3–4 feet tall.

EDIBLE PART: Leaves, used as a condiment for flavoring.

HARVESTABLE: Spring, summer, autumn.

FLAVOR: Strong spearmint gum flavor.

NOTES: Spearmint flavor can be useful for bringing moisture to your mouth on a hot day or if you are thirsty.

A tiny bit of leaf goes a long way.

Some people use the leaves to make a simple sauce or as a garnish for lamb or pork.

Used as a preservative and a medicinal and historically burned to create insect repellent smoke by the American Indians.

Artemisia tridentata

(BIG SAGEBRUSH)

STATES: Arizona, Colorado, Idaho, Montana, Nevada, New Mexico, Utah, Wyoming.

FLOWER: Yellow.

CHARACTERISTICS: Tall, round, or mound-shaped shrubs with woody trunks. The leaves of all artemisia in this book are strongly scented. The oils that cause this scent are highly flammable, so even green sagebrush burns well, but the scent intensifies as it burns.

HABITAT: Desert, alkaline soils.

FORM: Shrub, typically 4 feet tall but can be up to 15 feet tall in rare circumstances.

EDIBLE PART: Leaves, used as a condiment for flavoring.

HARVESTABLE: Spring, summer, autumn.

FLAVOR: Strong spearmint gum flavor.

NOTES: Spearmint flavor can be useful for bringing moisture to your mouth on a hot day or if you are thirsty.

A tiny bit of leaf goes a long way.

Some people use the leaves to make a simple sauce or as a garnish for lamb or pork.

Asclepias asperula

(SPIDER MILKWEED)

STATES: Arizona, Colorado, Idaho, Nevada, New Mexico, Utah.

FLOWER: White and green.

CHARACTERISTICS: Flowers of most *Asclepias* species bloom over many months, from March through October.

HABITAT: Disturbed, sunny locations, especially roadsides and field edges.

FORM: Native herbaceous perennial, spreading on rhizomes, typically 1–2 feet tall.

EDIBLE PARTS: Flowers, unopened flower buds, seeds, immature seed pods, brown sugar from flowers, roots, young sprouts.

HARVESTABLE: July, August, September.

FLAVOR: The flowers, buds, and young pods have a delicious sugary flavor that is both a surprise and a treat.

NOTES: This plant may be high in alkaloids and other chemicals and, like all plants in this book, should be eaten sparingly. **Avoid eating the milky sap.** The US Department of Agriculture says, "The sap contains a lethal brew of cardenolides (heart poison), which produces vomiting in low doses and death in higher doses." Eat just the flowers and not the flower stems to avoid the milk.

I pop the flower heads off one at a time. The young flower pods also delightfully pop in your mouth when eaten. However, flowers and other parts of the plant that are not young and tender may have a bitter flavor.

Some species of butterfly are said to depend on these plants for food, so you may want to harvest sparingly.

Tender shoots of the plant are eaten like asparagus in early spring, but this decimates the year's crop, so this use may be best only sparingly.

Other uses for all *Asclepias* species in this book: The mature, cottony down of the seed pods has been widely used as a cotton-like stuffing for mattresses, cloth dolls, pillows, and more, especially in times when cotton was expensive or unavailable. The down is also useful as a tinder for starting fires from sparks and can be gathered and stored for this purpose.

Various parts of the plant have medicinal uses. You can also use milkweed to create dye. The dry seed pods naturally split on their own and are a favorite toy boat for children. A type of rubber can be made from the milk of the plant, but people may have a skin allergy to the milk.

All milkweed species are important food sources for some butterflies, so harvest sparingly.

Asclepias cordifolia

(HEARTLEAF MILKWEED)

STATE: Nevada.

FLOWER: Red to purple petals with pinkish to purplish hoods.

HABITAT: Disturbed, sunny locations, especially roadsides and field edges.

FORM: Native herbaceous perennial, spreading on rhizomes, typically 2–5 feet tall.

EDIBLE PARTS: Flowers, unopened flower buds, seeds, immature seed pods, brown sugar from flowers, roots, young sprouts.

HARVESTABLE: July, August, September.

FLAVOR: The flowers, buds, and young pods have a delicious sugary flavor that is both a surprise and a treat.

NOTES: This plant may be high in alkaloids and other chemicals and, like all plants in this book, should be eaten sparingly. **Avoid eating the milky sap.** The US Department of Agriculture says, "The sap contains a lethal brew of cardenolides (heart poison), which produces vomiting in low doses and death in higher doses."

Asclepias erosa

(DESERT MILKWEED)

STATES: Arizona, Nevada, Utah.

FLOWER: Pale green with hoods that are greenish white to yellow-brown.

CHARACTERISTICS: Thick wooly leaves that become hairless as they age. The hoods of the flowers have been beautifully described as "hollow-cheeked hoods resembling corn kernels that yellow with age" by the Consortium of Midwest Herbaria. The flowers are fragrant.

HABITAT: Disturbed, sunny locations, especially roadsides and field edges.

FORM: Native herbaceous perennial, spreading on rhizomes, typically 2–5 feet tall.

EDIBLE PARTS: Flowers, unopened flower buds, seeds, immature seed pods, brown sugar from flowers, roots, young sprouts.

HARVESTABLE: July, August, September.

FLAVOR: The flowers, buds, and young pods have a delicious sugary flavor that is both a surprise and a treat.

   This plant may be high in alkaloids and other chemicals and, like all plants in this book, should be eaten sparingly. **Avoid eating the milky sap.** The US Department of Agriculture says, "The sap contains a lethal brew of cardenolides (heart poison), which produces vomiting in low doses and death in higher doses."

Asclepias fasciularis

(MEXICAN WHORLED MILKWEED)

STATES: Idaho, Nevada, Utah.

FLOWER: Green and pink, bicolor. Sometimes pale, almost white or pale gray, tinged with purple.

CHARACTERISTICS: Smooth plant stems. Leaves are smooth on top.

HABITAT: Disturbed, sunny locations, especially roadsides and field edges.

FORM: Native herbaceous perennial, spreading on rhizomes, typically 3 feet tall.

EDIBLE PARTS: Flowers, unopened flower buds, seeds, immature seed pods, brown sugar from flowers, roots, young sprouts.

HARVESTABLE: July, August, September.

FLAVOR: The flowers, buds, and young pods have a delicious sugary flavor that is both a surprise and a treat.

This plant may be high in alkaloids and other chemicals and, like all plants in this book, should be eaten sparingly. **Avoid eating the milky sap.** The US Department of Agriculture says, "The sap contains a lethal brew of cardenolides (heart poison), which produces vomiting in low doses and death in higher doses."

Asclepias incarnata

(SWAMP MILKWEED)

STATES: Colorado, Idaho, Montana, Nevada, New Mexico, Utah, Wyoming.

FLOWER: A bright pink-purple.

CHARACTERISTICS: Unlike most milkweeds, this species is found in marshy and wet soils, near water, thus its name.

HABITAT: Disturbed, sunny locations, especially roadsides and field edges.

FORM: Native herbaceous perennial, spreading on rhizomes, typically 2–5 feet tall.

EDIBLE PARTS: Flowers, unopened flower buds, seeds, immature seed pods, brown sugar from flowers, roots, young sprouts.

HARVESTABLE: July, August, September.

FLAVOR: The flowers, buds, and young pods have a delicious sugary flavor that is both a surprise and a treat.

    This plant may be high in alkaloids and other chemicals and, like all plants in this book, should be eaten sparingly. **Avoid eating the milky sap.** The US Department of Agriculture says, "The sap contains a lethal brew of cardenolides (heart poison), which produces vomiting in low doses and death in higher doses."

Asclepias involucrata

(DWARF MILKWEED)

STATES: Arizona, Colorado, New Mexico, Utah.

FLOWER: Petals that are greenish to purple with hoods that are white to yellow. Yellow is often but not always a dominant color of the flowers.

CHARACTERISTICS: The flowers of this species can vary highly in color. A semi-trailing or drooping form.

HABITAT: Disturbed, sunny locations, especially roadsides and field edges.

FORM: Native herbaceous perennial, spreading on rhizomes, typically 1–2 feet tall.

EDIBLE PARTS: Flowers, unopened flower buds, seeds, immature seed pods, brown sugar from flowers, roots, young sprouts.

HARVESTABLE: July, August, September.

FLAVOR: The flowers, buds, and young pods have a delicious sugary flavor that is both a surprise and a treat.

This plant may be high in alkaloids and other chemicals and, like all plants in this book, should be eaten sparingly. **Avoid eating the milky sap.** The US Department of Agriculture says, "The sap contains a lethal brew of cardenolides (heart poison), which produces vomiting in low doses and death in higher doses."

SYNONYM: *Asclepias macrosperma.*

Asclepias speciosa

(SHOWY MILKWEED)

STATES: Arizona, Colorado, Idaho, Montana, Nevada, New Mexico, Utah, Wyoming.

FLOWER: Pink or purplish petals with yellowish-brown hoods.

CHARACTERISTICS: The size of the flower combined with the bright pink color gives this showy flower its name. This species has the largest flowers of all *Asclepias* in North America. According to the Consortium of Midwest Herbaria, this plant was traditionally used as medicine for the eyes, for warts, for venereal diseases, and as a decoction of seeds for drawing poison from snake bites. It was eaten as a candy (which is how I think of all milkweeds) and "the immature fruits were peeled and the inner layer eaten along with young buds; stalks were cooked, flowers boiled, seeds eaten raw; also used to make string."

HABITAT: Disturbed, sunny locations, especially roadsides and field edges.

FORM: Native herbaceous perennial, spreading on rhizomes, typically 2–5 feet tall.

EDIBLE PARTS: Flowers, unopened flower buds, seeds, immature seed pods, brown sugar from flowers, roots, young sprouts.

HARVESTABLE: July, August, September.

FLAVOR: The flowers, buds, and young pods have a delicious sugary flavor that is both a surprise and a treat.

NOTES: This plant may be high in alkaloids and other chemicals and, like all plants in this book, should be eaten sparingly. **Avoid eating the milky sap.** The US Department of Agriculture says, "The sap contains a lethal brew of cardenolides (heart poison), which produces vomiting in low doses and death in higher doses."

Asclepias subverticillata

(HORSETAIL MILKWEED)

———

STATES: Arizona, Colorado, Idaho, Nevada, New Mexico, Utah, Wyoming

FLOWER: White, green, or grayish-purple petals with white or yellow hoods.

CHARACTERISTICS: The flowers of this species are highly variable. The Consortium of Midwest Herbaria says about this species, "the first buds eaten; the pods were eaten, used for clothing, and made into prayer sticks. Often considered to be highly poisonous."

HABITAT: Disturbed, sunny locations, especially roadsides and field edges.

FORM: Native herbaceous perennial, spreading on rhizomes, typically 2–5 feet tall.

EDIBLE PARTS: Flowers, unopened flower buds, seeds, immature seed pods, brown sugar from flowers, roots, young sprouts.

HARVESTABLE: July, August, September.

FLAVOR: The flowers, buds, and young pods have a delicious sugary flavor that is both a surprise and a treat.

NOTES: This plant may be high in alkaloids and, like all plants in this book, should be eaten sparingly. **Avoid eating the milky sap.** The US Department of Agriculture says, "The sap contains a lethal brew of cardenolides (heart poison), which produces vomiting in low doses and death in higher doses."

Some species of butterfly are said to depend on these plants for food, so you may want to harvest sparingly.

Asclepias syriaca

(COMMON MILKWEED)

STATES: Montana.

FLOWER: Pink, purple, and greenish petals with pale purple hoods.

CHARACTERISTICS: Usually found in moist soil. Known for highly variable leaf shapes. Found more commonly in other parts of the country because it likes moist soil.

HABITAT: Disturbed, sunny locations, especially roadsides and field edges.

FORM: Native herbaceous perennial, spreading on rhizomes, typically 2–5 feet tall.

EDIBLE PARTS: Flowers, unopened flower buds, seeds, immature seed pods, brown sugar from flowers, roots, young sprouts.

HARVESTABLE: July, August, September.

FLAVOR: The flowers, buds, and young pods have a delicious sugary flavor that is both a surprise and a treat.

NOTES: This plant may be high in alkaloids and other chemicals and, like all plants in this book, should be eaten sparingly. **Avoid eating the milky sap.** The US Department of Agriculture says, "The sap contains a lethal brew of cardenolides (heart poison), which produces vomiting in low doses and death in higher doses."

Asclepias verticillata

(WHORLED MILKWEED)

————

STATES: Arizona, Montana, New Mexico, Wyoming.

FLOWER: White or pale green.

CHARACTERISTICS: The whorled pattern of the leaves on slender stems gives this plant its name. Grows in clay or sandy soil.

HABITAT: Disturbed, sunny locations, especially roadsides and field edges.

FORM: Native herbaceous perennial, spreading on rhizomes, typically 2–5 feet tall.

EDIBLE PARTS: Flowers, unopened flower buds, seeds, immature seed pods, brown sugar from flowers, roots, young sprouts.

HARVESTABLE: July, August, September.

FLAVOR: The flowers, buds, and young pods have a delicious sugary flavor that is both a surprise and a treat.

NOTES: This plant may be high in alkaloids and other chemicals and, like all plants in this book, should be eaten sparingly. **Avoid eating the milky sap.** The US Department of Agriculture says, "The sap contains a lethal brew of cardenolides (heart poison), which produces vomiting in low doses and death in higher doses."

Asclepias viridiflora

(GREEN COMET MILKWEED)

———

STATES: Arizona, Colorado, Montana, New Mexico, Wyoming.

FLOWER: Green petals with greenish-yellow hoods that are sometimes tinged with purple.

CHARACTERISTICS: This species has been called rare, so if you find it, you may want to just take a picture instead of eating. The name *Asclepias* comes from *Asklepios*, the Greek god of healing. The roots of this species were used used historically for rashes, swelling, and sore throats, but see the notes below about the poisonous sap. *Viridiflora* means "green flowers."

HABITAT: Disturbed, sunny locations, especially roadsides and field edges.

FORM: Native herbaceous perennial, spreading on rhizomes, typically 2–5 feet tall.

EDIBLE PARTS: Flowers, unopened flower buds, seeds, immature seed pods, brown sugar from flowers, roots, young sprouts.

HARVESTABLE: July, August, September.

FLAVOR: The flowers, buds, and young pods have a delicious sugary flavor that is both a surprise and a treat.

NOTES: This plant may be high in alkaloids and other chemicals and, like all plants in this book, should be eaten sparingly. **Avoid eating the milky sap.** The US Department of Agriculture says, "The sap contains a lethal brew of cardenolides (heart poison), which produces vomiting in low doses and death in higher doses." Eat just the flowers and not the flower stems to avoid the milk.

Avena barbata

(SLENDER OAT)

STATES: Arizona, Montana, Nevada, New Mexico.

FLOWER: Green.

CHARACTERISTICS: The flowers, called "panicles" by botanists, can be erect or nodding (somewhat bent over or drooping). The grain can be ground for flour, soaked, sprouted, boiled, added to soup, used in multigrain bread, used with natural yeast, and more.

HABITAT: Found in disturbed and somewhat dry areas in heavy clay soil, and sometimes in drier meadows.

FORM: Annual, 2 feet tall, grasslike.

EDIBLE PART: Grain.

HARVESTABLE: July, August, September.

FLAVOR: Grain.

Avena fatua

(WILD OAT)

STATES: Arizona, Colorado, Idaho, Montana, Nevada, New Mexico, Utah, Wyoming.

FLOWER: Green.

CHARACTERISTICS: These wild oats are often found growing in farm fields of domestic oats and easily hybridize with farm oats (*A. sativa*). Has narrower leaf blades and weaker stems than *A. sativa*. Historically, the seeds were an important food source and were often gathered for winter use. They were sun-dried, boiled, pounded, or ground up. Pause for a moment to think of the work required to gather wild oats to feed a family through winter! Interestingly, *fatua* is Latin for "worthless," which is probably how you'd feel about this food while looking at a scant container of grain after a full day of hand-harvesting from the wild, because it would take a lot of work to get any useful quantity. The grain can be ground for flour, soaked, sprouted, boiled, added to soup, used in multigrain bread, used with natural yeast, and more.

HABITAT: Found in disturbed and somewhat dry areas in heavy clay soil, and sometimes in drier meadows.

FORM: Annual, 2 feet tall, grasslike.

EDIBLE PART: Grain.

HARVESTABLE: July, August, September.

FLAVOR: Grain.

Avena sativa

(COMMON OAT)

STATES: Arizona, Colorado, Idaho, Montana, Nevada, New Mexico, Utah, Wyoming.

FLOWER: Green.

CHARACTERISTICS: Often sowed by the government as a soil stabilizer after cutting or widening a roadway, or after a flash flood destabilizes an area. *Avena* is the Latin word for oats, and *sativa* is Latin for something that is sown or planted and can be indicative of some plants that have been long domesticated. The grain can be ground for flour, soaked, sprouted, boiled, added to soup, used in multigrain bread, used with natural yeast, and more.

HABITAT: Found in disturbed and somewhat dry areas in heavy clay soil, and sometimes in drier meadows.

FORM: Annual, 2 feet tall, grasslike.

EDIBLE PART: Grain.

HARVESTABLE: July, August, September.

FLAVOR: Grain.

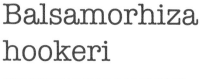

Balsamorhiza hookeri

(HOOKER'S BALSAMROOT)

———

STATES: Arizona, Colorado, Idaho, Montana, Nevada, Utah, Wyoming.

FLOWER: Yellow.

CHARACTERISTICS: There are at least dozens of look-alikes in the Rocky Mountain West, so if you decide to harvest this flower for eating, be sure you have the correct plant. Botanists acknowledge that classifying balsamroot plants is difficult, and there is debate over whether some species are actually varieties. The plants can be highly variable in small ways from region to region, which causes the classification problems. Some botanists argue that there are really only two species in the United States, with everything else being subspecies, but others disagree. Part of the problem may be that these plants are prone to natural hybridization or were at one time in history. Another theory is that they are prone to inbreeding, but then similar species (or subspecies, depending on who you ask) are found in isolation several states away. These plants are a botanical riddle. For most of us, they are just plain beautiful flowers.

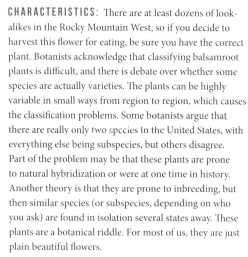

HABITAT: Sunny, open slopes and flatlands in heavy clay soil.

FORM: Herbaceous perennial, spring-growing flower, typically a foot tall.

EDIBLE PARTS: Root, shoots, leaves, flowers, seeds.

HARVESTABLE: Spring, summer, autumn.

FLAVOR: The root has the flavor and smell of balsam incense. The leaves are best cooked.

45

Balsamorhiza incana

(HOARY BALSAMROOT)

STATES: Idaho, Montana, Wyoming.

FLOWER: Yellow.

CHARACTERISTICS: Like *B. hookeri*, this species has strongly serrated, almost fern-like leaves. This species is usually distinguished by its wooly leaves, but the leaves are not always densely wooly. Leaves covered with dense matted hairs are called "tomentose" in botany. While some tomentose leaves are edible when cooked, they may be best avoided. Some people have allergic reactions to tomentose leaves.

HABITAT: Sunny, open slopes and flatlands in heavy clay soil.

FORM: Herbaceous perennial, spring-growing flower, typically a foot tall.

EDIBLE PARTS: Root, shoots, leaves, flowers, seeds.

HARVESTABLE: Spring, summer, autumn.

FLAVOR: The root has the flavor and smell of balsam incense. The leaves are best cooked.

NOTES: There are at least dozens of look-alikes in the Rocky Mountain West, so if you decide to harvest this flower for eating, be sure you have the correct plant.

Balsamorhiza sagittata

(ARROWLEAF BALSAMROOT)

———

STATES: Arizona, Colorado, Idaho, Montana, Nevada, Utah, Wyoming.

FLOWER: Yellow.

CHARACTERISTICS: This species has very different leaves than the other two species in this book, but it must be noted that *B. incana* and *B. sagittata* are known to easily naturally hybridize, so you can't always take the leaf shape as gospel for classification purposes.

HABITAT: Sunny, open slopes and flatlands in heavy clay soil.

FORM: Herbaceous perennial, spring-growing flower, typically a foot tall.

EDIBLE PARTS: Root, shoots, leaves, flowers, seeds.

HARVESTABLE: Spring, summer, autumn.

FLAVOR: The root has the flavor and smell of balsam incense. The leaves are best cooked.

NOTES: There are at least dozens of look-alikes in the Rocky Mountain West, so if you decide to harvest this flower for eating, be sure you have the correct plant.

Barbarea orthoceras

(AMERICAN YELLOWROCKET)

***

STATES: Arizona, Colorado, Idaho, Montana, Nevada, New Mexico, Utah, Wyoming.

FLOWER: Yellow or pale yellow.

CHARACTERISTICS: One of the distinctive identifying traits of this species, when compared to others in the genus, is that it is hairless and has no down, which is a smooth condition that botanists call "glabrous." Flowers have four petals.

HABITAT: Wet soils, especially along streams and creeks.

FORM: Herbaceous native perennial, up to 2 feet tall.

EDIBLE PART: Leaves.

HARVESTABLE: Spring, summer, autumn.

FLAVOR: Spicy hot.

NOTES: Edible oil can be extracted from the crushed seeds.

SYNONYM: *Barbarea americana.*

Barbarea verna

(LAND CRESS)

———

STATE: Montana.

FLOWER: Yellow or pale yellow.

CHARACTERISTICS: This species is mostly glabrous (smooth and hairless) except the lobes of the leaf blades, which sometimes have tiny hairs. Botanists call hairy or downy leaf lobes "blade auricles" (lobes) that are "ciliate" (have cilia, or small hairs). This is one of the defining characteristics of this species. In botany, the tiny details can make a big difference.

HABITAT: Wet soils, especially along streams and creeks.

FORM: Herbaceous native perennial, up to 2 feet tall.

EDIBLE PART: Leaves.

HARVESTABLE: Spring, summer, autumn.

FLAVOR: Spicy hot.

NOTES: Edible oil can be extracted from the crushed seed.

49

Barbarea vulgaris

(GARDEN YELLOWROCKET)

———

STATES: Colorado, Idaho, Montana, New Mexico, Utah, Wyoming.

FLOWER: Yellow or pale yellow.

CHARACTERISTICS: One identifier of this species is its protruding styles (part of the flower ovary) and stamens (the male flower organ). In the language of botany, protruding parts are called "exserted."

Barbarea is said to refer to St. Barbara, a patron saint of anyone who uses explosives, like artillerymen and miners, which kind of makes sense when you realize the flowers look kind of like explosions of yellow fire. The association also makes sense if you think that this plant occurs in places where military troops and miners would be working and eating in historic times. Wherever they went, they would have welcomed the sight of a known and prolific wild edible in days before grocery stores and canned or packaged food. Wild edibles were the fast food of historic times, especially when you were in the wild. The seeds might have been an important protein source because they were portable and storable. St. Barbara, according to legend, was a Greek child of a rich father who locked her in a tower to protect her virginity. She secretly converted to Christianity, and her angry father beheaded her. He was struck by lightning, and miracles happened at her tomb.

HABITAT: Wet soils, especially along streams and creeks.

FORM: Herbaceous native perennial, up to 2 feet tall.

EDIBLE PART: Leaves.

HARVESTABLE: Spring, summer, autumn.

FLAVOR: Spicy hot.

NOTES: Edible oil can be extracted from the crushed seed.

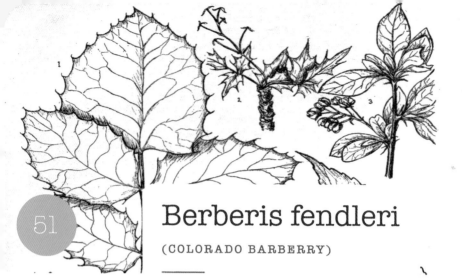

Berberis fendleri

(COLORADO BARBERRY)

STATES: Colorado, New Mexico, Utah.

FLOWER: Yellow.

CHARACTERISTICS: This species is believed to grow only in the Four Corners area.

HABITAT: Mountain slopes and ravines.

FORM: Flowering shrub.

BERRY: Red.

EDIBLE PARTS: Immature seeds, immature seedpod.

HARVESTABLE: Autumn.

FLAVOR: Sour and tart.

Brassica juncea

(BROWN MUSTARD)

STATES: Arizona, Colorado, Idaho, Montana, Nevada, New Mexico, Utah, Wyoming.

FLOWER: Yellow.

CHARACTERISTICS: Called brown mustard because its seeds are brown, but the seeds are sometimes also yellow, like other *Brassica* species. The brown mustard condiment is made from these seeds (not to be confused with yellow mustard condiment, which is made from the seeds of an unrelated species). This species is believed by botanists to be an ancient natural hybrid of *B. nigra* and *B. rapa*. The leaves are not clasping at the base.

HABITAT: Heavy, disturbed clay soils.

FORM: Herbaceous annual, typically growing 3–4 feet tall.

EDIBLE PARTS: Flowers, leaves, root, seeds.

HARVESTABLE: Spring, summer, autumn.

FLAVOR: Peppery.

NOTES: In addition to their wild forms, *Brassica juncea* and *Brassica rapa* both have sibling varieties that are commonly grown as vegetables. *Brassica* species in the wild can be difficult to distinguish.

Brassica napus

(RAPE MUSTARD)

STATES: Colorado, Idaho, Montana, Nevada, New Mexico.

FLOWER: Yellow.

CHARACTERISTICS: This species is believed to be an ancient hybrid of *B. oleracea* (which includes garden broccoli, cauliflower, kale, cabbage, and more) and *B. rapa*. *Brassica* is the Latin word for "cabbage." The garden rutabaga is a subspecies of *B. napus*, but the edible bulb rarely occurs in the wild, especially in the arid Rocky Mountains. Kale, cabbage, rutabaga, and other *Brassica* seeds are available on my website, SeedRenaissance.com.

HABITAT: Heavy, disturbed clay soils.

FORM: Herbaceous annual, typically growing 3–4 feet tall.

EDIBLE PARTS: Flowers, leaves, root, seeds.

HARVESTABLE: Spring, summer, autumn.

FLAVOR: Peppery.

NOTES: In addition to their wild forms, *Brassica juncea* and *Brassica rapa* both have sibling varieties that are commonly grown as vegetables. *Brassica* species in the wild can be difficult to tell apart.

Brassica nigra

(BLACK MUSTARD)

STATES: Colorado, Idaho, Montana, Nevada, New Mexico, Utah.

FLOWER: Yellow.

CHARACTERISTICS: Called black mustard because of the color of the seeds. A special black mustard condiment is made from the seeds of this species. The leaves are not clasping at the base. Historically this species was widely used medicinally as a tea infusion or poultice to treat asthma, palsy, coughs, fever, and more. Some people believe that the black mustard condiment contains some of these health benefits.

HABITAT: Heavy, disturbed clay soils.

FORM: Herbaceous annual, typically growing 3–4 feet tall.

EDIBLE PARTS: Flowers, leaves, root, seeds.

HARVESTABLE: Spring, summer, autumn.

FLAVOR: Peppery.

NOTES: In addition to their wild forms, *Brassica juncea* and *Brassica rapa* both have sibling varieties that are commonly grown as vegetables. *Brassica species* in the wild can be difficult to tell apart.

Brassica rapa

(FIELD MUSTARD)

STATES: Arizona, Colorado, Idaho, Montana, Nevada, New Mexico, Utah, Wyoming.

FLOWER: Yellow.

CHARACTERISTICS: Seeds of this species can be black, brown, or red in color, even from the same plant. Canola oil, pak choi salad greens, and turnips are all subspecies of *B. rapa*. There are many popular garden greens in this species that I grow in my garden that are more popular in Asia than the United States. Mizuna is the salad green from this species that I love the most. You can find mizuna seeds at my website, SeedRenaissance.com.

HABITAT: Heavy, disturbed clay soils.

FORM: Herbaceous annual, typically growing 3–4 feet tall.

EDIBLE PARTS: Flowers, leaves, root, seeds.

HARVESTABLE: Spring, summer, autumn.

FLAVOR: Peppery.

NOTES: In addition to their wild forms, *Brassica juncea* and *Brassica rapa* both have sibling varieties that are commonly grown as vegetables. *Brassica* species in the wild can be difficult to distinguish.

55

Bromus breviaristatus

(MOUNTAIN BROME)

STATES: Arizona, Colorado, Idaho, Montana, Nevada, New Mexico, Utah, Wyoming.

FLOWER: Green.

CHARACTERISTICS: Some botanists call this a synonym for *B. carinatus*, while others disagree. Some experts say the scientific name *Bromus marginatus* is a synonym for *Bromus breviaristatus*. All *Bromus* species can be difficult to tell apart, and difficult for experts to agree on classification, so don't feel bad if you are unsure which species you've found.

HABITAT: Dry open slopes, plains, roadsides, and disturbed areas.

FORM: Annual invasive grass that relies on early spring moisture for germination.

EDIBLE PART: Seeds.

HARVESTABLE: Summer, autumn.

NOTES: The seeds can be ground for flour.

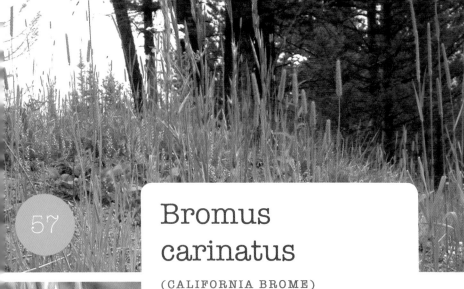

Bromus carinatus

(CALIFORNIA BROME)

STATES: Colorado, New Mexico.

FLOWER: Green.

CHARACTERISTICS: Often found in moist areas, while other *Bromus* species tolerate more arid conditions. *Bromus marginatus* is considered a subspecies of *B. carinatus* by some experts and others argue no.

HABITAT: Dry open slopes, plains, roadsides, and disturbed areas.

FORM: Annual invasive grass that relies on early spring moisture for germination.

EDIBLE PART: Seeds.

HARVESTABLE: Summer, autumn.

NOTES: The seeds can be ground for flour.

Bromus diandrus

(RIPGUT BROME)

STATES: Arizona, Colorado, Idaho, Montana, Nevada, New Mexico, Utah.

FLOWER: Green.

CHARACTERISTICS: The name "ripgut" means that ranchers should avoid letting horses, cattle, and stock animals eat this plant as its sharp seed parts, called "florets," can rip the guts. *B. diandrus* may be a synonym for *B. rigidus*, depending on which expert you ask. Native Americans tied the dried stalks of many *Bromus* species together to make hair combs or used the full bundled grasses as brooms.

HABITAT: Dry open slopes, plains, roadsides, and disturbed areas.

FORM: Annual invasive grass that relies on early spring moisture for germination.

EDIBLE PART: Seeds.

HARVESTABLE: Summer, autumn.

NOTES: The seeds can be ground for flour.

Bromus japonicus

(JAPANESE BROME, FIELD BROME)

STATES: Arizona, Colorado, Idaho, Montana, Nevada, New Mexico, Utah, Wyoming.

FLOWER: Green.

CHARACTERISTICS: *B. japonicus* may be a synonym for *Bromus commutatus*, depending on which expert you consult. The panicles (flowers) of this species have sort of a stacked pyramid look. *Japonicus* could be a nod to the stacked pagoda shape of the panicle, or it could mean that at some point someone thought this grass originated from Asia. It is believed to be an introduced species that has naturalized in the United States.

HABITAT: Dry open slopes, plains, roadsides, and disturbed areas.

FORM: Annual invasive grass that relies on early spring moisture for germination.

EDIBLE PART: Seeds.

HARVESTABLE: Summer, autumn.

NOTES: The seeds can be ground for flour.

Bromus marginatus

(MOUNTAIN BROME)

STATES: Arizona, Colorado, Idaho, Montana, Nevada, New Mexico, Utah, Wyoming.

FLOWER: Green.

CHARACTERISTICS: This species name might botanically conflated with about a dozen other *Bromus* species, and these professional arguments will likely never be settled. Competing botanists seem to publish their own classifications, arguing their small reasons for their classification opinions. Most laypeople ignore the professional drama and don't worry too much about the finer details of classification.

HABITAT: Dry open slopes, plains, roadsides, and disturbed areas.

FORM: Annual invasive grass that relies on early spring moisture for germination.

EDIBLE PART: Seeds.

HARVESTABLE: Summer, autumn.

NOTES: The seeds can be ground for flour.

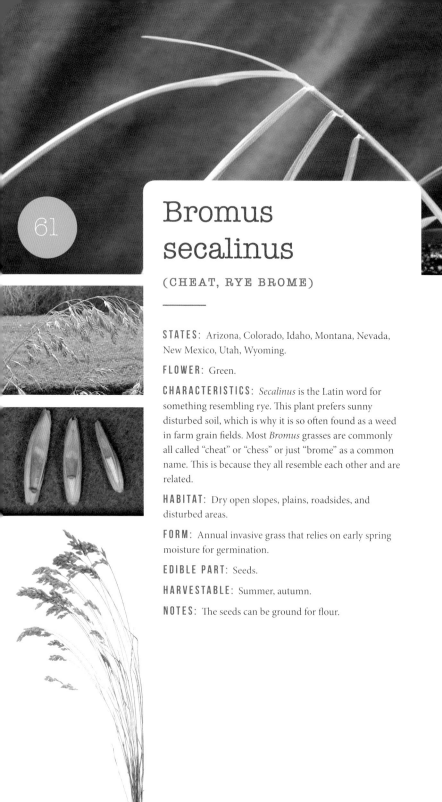

Bromus secalinus

(CHEAT, RYE BROME)

STATES: Arizona, Colorado, Idaho, Montana, Nevada, New Mexico, Utah, Wyoming.

FLOWER: Green.

CHARACTERISTICS: *Secalinus* is the Latin word for something resembling rye. This plant prefers sunny disturbed soil, which is why it is so often found as a weed in farm grain fields. Most *Bromus* grasses are commonly all called "cheat" or "chess" or just "brome" as a common name. This is because they all resemble each other and are related.

HABITAT: Dry open slopes, plains, roadsides, and disturbed areas.

FORM: Annual invasive grass that relies on early spring moisture for germination.

EDIBLE PART: Seeds.

HARVESTABLE: Summer, autumn.

NOTES: The seeds can be ground for flour.

Bromus tectorum

(DOWNY BROME, CHEAT GRASS)

STATES: Arizona, Colorado, Idaho, Montana, Nevada, New Mexico, Utah, Wyoming.

FLOWER: Green.

CHARACTERISTICS: At some point during the settlement of the West, this grass was (likely accidentally) imported from Europe and has now vastly populated the western United States. This grass has caused ecological havoc because it spreads aggressively and easily and dries out very early in summer, making it perfect wildfire fodder. It quickly and aggressively spreads after a fire, creating more fodder. The results are that this invasive species has single-handedly caused more wildfires in the West than perhaps any other source. It can easily ignite with a discarded cigarette or a spark from a vehicle, a target practice bullet, or a small firework. This grass is famous for sticking in the socks, shoes, and laces of hikers and farm workers. I've found this plant at 11,000 feet and higher, staking a claim on the sides of hiking trails, no doubt brought in on someone's clothes. I try to pull it out when I find it in otherwise pristine hiking area, but it's probably a losing battle and wherever it colonizes, wildfires are sure to follow. If we would all eat this fiddly grain, instead of letting the grains sow themselves, we'd be exacting a perfect revenge.

HABITAT: Dry open slopes, plains, roadsides, and disturbed areas.

FORM: Annual invasive grass that relies on early spring moisture for germination.

EDIBLE PARTS: Seeds.

HARVESTABLE: Summer, autumn.

NOTE: The seeds can be ground for flour.

Calandrinia ciliata

(REDMAIDS)

———

STATES: Arizona, Idaho, Nevada, New Mexico.

FLOWER: Red, purple, and sometimes white or bicolor.

HABITAT: Open grassland, fields, and disturbed soils.

FORM: Annual, low-growing, spreading herbaceous flower.

EDIBLE PARTS: Leaves, seeds.

HARVESTABLE: Spring, early summer.

FLAVOR: *Strong lemon.*

NOTES: Like all strongly lemon-flavored wild edibles, redmaids should be eaten only in small amounts. Some sources say the seeds were prized by the Native Americans for making small pressed cakes, but since these plants don't produce many seeds, this must have been a rare treat. Some sources also say the Native Americans ate the roots and stems too. Most modern sources agree that the genus name *Calandrinia* is named in honor of Jean-Louis Calandrini (1703–1758). Most modern sources agree he was from Geneva, Switzerland, but historically he was reported to be from Italy, Germany, or Switzerland. He has been called a botanist, but he was actually a published mathematician and astronomer. I have not yet found any information on why this genus was named in his honor, but I would like to know.

63

Callirhoe involucrata

(BUFFALO ROSE, WINECUP POPPY MALLOW)

STATES: Arizona, Colorado, New Mexico, Wyoming.

FLOWER: Red.

CHARACTERISTICS: Grows in the Moab, Utah, area. Overharvesting could decimate populations of this beautiful wild flower, which deserves a spot in the spring home-landscaping garden. I am working to (hopefully) make seeds available at SeedRenaissance.com.

HABITAT: Sunny, open, dry ground and roadsides.

FORM: Low-growing perennial flower blooming in mid-spring.

EDIBLE PARTS: Leaves, root.

HARVESTABLE: Spring, summer, autumn.

FLAVOR: The root is said to taste like sweet potato. However, this plant is not widely found.

Calochortus ambiguus

(DOUBTING MARIPOSA LILY)

STATES: Arizona, New Mexico, Utah.

FLOWER: White petals with a longitudinal purple stripe and yellow, greenish, gray, or gray-blue base, sometimes with with purple dots at the base of the petals. The flower coloring can be variable, and the stripe is not always present.

CHARACTERISTICS: *Ambiguus* means doubtful or uncertain, which could be a reference to the variability of the flower coloring. All *Calochortus* species can be highly variable in the coloring and pattern of the petals.

HABITAT: Alkaline slopes, plains, and desert lands.

FORM: Small flower.

EDIBLE PARTS: Flowers, bulb, stem, leaves

HARVESTABLE: Spring, summer, autumn.

FLAVOR: *Sweet.*

NOTES: Before the flower emerges, almost all *Calochortus* look nearly identical to death camas, one of the most poisonous plants in the West. Death camas also has a bulb, and confusing the two bulbs could be deadly. All parts of death camas are poisonous, so even confusing the grasslike leaves could be deadly. There are dozens of species of *Calochortus*, with about a third of them found only in California, and none of those are included in this book. The American Indians heavily relied on *Calochortus* as a food supply, probably especially during the hunger gap of early spring, and they must have been expert at telling *Calochortus* apart from death camas at that stage. They ate the bulbs raw, roasted, steamed, and boiled and often cooked them directly in the hot ash of their campfires.

Calochortus apiculatus

(POINTEDTIP MARIPOSA LILY)

STATES: Idaho, Montana, Wyoming.

FLOWER: White or pink petals with a pale yellow base.

CHARACTERISTICS: The flower petals are often densely hairy, with the hairs being the same color as the petals. There are sometimes purple tinges or streaks on the petals. Flowers in summer. All *Calochortus* species can be highly variable in the coloring and pattern of the petals.

HABITAT: Alkaline slopes, plains, and desert lands.

FORM: Small flower.

EDIBLE PARTS: Flowers, bulb, stem, leaves.

HARVESTABLE: Spring, summer, autumn.

FLAVOR: Sweet.

NOTES: Before the flower emerges, almost all *Calochortus* look nearly identical to death camas, one of the most poisonous plants in the West.

Calochortus aureus

(GOLDEN MARIPOSA LILY)

STATES: Arizona, Colorado, New Mexico, Utah.

FLOWER: Lemon yellow, often with a small rainbow-shaped red arch at the base of each petal in the center of the flower.

CHARACTERISTICS: There are sometimes lemon-yellow hairs at the center of the flower. *Aureus* is Latin for gold, which reflects the color of the petals. Often found in clay or dry, sandy soils. Blooms in early summer. All *Calochortus* species can be highly variable in the coloring and pattern of the petals.

HABITAT: Alkaline slopes, plains, and desert lands.

FORM: Small flower.

EDIBLE PARTS: Flowers, bulb, stem, leaves.

HARVESTABLE. Spring, summer, autumn.

FLAVOR: *Sweet.*

NOTES: Before the flower emerges, almost all *Calochortus* look nearly identical to death camas, one of the most poisonous plants in the West.

Calochortus bruneaunis

(BRUNEAU MARIPOSA LILY)

STATES: Idaho, Montana, Nevada, Utah.

FLOWER: White or lilac with a with red or purple spot near the base of the petals in the center of the flower and a longitudinal green stripe near the base with a red or purple crescent.

CHARACTERISTICS: Sometimes found with yellow hairs at the center of the flower. Flowers in late spring or early summer in dry, open areas or sometimes in pine forest areas. All *Calochortus* species can be highly variable in the coloring and pattern of the petals.

HABITAT: Alkaline slopes, plains, and desert lands.

FORM: Small flower.

EDIBLE PARTS: Flowers, bulb, stem, leaves.

HARVESTABLE: Spring, summer, autumn.

FLAVOR: Sweet.

NOTES: Before the flower emerges, almost all *Calochortus* look nearly identical to death camas, one of the most poisonous plants in the West.

Calochortus elegans

(ELEGANT MARIPOSA LILY)

STATES: Idaho, Montana.

FLOWER: White or pale green petals with a purple crescent at the base of the flower center.

CHARACTERISTICS: Often densely hairy in the center of the flower. This flower is somewhat rare, so if you find it, instead of eating it, you might want to just take pictures. All *Calochortus* species can be highly variable in the coloring and pattern of the petals.

HABITAT: Alkaline slopes, plains, and desert lands.

FORM: Small flower.

EDIBLE PARTS: Flowers, bulb, stem, leaves.

HARVESTABLE: Spring, summer, autumn.

FLAVOR: *Sweet.*

NOTES: Before the flower emerges, almost all *Calochortus* look nearly identical to death camas, one of the most poisonous plants in the West.

Calochortus eurycarpus

(WHITE MARIPOSA LILY)

————

STATES: Idaho, Montana, Nevada, Utah, Wyoming.

FLOWER: White or lavender petals with a red or purple spot in the center of each petal and sometimes a yellow spot under this spot.

CHARACTERISTICS: Hairs are often found at the center of the flower. Often found in open areas of wild grasses. Blooms in early summer. All *Calochortus* species can be highly variable in the coloring and pattern of the petals.

HABITAT: Alkaline slopes, plains, and desert lands.

FORM: Small flower.

EDIBLE PARTS: Flowers, bulb, stem, leaves.

HARVESTABLE: Spring, summer, autumn.

FLAVOR: *Sweet.*

NOTES: Before the flower emerges, almost all *Calochortus* look nearly identical to death camas, one of the most poisonous plants in the West.

Calochortus flexuosus

(WINDING MARIPOSA LILY)

———

STATES: Arizona, Colorado, Nevada, New Mexico, Utah.

FLOWER: White petals, often with a lilac blush at the ends. The center of the flower is often yellow, and sometimes there is a red blotch at the base of each petal.

CHARACTERISTICS: Flowers in spring or early summer, often in stony alkaline soil in sagebrush areas or mesas. The Consortium of Midwest Herbaria says that "the bulbs were roasted in ash pits and steamed before eating" when historically consumed by Native Americans. All *Calochortus* species can be highly variable in the coloring and pattern of the petals.

HABITAT: Alkaline slopes, plains, and desert lands.

FORM: Small flower.

EDIBLE PARTS: Flowers, bulb, stem, leaves.

HARVESTABLE: Spring, summer, autumn.

FLAVOR: Sweet.

NOTES: Before the flower emerges, almost all *Calochortus* look nearly identical to death camas, one of the most poisonous plants in the West.

Calochortus gunnisonii

(GUNNISON'S MARIPOSA LILY)

———————

STATES: Arizona, Colorado, Montana, New Mexico, Utah, Wyoming.

FLOWER: Petals are white or pale purple or even bright purple, often with a longitudinal band of dark purple near the base of each petal. The center of the flower is often yellow or yellowish green with purple splotches.

CHARACTERISTICS: The center of the flower below the purple band is often covered in yellow or yellowish-green hairs. If the petals are fully purple, sometimes there is a band of white above the longitudinal dark purple stripe. This variety sometimes appears with pale yellow petals in New Mexico but not in other areas. All *Calochortus* species can be highly variable in the coloring and pattern of the petals.

HABITAT: Alkaline slopes, plains, and desert lands.

FORM: Small flower.

EDIBLE PARTS: Flowers, bulb, stem, leaves.

HARVESTABLE: Spring, summer, autumn.

FLAVOR: *Sweet.*

NOTES: Before the flower emerges, almost all *Calochortus* look nearly identical to death camas, one of the most poisonous plants in the West.

Calochortus invenustus

(PLAIN MARIPOSA LILY)

STATE: Nevada.

FLOWER: Petals are white, pale lavender, or blushed lavender near the tips or fully bright purple. Centers are often yellow.

CHARACTERISTICS: The center of the flower often has yellow hairs. The organs at the center of the flower are often blue or purple. Flowers bloom in late spring or through the summer. Often found in arid soil.

HABITAT: Alkaline slopes, plains, and desert lands.

FORM: Small flower.

EDIBLE PARTS: Flowers, bulb, stem, leaves.

HARVESTABLE: Spring, summer, autumn.

FLAVOR: Sweet.

NOTES: Before the flower emerges, almost all *Calochortus* look nearly identical to death camas, one of the most poisonous plants in the West.

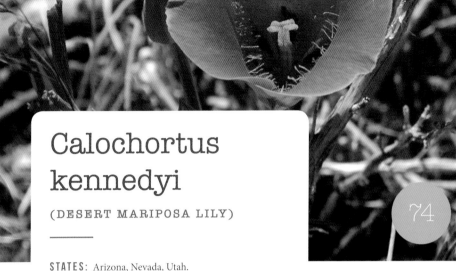

Calochortus kennedyi

(DESERT MARIPOSA LILY)

STATES: Arizona, Nevada, Utah.

FLOWER: Petals are often a stunning bright orange or red or bright lemon yellow. There is often a dark brown blotch of color at the base of each petal.

CHARACTERISTICS: The organs (anthers) in the center of the flower are sometimes a contrasting bright purple, making this flower truly a sight to see. The center of the flower is often hairy. The variable colors of the petals may make classification a chore, but the gorgeous photogenic qualities make this a flower for the ages. Often found on gravelly or stony slopes or mesas. This species was first collected in California by William Ledlie Kennedy, who was a well-known owner of stores and mills in Kern County, California, with a fascination for botany. In 1876, he sent some specimens to the Smithsonian, which led to several species, including this one, being named in his honor. His botanical contributions deserve more attention.

HABITAT: Alkaline slopes, plains, and desert lands.

FORM: Small flower.

EDIBLE PARTS: Flowers, bulb, stem, leaves.

HARVESTABLE: Spring, summer, autumn.

FLAVOR: *Sweet.*

NOTES: Before the flower emerges, almost all *Calochortus* look nearly identical to death camas, one of the most poisonous plants in the West.

Calochortus leichtlinii

(SMOKEY MARIPOSA LILY)

———————

STATES: Nevada, California.

FLOWER: Petals are white or pale blue, sometimes blushing pink at the ends. There is often a red or purple or black spot at the base of each petal.

CHARACTERISTICS: The center of the flower is often yellow, with a few hairs. The anthers at the center are often white or pale colored. This flower was featured in *Curtis's Botanical Magazine*: *Comprising the Plants of the Royal Gardens of Kew*, which was in print from the 1870s and can be found online at Archive.org. In October 1870, the magazine reported that this species "was discovered by Mr. Roezl in the Sierra Nevada of California" who told another botanist, who sent bulbs to the Royal Gardens in Kew, where botanists grew out the bulbs and then included hand-colored drawings of the plant in the magazine! It makes you appreciate what botany was like in the days before photography.

HABITAT: Alkaline slopes, plains, and desert lands.

FORM: Small flower.

EDIBLE PARTS: Flowers, bulb, stem, leaves.

HARVESTABLE: Spring, summer, autumn.

FLAVOR: Sweet.

NOTES: Before the flower emerges, almost all *Calochortus* look nearly identical to death camas, one of the most poisonous plants in the West.

Calochortus macrocarpus

(SAGEBRUSH MARIPOSA LILY)

STATES: Idaho, Montana, Nevada.

FLOWER: Purple or lilac or pink petals, sometimes with a green or red longitudinal stripe near the base. The center of the flower is yellow or yellowish green with white splotches.

CHARACTERISTICS: The center of the flower often has yellow or pale green hairs. *Calochortus cyaneus* is a synonym. This is said to be one of the most prolific of the mariposa lilies. It sometimes has a red stripe when found in Idaho. Blooms in summer in arid soil in sunny locations.

HABITAT: Alkaline slopes, plains, and desert lands.

FORM: Small flower.

EDIBLE PARTS: Flowers, bulb, stem, leaves.

HARVESTABLE: Spring, summer, autumn.

FLAVOR: Sweet.

NOTES: Before the flower emerges, almost all *Calochortus* look nearly identical to death camas, one of the most poisonous plants in the West.

Calochortus nitidus

(BROADFRUIT MARIPOSA LILY)

———

STATE: Idaho.

FLOWER: Lavender petals with a purple crescent near the base.

CHARACTERISTICS: The flower is often hairy in the center. This flower is somewhat rare, so it may be best to photograph it instead of eating the bulb if you find it.

HABITAT: Alkaline slopes, plains, and desert lands.

FORM: Small flower.

EDIBLE PARTS: Flowers, bulb, stem, leaves.

HARVESTABLE: Spring, summer, autumn.

FLAVOR: Sweet.

NOTES: Before the flower emerges, almost all *Calochortus* look nearly identical to death camas, one of the most poisonous plants in the West.

Calochortus nuttallii

(SEGO LILY)

————

STATES: Arizona, Colorado, New Mexico, Utah.

FLOWER: White petals blushing lilac or sometimes red at the tips. Yellow or sometimes white or pale green center with a red, brown, or purple crescent at the base of each petal.

CHARACTERISTICS: The anthers are often yellow, and there are often small yellow hairs at the center of the flower. This is the official state flower of Utah and is widely and easily found in Utah's alkaline deserts. In March of 1911, this flower was made the official state flower of Utah because of its role in saving the pioneers from starvation. Kate C. Snow, president of the Daughters of Utah Pioneers, wrote in 1930 that between 1840 and 1851, Utah residents were forced to ration food. "During this time they learned to dig for and to eat the soft, bulbous root of the sego lily. The memory of this use, quite as much as the natural beauty of the flower, caused it to be selected in after years by the Legislature as the floral emblem of the state" (source: Utah.gov). Other sources credit Native Americans for teaching the pioneers to eat these roots, saving the settlers from starvation.

HABITAT: Alkaline slopes, plains, and desert lands.

FORM: Small flower.

EDIBLE PARTS: Flowers, bulb, stem, leaves.

HARVESTABLE: Spring, summer, autumn.

FLAVOR: Sweet.

NOTES: Before the flower emerges, almost all *Calochortus* look nearly identical to death camas, one of the most poisonous plants in the West.

78

Calochortus panamintensis

(PANAMINT MOUNTAIN MARIPOSA LILY)

————

STATE: Nevada.

FLOWER: White petals blushing to lilac or pink. Yellow center with one or more red or purple crescents at the base of each petal.

CHARACTERISTICS: This is a rare flower, found only in a small area of California and Nevada, and if you find it, it may be best to photograph it instead of eating it.

HABITAT: Alkaline slopes, plains, and desert lands.

FORM: Small flower.

EDIBLE PARTS: Flowers, bulb, stem, leaves.

HARVESTABLE: Spring, summer, autumn.

FLAVOR: Sweet.

NOTES: Before the flower emerges, almost all *Calochortus* look nearly identical to death camas, one of the most poisonous plants in the West.

79

Calochortus striatus

(ALKALI MARIPOSA LILY)

STATE: Nevada.

HABITAT: Alkaline slopes, plains, and desert lands.

FLOWER: White, pink, lilac, or purple petals with many thin dark purple stripes running up and down the petal. Pale yellow or white center.

CHARACTERISTICS: This flower often has white or pink hairs in the center. This is a rare flower and it may be best, if you find it, to photograph it instead of tasting the bulb.

FORM: Small flower.

EDIBLE PARTS: Flowers, bulb, stem, leaves.

HARVESTABLE: Spring, summer, autumn.

FLAVOR: Sweet.

NOTES: Before the flower emerges, almost all *Calochortus* look nearly identical to death camas, one of the most poisonous plants in the West.

Calypso bulbosa

(FAIRY SLIPPER)

STATES: Arizona, Colorado, Idaho, Montana, New Mexico, Utah, Wyoming.

FLOWER: Pink, purple, and yellow.

CHARACTERISTICS: Usually not recommended for harvest because it is scarce. Part of the reason this flower is not widely found is that it is hemi-mycoheterotrophic, which means it is symbiotic with a specific fungus, relying on the underground plant to provide part of its nutrients.

The Lady Bird Johnson Wildflower Center says the genus name comes from the sea nymph Calypso of Homer's Odyssey, "who detained the willing Odysseus on his return from Troy; like Calypso, the plant is beautiful and prefers secluded haunts."

HABITAT: Moist, shady, alkaline soil.

FORM: Small, perennial, herbaceous flower.

EDIBLE PART: Root.

FLAVOR: Buttery flavor, especially in spring.

Calystegia sepium

(HEDGE BINDWEED)

STATES: Arizona, Colorado, Idaho, Montana, Nevada, New Mexico, Utah, Wyoming.

FLOWER: White, sometimes blushing pink or purple.

HABITAT: Moist soil, including lawns, gardens, roadsides, and mountainsides.

FORM: Annual twining vine with funnel-shaped flowers; this plant resembles but is not related to morning glory.

EDIBLE PARTS: Leaves, root, stalks, shoots; all should be eaten only in small amounts.

HARVESTABLE: Summer, autumn.

FLAVOR: Mild, lightly sweet.

Camelina microcarpa

(LESSER GOLD OF PLEASURE)

———

STATES: Arizona, Colorado, Idaho, Montana, Nevada, New Mexico, Utah, Wyoming.

FLOWER: Yellow.

CHARACTERISTICS: Produces small (1/3-inch) kiwi-shaped pods filled with seeds. In botany, these pods are called "pyriform" fruits. *Pyriform* means pear-shaped, but I think the shape (and color when dry) more resemble tiny kiwis in this instance.

HABITAT: Full sun; tolerates a wide range of soils and conditions.

FORM: Annual, with branched stems growing 1–3 feet tall.

EDIBLE PART: Seeds.

HARVESTABLE: August, September.

FLAVOR: A nutty, slightly oily flavor.

Camelina sativa

(GOLD OF PLEASURE)

STATES: Arizona, Idaho, Montana, New Mexico, Utah, Wyoming.

FLOWER: Yellow.

CHARACTERISTICS: Looks almost identical to *Camelina microcarpa*, but *C. sativa* has larger seed pods.

HABITAT: Full sun; tolerates a wide range of soils and conditions.

FORM: Annual, with branched stems growing 1–3 feet tall.

EDIBLE PART: Seeds.

HARVESTABLE: August, September.

FLAVOR: A nutty, slightly oily flavor.

NOTE: We grow *Camelina sativa* in our garden as a grain for home use. *Camelina* is being touted as the next quinoa, a healthy grain that deserves to be more widely eaten because it is high in protein and natural omega-3 fatty acids.

Beyond its health benefits and great flavor, *Camelina* has two other hugely important assets. First, it is one of the easiest grains in the world to harvest and clean. The inflated pods break open easily when dried and are smoothly separated from the grain by sieve. What's more, the pods contain lots of seeds. There is no manual rubbing or cleaning necessary, as is required with wheat, oats, barley, and other common grains.

Second, the grain grows well in rich or poor soils, so it can be sowed in the family garden or in heavy clay soil. The seeds can be planted in late fall for spring germination or in early spring, and only need to be lightly raked into the soil. In some areas, these plants may be dry-farmed, meaning they don't need additional water. The plants can be grown thickly to maximize the grain harvest.

Camelina seeds are available at SeedRenaissance.com. The seeds are 30–40 percent oil and 40 percent protein, according to the National Resource Conservation Center Plant Guide (https://plants.usda.gov/plantguide/pdf/pg_casa2.pdf).

Campanula rapunculoides

(CREEPING BELLFLOWER)

STATES: Colorado, Idaho, Montana, Nevada, New Mexico, Utah, Wyoming.

FLOWER: Purple.

CHARACTERISTICS: We grow this plant in our yard as a beautiful, showy July landscaping plant with spikes of purple flowers. These flowers are drought tolerant and will colonize an area if given regular water, making them a good, tall choice for the back of perennial flower beds. The leaves are best before the flowers open; afterward, they get somewhat tough. Plants that get regular water taste better than plants tolerating drought. Seeds are available at SeedRenaissance.com.

HABITAT: Prefers shade in dry areas.

FORM: Spreading herbaceous perennial flower that can grow 5 feet tall.

EDIBLE PARTS: Leaves, root, flower.

HARVESTABLE: July, August.

FLAVOR: Mild, pleasant. Roots have a slight sweetness.

Capsella bursa-pastoris

(SHEPHERD'S PURSE)

———

STATES: Arizona, Colorado, Idaho, Montana, Nevada, New Mexico, Utah, Wyoming.

FLOWER: White.

CHARACTERISTICS: The heart-shaped leaves are not true leaves: they are actually seed pods.

HABITAT: Sunny, heavy soil.

FORM: Herbaceous annual.

EDIBLE PARTS: The heart-shaped leaves are 3 percent protein; flowers, roots, seeds.

HARVESTABLE: March, April, May.

FLAVOR: Mild and slightly sweet.

Cardamine hirsuta

(HAIRY BITTERCRESS)

STATES: Arizona, New Mexico.

FLOWER: White petals with green or rarely green-purplish sepals (the part that encloses the flower).

CHARACTERISTICS: The flower petals are sometimes entirely absent. Flowers bloom in April, May, and early June. Leaf stalks are hairy.

HABITAT: Grows in water or wet ground.

FORM: White, pink, blue.

EDIBLE PARTS: Leaves, roots, flowers.

HARVESTABLE: Spring.

FLAVOR: Hot, spicy, and bitter, as the "cress" name implies.

Cardamine oligosperma

(SPRING CRESS)

────────

STATES: Colorado, Idaho, Montana, Nevada, Utah, Wyoming.

FLOWER: White and tiny.

CHARACTERISTICS: Found in wet and moist soil and sometimes in dry soil too. Flowers bloom from March through July. The plant grows from a taproot.

HABITAT: Grows in water or wet ground.

FORM: Herbaceous flower, growing 18 inches tall.

FLOWER: White, pink, blue.

EDIBLE PARTS: Leaves, roots, flowers.

HARVESTABLE: Spring.

FLAVOR: Hot, spicy, and bitter, as the "cress" name implies.

Cardamine pensylvanica

(PENNSYLVANIA BITTERCRESS)

———

STATES: Colorado, Idaho, Montana, Nevada, New Mexico, Utah, Wyoming.

FLOWER: White.

CHARACTERISTICS: Blooms in spring and early summer. Typically found in moist soils.

HABITAT: Grows in water or wet ground.

FORM: Herbaceous flower, growing 18 inches tall.

EDIBLE PARTS: Leaves, roots, flowers.

HARVESTABLE: Spring and early summer.

FLAVOR: Hot, spicy, and bitter, as the "cress" name implies.

Cardaria draba

(WHITETOP, HOARY CRESS)

STATES: Arizona, Colorado, Idaho, Montana, Nevada, New Mexico, Utah, Wyoming.

FLOWER: White.

HABITAT: Roadsides, ditch banks, fields.

FORM: Herbaceous perennial flower, growing up to 24 inches tall.

EDIBLE PARTS: Leaves, seeds.

HARVESTABLE: Spring.

FLAVOR: Spicy radish or cress flavor. The seeds are used as a pepper substitute.

NOTES: This plant is commonly found growing thickly on roadsides and ditch banks in spring, but harvesting from any place where the plants may have been exposed to pesticides, herbicides, or car exhaust is not recommended. Because this plant is so spicy, it is not one of my favorites, but people who love horseradish often love this vegetable.

91

Carduus nutans

(MUSK THISTLE)

STATES: Arizona, Colorado, Idaho, Montana, Nevada, New Mexico, Utah, Wyoming.

FLOWER: Purple.

HABITAT: Open spaces; disturbed soil.

FORM: One to seven spiny-branched stems, growing up to six feet tall.

EDIBLE PARTS: The pith of the stems can be eaten boiled; the young flower is used as milk rennet.

HARVESTABLE: Late spring, early summer.

FLAVOR: Mild.

NOTES: The flowers of this and most large purple-flowered thistles can be used to curdle milk for making soft cheeses at home.

HOMEMADE SOFT CHEESE

1. Pick the flower head just as the petals begin to appear, before the flower opens.
2. Rinse, place in a gallon of milk, and leave at room temperature until the milk has turned thick and begun to separate into curds and whey. Remove flower head.
3. Line a sieve with a straining cloth. Pour curd and whey into the sieve and allow whey to drain into a bowl.
4. When the whey is drained, the condensed curd that remains in the sieve is a soft cheese that can be used immediately or refrigerated for several days.

For instructions to make hard cheese and other recipes and information, see my book *Make Your Own Cheese: 12 Recipes for Cheddar, Parmesan, Mozzarella, Self-Reliant Cheese, and More!*

Carum carvi

(COMMON CARAWAY)

STATES: Colorado, Idaho, Montana, New Mexico, Utah, Wyoming.

FLOWER: White.

CHARACTERISTICS: This is a common spice, sold in grocery stores worldwide.

HABITAT: Fields, roadsides, disturbed soil.

FORM: Biennial flower, growing up to 4 feet tall.

EDIBLE PARTS: Leaves, root, seeds.

HARVESTABLE: Root is best in the first year. Leaves are best when young and tender.

FLAVOR: Savory.

Castilleja angustifolia

(NORTHWESTERN INDIAN PAINTBRUSH)

———

STATES: Arizona, Colorado, Idaho, Montana, Nevada, New Mexico, Utah, Wyoming.

FLOWER: Red or sometimes pinkish.

CHARACTERISTICS: Found typically in rocky or sandy soils and sometimes in clay. Used historically for medicinal purposes, including regulating menstruation. This species has a handful of synonyms, which represents that fact that many *Castilleja* species are difficult to tell apart and that there is debate about whether some species are distinct or simply subspecies (varieties).

HABITAT: Desert, alkaline soil, roadsides, sagebrush plains.

FORM: Showy spring perennial flower, growing up to 30 inches tall.

EDIBLE PARTS: Flowers, nectar.

HARVESTABLE: Spring, summer (depending on elevation and shade).

FLAVOR: Pleasant.

NOTES: Beautiful spikes of this spring flower grow abundantly on my farm in the desert and may seem too beautiful to pick, but the flowers are worth tasting. They may not be a meal in themselves, but they brighten any salad and serve as a conversation-worthy garnish.

There are some reports that the flowers of all *Castilleja* species can be high in selenium, so do not eat many, especially if you are already taking selenium as a supplement.

Castilleja applegatei Fernald

(WAVYLEAF INDIAN PAINTBRUSH)

STATES: Idaho, Nevada, Utah, Wyoming.

FLOWER: Red.

CHARACTERISTICS: This species was historically used to make an adult beverage, which may explain why one of its synonyms is *C. martinii*. *Castilleja* species are difficult to tell apart, and there is debate about whether some species are distinct or simply subspecies (varieties).

HABITAT: Desert, alkaline soil, roadsides, sagebrush plains.

FORM: Showy spring perennial flower, growing up to 30 inches tall.

EDIBLE PARTS: Flowers, nectar.

HARVESTABLE: Spring, summer (depending on elevation and shade).

FLAVOR: Pleasant.

Castilleja aquariensis

(INDIAN PAINTBRUSH)

———

STATE: Utah.

FLOWER: Yellow.

CHARACTERISTICS: This yellow flower color is rare among *Castilleja* species. This plant is fairly rare, and if you find it, it may be best to take pictures instead of harvesting for eating. At the time of printing, there were only about 75,000 plants known to exist. The flowers are so beautiful that it should be commercially cultivated.

HABITAT: Desert, alkaline soil, roadsides, sagebrush plains.

FORM: Showy spring perennial flower, growing up to 30 inches tall.

EDIBLE PARTS: Flowers, nectar.

HARVESTABLE: Spring, summer (depending on elevation and shade).

FLAVOR: Pleasant.

95

Castilleja hispida

(HARSH INDIAN PAINTBRUSH)

STATES: Idaho, Montana, Nevada.

FLOWER: Red and rarely yellow.

CHARACTERISTICS: This flower has a more chunky, sectional pattern than other *castillejas*.

HABITAT: Desert, alkaline soil, roadsides, sagebrush plains.

FORM: Showy spring perennial flower, growing up to 30 inches tall.

EDIBLE PARTS: Flowers, nectar.

HARVESTABLE: Spring, summer (depending on elevation and shade).

FLAVOR: Pleasant.

Castilleja linariifolia

(WYOMING INDIAN PAINTBRUSH)

———————

STATES: Arizona, Colorado, Idaho, Montana, Nevada, New Mexico, Utah, Wyoming.

FLOWER: Red.

CHARACTERISTICS: Some of the flowers have yellow-green "beaks," which is an unusual form of flower that looks exactly as it sounds—a flower with a beak sticking out.

HABITAT: Desert, alkaline soil, roadsides, sagebrush plains.

FORM: Showy spring perennial flower, growing up to 30 inches tall.

EDIBLE PARTS: Flowers, nectar.

HARVESTABLE: Spring, summer (depending on elevation and shade).

FLAVOR: Pleasant.

Castilleja miniata

(GIANT RED INDIAN PAINTBRUSH)

———

STATES: Arizona, Colorado, Idaho, Montana, Nevada, New Mexico, Utah, Wyoming.

FLOWER: Red, orange, or occasionally yellow.

CHARACTERISTICS: Unlike some of its cousins, this plant tends to grow in moist soil. The Consortium of Midwest Herbaria notes that historically, the bark of the roots of this plant has been used by Native Americans to dye deerskin.

HABITAT: Desert, alkaline soil, roadsides, sagebrush plains.

FORM: Showy spring perennial flower, growing up to 4 feet tall, which is taller than most of its cousins.

EDIBLE PARTS: Flowers, nectar.

HARVESTABLE: Spring, summer (depending on elevation and shade).

FLAVOR: Pleasant.

Castilleja sessiliflora

(DOWNY PAINTEDCUP)

———————

STATES: Arizona, Colorado, Montana, New Mexico, Wyoming.

FLOWER: Mostly pink or red with one yellowish-green flower per cluster.

CHARACTERISTICS: Prefers sandy soil. Native Americans drank the nectar of the flowers.

HABITAT: Desert, alkaline soil, roadsides, sagebrush plains.

FORM: Showy spring perennial flower, growing up to 30 inches tall.

EDIBLE PARTS: Flowers, nectar.

HARVESTABLE: Spring, summer (depending on elevation and shade).

FLAVOR: Pleasant.

Celtis laevigata

(SOUTHERN HACKBERRY,
SUGARBERRY)

———

100

STATES: Arizona, Colorado, Idaho, Nevada, New Mexico, Utah, Wyoming.

FLOWER: Green and white.

CHARACTERISTICS: The fleshy fruit, called a "drupe," is orange or brown before turning red when ripe. According to the Consortium of Midwest Herbaria, the bark was used by Native Americans to treat sore throats and venereal diseases.

HABITAT: Sandy or rocky soils near water.

FORM: Tree, growing up to 80 feet tall.

BERRY: Brown, red, orange, black, or purple depending on location, condition, and subspecies.

EDIBLE PART: Berry-sized fruit.

HARVESTABLE: Early autumn.

FLAVOR: Sweet.

NOTES: This tree grows as a shrub, small tree, or huge tree depending on conditions. Hackberry prefers locations with access to water and grows larger in those locations.

While the flavor is good, the problem with hackberries is that each berry is a thin amount of flesh around a large pit; otherwise, they might be sold commercially.

Like many of the species in this book, there are cousins of these plants worth trying that grow in other areas of the country, but I don't list them here because they don't grow in the Rocky Mountain West.

Celtis occidentalis

(COMMON HACKBERRY)

STATES: Colorado, Montana, New Mexico, Utah, Wyoming.

FLOWER: Green and white.

CHARACTERISTICS: The young berries, called drupes, are orange before becoming fully ripe and then turn purple or black when ripe.

HABITAT: Sandy or rocky soils near water.

FORM: Tree, growing up to 80 feet tall.

BERRY: Brown, red, orange, black, or purple depending on location, condition, and subspecies.

EDIBLE PART: Berry-sized fruit.

HARVESTABLE: Early autumn.

FLAVOR: Sweet.

NOTES: This tree grows as a shrub, small tree, or huge tree depending on conditions. Hackberry prefers locations with access to water and grows larger in those locations.

While the flavor is good, the problem with hackberries is that each berry is a thin amount of flesh around a large pit; otherwise, they might be sold commercially.

Celtis reticulata

(NETLEAF HACKBERRY)

STATES: Arizona, Colorado, Idaho, Nevada, New Mexico, Utah, Wyoming.

FLOWER: Green and white.

CHARACTERISTICS: The young fruits, called drupes, are orange before being ripe and then red or red-black when ripe.

HABITAT: Sandy or rocky soils near water.

FORM: Tree, growing up to 80 feet tall.

BERRY: Brown, red, orange, black, or purple depending on location, condition, and subspecies.

EDIBLE PARTS: Berry-sized fruit.

HARVESTABLE: Early autumn.

FLAVOR: Sweet.

103

Cenchrus longispinus

(LONGSPINE SANDBUR)

———

STATES: Arizona, Colorado, Montana, Nevada, New Mexico, Utah, Wyoming.

FLOWER: Green.

CHARACTERISTICS: Its seems to me that when a plant is as hated as this one is, our best revenge is to feast upon it. However, feast carefully, because to get to the seeds, you have to go through the burs. Inside each bur are one to three tiny edible seeds. This plant is extra horrible because research has shown that some of the seeds germinate the first year, and others germinate in later years, making this painful plant extra hard to eradicate.

HABITAT: Heavy, disturbed soils, roadsides, fields.

FORM: Spiny, spreading low-growing grass.

EDIBLE PART: Seeds.

HARVESTABLE: Summer, autumn.

FLAVOR: Mild.

Centaurea cyanus

(GARDEN CORNFLOWER)

STATES: Arizona, Colorado, Idaho, Montana, Nevada, New Mexico, Utah, Wyoming.

FLOWER: Blue. Natural hybrids are the cause of some of the flower color variety.

CHARACTERISTICS: Dried flower petals are sold to make a tea that is a widely used medicinal. Also, an edible blue dye can be made from the flower.

HABITAT: Roadsides, plains, meadows.

FORM: Slender annual flower, typically 2–3 feet tall.

EDIBLE PART: Flower.

HARVESTABLE: Early summer.

FLAVOR: Mild.

Centaurea jacea

(BROWN KNAPWEED)

STATES: Idaho, Montana, Utah.

FLOWER: Pink, purple, or pale blue. Natural hybrids are the cause of some of the flower color variety.

HABITAT: Roadsides, plains, meadows.

FORM: Slender annual flower, typically 2–3 feet tall.

EDIBLE PART: Cooked young leaves.

HARVESTABLE: Early summer.

FLAVOR: Mild.

Chamerion angustifolium

(FIREWEED)

STATES: Arizona, Colorado, Idaho, Montana, Nevada, New Mexico, Utah, Wyoming.

FLOWER: Red, purple.

CHARACTERISTICS: I often eat the leaves when hiking in summer. They are pleasant and more substantial than most greens. The flowers also have a mild flavor and are fun to pop in your mouth as you walk along a trail.

HABITAT: Mountains near water.

FORM: Slender, showy flower growing up to 5 feet tall.

EDIBLE PARTS: Flowers, leaves, root, stem.

HARVESTABLE: Summer

FLAVOR: Mild.

SYNONYM: *Epilobium angustifolium*.

Chamerion latifolium

(DWARF FIREWEED)

———

STATES: Colorado, Idaho, Montana, Nevada, Utah, Wyoming.

FLOWER: Red, purple.

CHARACTERISTICS: The flowers of this plant look very similar to its cousin, *Chamerion angustifolium*, but it is much smaller in overall height.

HABITAT: Mountains near water.

FORM: Slender, showy flower growing 6–18 inches tall.

EDIBLE PARTS: Flowers, leaves, root, stem.

HARVESTABLE: Summer.

FLAVOR: Mild.

SYNONYM: *Epilobium latifolium.*

Chenopodium album

(LAMBSQUARTERS, WILD SPINACH)

STATES: Arizona, Colorado, Idaho, Montana, Nevada, New Mexico, Utah, Wyoming.

FLOWER: Green.

CHARACTERISTICS: The flowers are somewhat unusual because they do not have petals. Some botanists say that because *Chenopodium* species can look so similar, sometimes comparing seeds is the best way to tell them apart. In addition to having a long history of being eaten raw as salad and the seed ground for mush, the plant also has many historical medicinal uses.

HABITAT: Sunny, open spaces in heavy soils.

FORM: Herbaceous plant typically growing 4–5 feet tall.

EDIBLE PARTS: Leaves, seeds.

HARVESTABLE: Spring, summer.

FLAVOR: Mild.

NOTES: Lambsquarters is one of the wild greens I eat the most, simply because it grows so prolifically on our property.

Chenopodium berlandieri

(GOOSEFOOT, NETSEED LAMBSQUARTERS)

———————

STATES: Arizona, Colorado, Idaho, Montana, Nevada, New Mexico, Utah, Wyoming.

FLOWER: Green.

CHARACTERISTICS: *Berlandieri* is in honor of Jean-Louis Berlandier (1805–1851), a botanist born in Geneva, Switzerland, who came to Mexico and Texas at age twenty as part of a botanical expedition. He never went home. His important original sketches and writings are today found in museums and in the Library of Congress. Because he knew the borderlands of Texas and Mexico so well, in 1850, he was asked to join a committee to define the US–Mexico border. Sadly, a year later, he drowned in a river in Mexico, but his contribution to botanical knowledge lives on in this and other plants.

HABITAT: Sunny, open spaces in heavy soils.

FORM: Herbaceous plant typically growing 4–5 feet tall.

EDIBLE PARTS: Leaves, seeds.

HARVESTABLE: Spring, summer.

FLAVOR: Mild.

Chenopodium murale

(NETTLELEAF GOOSEFOOT)

STATES: Arizona, Idaho, Montana, Nevada, New Mexico, Utah, Wyoming.

FLOWER: Green.

CHARACTERISTICS: The seeds of this plant have sharp edges, unlike the other *Chenopodium* species in this book. *Chenopodium* is Latin for "goosefoot," which is the shape of the leaves of this plant and its cousins.

HABITAT: Sunny, open spaces in heavy soils.

FORM: Herbaceous plant typically growing 4–5 feet tall.

EDIBLE PARTS: Leaves, seeds.

HARVESTABLE: Spring, summer.

FLAVOR: Mild.

Chorispora tenella

(BLUE MUSTARD)

STATES: Arizona, Colorado, Idaho, Montana, Nevada, New Mexico, Utah, Wyoming.

FLOWER: Blue, purple.

CHARACTERISTICS: It is not unusual to find this species growing in a massive purple carpet in spring, covering waste spaces, pastures, roadsides, or fields. It can be very beautiful.

HABITAT: Disturbed soils.

FORM: Small, low-growing herbaceous flower.

EDIBLE PARTS: Leaves, flowers seedpod.

HARVESTABLE: Spring.

FLAVOR: Radish, spicy flavor.

Chrysothamnus nauseosus

(RUBBER RABBITBRUSH)

STATES: Arizona, New Mexico, Utah.

FLOWER: Yellow.

CHARACTERISTICS: There are almost two dozen known varieties of this species, and it also easily creates natural hybrids with its cousins. Because it has so many varieties, it can vary widely in size, shape, and the color of the stems, but the flowers are usually yellow. There is much discussion about how to classify species and varieties. The US Forest Service says this plant gets its name because the sap contains rubber. "Rabbitbrush was first tested as a source of high-quality rubber during World War II. In recent decades, there has been renewed interest in its potential for production of rubber, resins, and other chemicals. Compounds in rubber rabbitbrush are being evaluated for nematicides, anti-malarial properties, and insect repellents. Rubber rabbitbrush has also been identified as a potential source of biomass and biocrude fuels."

HABITAT: Desert, alkaline soils.

FORM: Flowering bush.

EDIBLE PARTS: Leaves, gum.

HARVESTABLE: Spring, summer, autumn.

FLAVOR: Mint.

NOTES: This bush can be used as a landscape plant because it produces an attractive mass of yellow flowers through most of summer and autumn.

SYNONYM: *Ericameria nauseosa.*

Chrysothamnus viscidiflorus

(DOUGLAS RABBITBRUSH, GREEN RABBITBRUSH)

STATES: Arizona, Nevada, New Mexico, Utah.

FLOWER: Yellow.

CHARACTERISTICS: This plant has green stems and leaves, unlike its cousin *Chrysothamnus nauseosus*. The Consortium of Midwest Herbaria says this plant has many historical uses, including various medicinal uses, using the root as chewing gum, using the branches as thatching, and using the flowers to make a yellow-orange dye.

HABITAT: Desert, alkaline soils.

FORM: Flowering bush.

EDIBLE PARTS: Leaves, gum.

HARVESTABLE: Spring, summer, autumn.

FLAVOR: Mint.

NOTES: This bush can be used as a landscape plant because it produces an attractive mass of yellow flowers through most of summer and autumn.

Cichorium intybus

(CHICORY)

———

STATES: Arizona, Colorado, Idaho, Montana, Nevada, New Mexico, Utah, Wyoming.

FLOWER: Blue.

NOTES: Flowers open until noon and are a rare shade of blue and showy. Inulin, a prebiotic fiber, is found in the roots; it is naturally sweet, has a good glycemic load, and is found in many commercial yogurts. This plant has infested our backyard pasture and is almost impossible to get rid of. It is extremely drought tolerant.

HABITAT: Disturbed soils in sunny, dry locations.

FORM: Slender, wiry flower, typically growing 3 feet tall.

EDIBLE PARTS: Root, leaves.

HARVESTABLE: Spring, summer.

FLAVOR: The leaves have a mild flavor. The root has a grasslike flavor with a mildly bitter aftertaste, especially when it has been exposed to drought; tastes best roasted. Flowers are edible but bitter.

The stalks of the plant can be almost wiry, and the fiber has been used to make rope, paper, and fabric.

Cirsium arvense

(CANADA THISTLE)

STATES: Arizona, Colorado, Idaho, Montana, Nevada, New Mexico, Utah, Wyoming.

FLOWER: Purple.

CHARACTERISTICS: This is an aggressive weed. The US National Agricultural Library says it was likely introduced in the United States in the 1600s, possibly as an accidental addition to imported farm seeds.

HABITAT: Strongly invasive in disturbed soil, wastelands, and roadsides.

FORM: Spreads branching, spiny stems growing up to 7 feet tall.

EDIBLE PARTS: Roots of first year, leaves minus spines, stems peeled.

HARVESTABLE: Spring, summer.

FLAVOR: Lemony.

NOTES: Seeds can be roasted for eating.

OTHER USES: Thistle down is easily lit by a flint and steel and makes excellent fire-starting tinder.

The flower head, picked just as the petals begin to open, can be rinsed and used to curdle milk to make cheese. See recipe under musk thistle (edible plant #91).

Cirsium ochrocentrum

(YELLOWSPINE THISTLE)

STATES: Arizona, Colorado, New Mexico, Utah, Wyoming.

FLOWER: Red or pink; occasionally purple.

CHARACTERISTICS: Shorter than most other *Cirsium* species.

HABITAT: Strongly invasive in disturbed soil, wastelands, and roadsides.

FORM: Spreads branching, spiny stems growing up to 7 feet tall.

EDIBLE PARTS: Roots of first year, leaves minus spines, stems peeled.

HARVESTABLE: Spring, summer.

FLAVOR: Lemony.

NOTES: Seeds can be roasted for eating.

OTHER USES: Thistle down is easily lit by a flint and steel and makes excellent fire-starting tinder.

The flower head, picked just as the petals begin to open, can be rinsed and used to curdle milk to make cheese. See recipe under musk thistle (edible plant #91).

Cirsium vulgare

(COMMON THISTLE, BULL
THISTLE)

STATES: Arizona, Colorado, Idaho, Montana, Nevada, New Mexico, Utah, Wyoming.

FLOWER: Purple and occasionally white.

CHARACTERISTICS: This plant is a host for the larvae of some butterfly species, and some botanists have noted that this may help keep the populations in check. It is also an important source of food for many species of bees, bumblebees, and moths.

HABITAT: Strongly invasive in disturbed soil, wastelands, and roadsides.

FORM: Spreads branching, spiny stems growing up to 7 feet tall.

EDIBLE PARTS: Roots of first year, leaves minus spines, stems peeled.

HARVESTABLE: Spring, summer.

FLAVOR: Lemony.

NOTES: Seeds can be roasted for eating.

OTHER USES: Thistle down is easily lit by a flint and steel and makes excellent fire-starting tinder.

The flower head, picked just as the petals begin to open, can be rinsed and used to curdle milk to make cheese. See recipe under musk thistle (edible plant #91).

Claytonia perfoliata

(MINER'S LETTUCE, WINTER PURSLANE)

STATES: Arizona, Colorado, Idaho, Montana, Nevada, Utah, Wyoming.

FLOWER: White.

CHARACTERISTICS: Claytonia is also available from some garden seed companies for growing in the home garden and does particularly well in winter greenhouses and cold frames. Very cold-hardy vegetable.

HABITAT: Grows in water or wet soil.

FORM: Low-growing, flowering herb, up to 12 inches tall.

EDIBLE PARTS: Flowers, leaves, root.

HARVESTABLE: Spring, summer.

FLAVOR: Crunchy, juicy, and mild when grown in cool to cold temperatures but becomes bitter when exposed to heat.

Cleome serrulata

(ROCKY MOUNTAIN BEE PLANT)

STATES: Arizona, Colorado, Idaho, Montana, Nevada, New Mexico, Utah, Wyoming.

FLOWER: Purple.

CHARACTERISTICS: One of the most beautiful of all wildflowers of the West. This is a huge, showy plant in August and definitely should be grown more as a landscape plant.

This is the hottest wild edible I have ever tasted. The heat is immediate and painful from leaves, flowers, and seed pods—so hot that my tongue felt slightly burned for days afterward. Yikes! It is possible the heat may be dissipated by cooking, but I'm not going to test my theory to find out.

If you love hot, hot peppers, maybe this plant is for you! Seeds are available at SeedRenaissance.com.

HABITAT: Wastelands, roadsides in open, sunny locations.

FORM: Branching, stemmed flower, growing up to 4 feet tall.

EDIBLE PARTS: Petals, leaves, seeds, seedpods.

HARVESTABLE: Summer.

FLAVOR: Hot.

Convolvulus arvensis

(FIELD BINDWEED)

STATES: Arizona, Colorado, Idaho, Montana, Nevada, New Mexico, Utah, Wyoming.

FLOWER: White.

HABITAT: Disturbed land, gardens, yards, fences, roadsides.

FORM: Slender, twining vine.

EDIBLE PARTS: Leaves, flowers.

HARVESTABLE: Summer, autumn

FLAVOR: Mild.

NOTES: The argument over whether the various species of bindweed are edible or not will probably never stop. Experts agree they have high levels of alkaloids in them, like rhubarb and many other plants, and everyone agrees that alkaloids can be difficult to remove from the body and can damage organ function over the long term.

I eat field bindweed sparingly. I've never had any problems with it, but this doesn't mean that it's not dangerous. There are many herbs and spices sold in the grocery store that are toxic at high levels, and no one bats an eye at them because everyone just understands that cinnamon, for example, is something you only eat in small amounts. I eat field bindweed the same way—sparingly.

Many people in the edible wild greens movement eat field bindweed, but many other people think we are crazy. (In my experience, the people who think that also tend to drink soda, which is dangerously unhealthy, so there we are.)

Conyza canadensis

(HORSEWEED)

STATES: Arizona, Colorado, Idaho, Montana, Nevada, New Mexico, Utah, Wyoming.

FLOWER: White.

HABITAT: Disturbed soil and waste spaces.

FORM: Branched single-stem flower, growing up to 3 feet tall.

EDIBLE PART: Leaves.

HARVESTABLE: Spring, summer.

FLAVOR: Onion.

NOTES: Native, and one of the rare plants in this book that is found in every state in America.

SYNONYM: *Erigeron canadensis.*

Cornus canadensis

(CREEPING DOGWOOD)

STATES: Colorado, Idaho, Montana, New Mexico, Wyoming.

FLOWER: White.

CHARACTERISTICS: Because of its beautiful flowers, berries, leaves, and low-growing habit, this plant is sometimes used as a landscape plant. This plant is somewhat rare in nature, unlike its cousin the western dogwood, which is prolific. Produces red berries.

HABITAT: Mountainsides, shady areas.

FORM: Shrub.

EDIBLE PART: Fruit.

HARVESTABLE: Summer.

FLAVOR: Slightly sweet, mealy; many people say tasteless unless exactly ripe.

OTHER USES: Dogwood berries are high in natural pectin, and you can use them to make pectin.

Cornus sericea

(WESTERN DOGWOOD)

STATES: Arizona, Colorado, Idaho, Montana, Nevada, New Mexico, Utah, Wyoming.

FLOWER: White.

CHARACTERISTICS: In the West, this wild native is widely used as a landscape plant, including in my own yard, because of its beautiful bright red branches. In summer, it is a green bush, but in winter, the leaves are shed, leaving a stunning sculptural centerpiece, adding a splash of color on gray snowy days. As I write this, the snow is gently piling up outside my window and the dogwood only becomes more pleasing to see. My wife and I use many wild natives as decorative landscape plants on our large property. The white berries with their creamy, smooth texture are also visually interesting in the summer. When I take students into the canyons in summer for wild berry classes, I try to avoid dogwood berries because time is short, but I always get asked about them. Students find them fascinating. But when they taste them, the love goes away. One student said dogwood berries tasted like something you would use to clean your bathroom: astringent, bitter, and sour all at once.

HABITAT: Mountainsides, shady areas.

FORM: Shrub.

EDIBLE PART: Fruit.

HARVESTABLE: Summer.

FLAVOR: Bitter.

NOTES: Produces white berries. As a general rule, eating white berries is not a good idea, because many of them are poisonous.

OTHER USES: Dogwood berries are high in natural pectin, and you can use them to make pectin.

123

Cornus unalaschkensis

(BUNCHBERRY)

———

STATE: Idaho.

FLOWER: White.

CHARACTERISTICS: Some experts believe this is the same as *Cornus canadensis*, while others disagree.

HABITAT: Mountainsides, shady areas.

FORM: Shrub.

EDIBLE PART: Fruit.

HARVESTABLE: Summer.

FLAVOR: Slightly sweet if exactly ripe. Some people say boiling these berries improves the flavor and texture. If you were going to go to the trouble of boiling them, you might as well add some natural stevia sugar or birch sugar and make jam from them. For jam recipes using stevia and birch sweeteners, see my book *The Stevia Solution*.

NOTES: Produces red berries.

OTHER USES: Dogwood berries are high in natural pectin, and you can use them to make pectin.

Corylus cornuta

(BEAKED HAZELNUT)

125

STATES: Colorado, Idaho, Montana, Wyoming.

FLOWER: Yellow.

CHARACTERISTICS: The name comes from the husk, which extends beyond the nut to form a beak. These nuts are 15 percent protein by weight, making them a healthy, high-energy food. This bush is often found as an understory plant in aspen and pine forests and grows quite dense if there is somewhat regular water. The bushes that get better light and water produce the most nuts. The bush flowers in early spring, but the nuts are not ripe until early autumn. Once they are ripe, they begin falling to the ground. All kinds of animals rely on the nuts for food, so you might want to leave enough to share if you harvest these. In the shell, the nuts can be up to the size of a quarter. The flower of this bush is a long catkin. Foraging for these nuts is a popular pastime because the flavor is delicious, they are easy to get off the bush, and they can even be harvested off the ground if you can get them before the wildlife. Some people mix wild elderberries with wild hazelnuts to make ice cream pie, which sounds like a perfect treat to me. These bushes are sold commercially too, and we have made space to add them to our property, but as with most nut trees, it takes about five years for them to start producing a good harvest of nuts and it is necessary to plant at least two for pollination.

HABITAT: Mountainsides, shady areas.

FORM: Shrubby deciduous thicket, typically 10–20 feet tall.

EDIBLE PART: Nuts.

HARVESTABLE: Autumn.

FLAVOR: Nut.

Crataegus chrysocarpa

(RED HAW TREE, FIREBERRY HAWTHORN)

STATES: Colorado, Idaho, Montana, New Mexico, Utah, Wyoming.

FLOWER: White.

CHARACTERISTICS: Produces thorny, smooth twigs.

FRUIT: Red, black.

HABITAT: Mountainsides.

FORM: Native tree or tall shrub, growing up to 20 feet tall.

EDIBLE PARTS: Fruit, flowers.

HARVESTABLE: Autumn.

FLAVOR: Mildly sweet. Some people describe the flavor as overripe apple.

NOTES: American Indians commonly gathered the berry-sized fruits for eating fresh and drying as pressed cakes for winter use. The dried berries are also widely used medicinally today.

Hawthorns don't come by their name without reason. Depending on the species, **they have straight or curved thorns an inch or more long, so beware!** To add insult to injury, some people have allergic reactions when punctured by these thorns.

In the legend of lumberjack Paul Bunyan, he uses the thorny hawthorn as a back scratcher.

Hawthorns are also noted for their beautiful autumn leaf-color display: they turn scarlet, orange, and purple.

Birds and animals strongly favor the fruit and often clean up the whole tree, so there is little litter on the ground.

Some experts say not to eat the seeds of hawthorn fruits, while others disagree.

Crataegus douglasii

(BLACK HAWTHORN)

STATES: Idaho, Montana, Nevada, Wyoming.

FLOWER: White.

CHARACTERISTICS: Produces smooth twigs often with thorns but sometimes without. The flowers attract butterflies. *Douglasii* is in honor of Scottish botanist David Douglas (1799–1834), who made three botanical collecting trips to America at a time when Great Britain's horticulture community was fascinated by what could be discovered in the United States. Douglas visited the eastern and western United States and even Hawaii. He cultivated 240 US species in Britain and was famous for his work growing US pine trees there.

FRUIT: Red, black.

HABITAT: Mountainsides.

FORM: Native tree, growing up to 35 feet tall.

EDIBLE PARTS: Fruit, flowers.

HARVESTABLE: Autumn.

FLAVOR: Mildly sweet. Some people describe the flavor as overripe apple.

NOTES: American Indians commonly gathered the berry-sized fruits for eating fresh and drying as pressed cakes for winter use. The dried berries are also widely used medicinally today.

Crataegus erythropoda

(CERRO HAWTHORN)

———

STATES: Arizona, Colorado, New Mexico, Utah, Wyoming.

FLOWER: White.

CHARACTERISTICS: This tree was once sold under the commercial name "chocolate haw" but is less available to purchase today. Produces smooth twigs with 1-inch thorns. Flowers in May and June like most *Crataegus* species.

FRUIT: Red, black.

HABITAT: Mountainsides.

FORM: Native tree.

EDIBLE PARTS: Fruit, flowers.

HARVESTABLE: Autumn.

FLAVOR: Mildly sweet. Some people describe the flavor as overripe apple.

129

Crataegus monogyna

(COMMON HAWTHORN, ENGLISH HAWTHORN, ONE-SEED HAWTHORN)

STATES: Montana, Utah.

FLOWER: White, occasionally pink.

CHARACTERISTICS: Like most hawthorns, this tree can produce 2,000 berries, called "haws."

FRUIT: Red, black.

HABITAT: Mountainsides.

FORM: Native tree, growing up to 35 feet tall, but they sometimes grows 10 feet tall or lower as a shrub, often depending on water.

EDIBLE PARTS: Fruit, flowers.

HARVESTABLE: Autumn.

FLAVOR: Mildly sweet. Some people describe the flavor as overripe apple.

Crataegus rivularis

(RIVER HAWTHORN)

STATES: Arizona, Colorado, Idaho, Montana, Nevada, New Mexico, Utah, Wyoming.

FLOWER: White.

CHARACTERISTICS: Ray Mears, a naturalist, has a great video online showing how to harvest haws and make no-cook haw jelly and traditional haw fruit leather—just make sure your hands are clean! A small improvement on his technique would be to take the berries in the kitchen and use a strainer. The American Indians widely ate raw and preserved haw fruit and likely made haw fruit leather much as Mears does in his video—and it is surprising that you can collect the berries and have the leather ready to dry without cooking or electricity in less than fifteen minutes. His technique—gather the ripe berries, mash them in a bowl, let the natural pectin set up for a few minutes, then slice and air dry—works with the berries of any haw species. Haw flakes are a traditional Chinese wafer candy made from haw fruit and are available in the United States on Amazon.com for the adventurous eater.

FRUIT: Red, black.

HABITAT: Mountainsides.

FORM: Native tree.

EDIBLE PARTS: Fruit, flowers.

HARVESTABLE: Autumn.

FLAVOR: Mildly sweet. Some people describe the flavor as overripe apple.

Some experts say not to eat the seeds of hawthorn fruits, while others disagree.

Crataegus saligna

(WILLOW HAWTHORN)

———

STATES: Colorado, Utah.

FLOWER: White.

CHARACTERISTICS: This species of haw is rare in the wild, partially because it only exists in the arid West and grows only along rivers where there is constant access to water. It was discovered in 1896 by botanist Edward Lee Greene along the lower Cimarron River, Colorado. Greene (1843–1915), who named more than 4,400 species in his career, is a hugely important figure in the history of American botany. He published near 500 papers, wrote an important botany book called *Landmarks of Botanical History*, and was the first-ever professor of botany at the University of California, Berkeley.

FRUIT: Red, black.

HABITAT: Mountainsides.

FORM: Native tree.

EDIBLE PARTS: Fruit, flowers.

HARVESTABLE: Autumn.

FLAVOR: Mildly sweet. Some people describe the flavor as overripe apple.

Crataegus succulenta

(FLESHY HAWTHORN FRUIT)

STATES: Arizona, Colorado, Idaho, Montana, New Mexico, Utah, Wyoming.

FLOWER: White.

CHARACTERISTICS: One expert has called this the most wide-ranging hawthorn in North America because it is wild in most of the United States and Canada.

FRUIT: Red, black.

HABITAT: Mountainsides.

FORM: Native tree, growing up to 25 feet tall, but it is more often half that size.

EDIBLE PARTS: Fruit, flowers.

HARVESTABLE: Autumn.

FLAVOR: Mildly sweet. Some people describe the flavor as overripe apple.

SYNONYM: *Crataegus macracantha*.

Crepis acuminata

(TAPERTIP HAWKSBEARD)

STATES: Arizona, Colorado, Idaho, Montana, Nevada, New Mexico, Utah, Wyoming.

FLOWER: Yellow.

CHARACTERISTICS: The classification differences between many *Crepis* species can be as small as slightly different leaves, which is why there is also disagreement among experts about whether different plants are different species or simply different varieties. It's useful to remember that at this level of detail, classifications are simply humans trying to describe what Mother Nature has created. To her, our attempts to define her work are probably futile.

HABITAT: Desert, strongly alkaline soil.

FORM: Herbaceous flower, typically growing about 12 inches tall.

EDIBLE PART: Leaves.

HARVESTABLE: Spring.

FLAVOR: Mild.

NOTES: In early spring, when the plants have just emerged from the ground, *Crepis* species can look somewhat like salsify species, which emerge at the same time. Hawksbeards are toothier at this stage than salsify, while salsify is more frilly, but both create an almost perfect circle of leaves low against the ground. Luckily, both salsify and hawksbeard are equally edible and delicious at this early stage, so even if you struggle to tell them apart, you can eat them. However, don't harvest the salsify leaves too much because then they won't form the parsnip-like root that they are prized for.

Crepis atribarba

(SLENDER HAWKSBEARD)

STATES: Colorado, Idaho, Montana, Nevada, Utah, Wyoming.

FLOWER: Yellow.

CHARACTERISTICS: This is another species where even experts admit it might simply be a variety and not a species at all. The Consortium of Midwest Herbaria says this species is actually a "variable mixture" that easily creates natural hybrids, and some are "difficult to distinguish in practice." When the people who make up the definitions tell you that even they can't sometimes tell them apart, you begin to wonder if some of modern botany, without much left to discover, is just busy-work. (But I'm probably being too harsh.)

HABITAT: Desert, strongly alkaline soil.

FORM: Herbaceous flower, typically growing about 12 inches tall.

EDIBLE PART: Leaves.

HARVESTABLE: Spring.

FLAVOR: Mild.

Crepis capillaris

(SMOOTH HAWKSBEARD)

STATES: Colorado, Idaho, Montana, Nevada, Utah.

FLOWER: Yellow.

CHARACTERISTICS: The flowers of this species are more dense than other species, meaning they have petals but are smaller in diameter.

HABITAT: Desert, strongly alkaline soil.

FORM: Herbaceous flower, typically growing about 12 inches tall.

EDIBLE PART: Leaves.

HARVESTABLE: Spring.

FLAVOR: Mild.

Crepis intermedia

(LIMESTONE HAWKSBEARD)

STATES: Arizona, Colorado, Idaho, Montana, Nevada, New Mexico, Utah, Wyoming.

FLOWER: Yellow.

CHARACTERISTICS: This is another *Crepis* species experts say look much like many others and can be difficult to distinguish in reality. This species "combines the features" of at least four other local *Crepis* species, according to the Consortium of Midwest Herbaria.

HABITAT: Desert, strongly alkaline soil.

FORM: Herbaceous flower, typically growing about 12 inches tall.

EDIBLE PART: Leaves.

HARVESTABLE: Spring.

FLAVOR: Mild.

Crepis modocensis

(MODOC HAWKSBEARD)

STATES: Colorado, Idaho, Montana, Nevada, Utah, Wyoming.

FLOWER: Yellow.

CHARACTERISTICS: This species is mainly differentiated by its bristly stems. However, I will say I love the name. It got this name from botanist Edward Lee Greene, who first published the discovery in his botanical journal titled *Erythea* in 1895. He gave the species this name because it was first collected from nature in Modoc County, California, found growing on lava beds by a Mrs. R. M. Austin, according to an 1896 US Department of Agriculture pamphlet *"Crepis Occidentalis* and Its Allies" by Frederick Vernon Coville. Sometimes I feel I was born in the wrong time and I definitely missed the golden age of botanical discovery in America. Had I been alive, I would have been stalking the hills of the West looking for new species. I still look, but I've only ever found one thing that might be a new species (and I haven't been able to confirm that yet).

HABITAT: Desert, strongly alkaline soil.

FORM: Herbaceous flower, typically growing about 12 inches tall.

EDIBLE PART: Leaves.

HARVESTABLE: Spring.

FLAVOR: Mild.

137

Crepis occidentalis

(LARGEFLOWER HAWKSBEARD)

STATES: Arizona, Colorado, Idaho, Montana, Nevada, New Mexico, Utah, Wyoming.

FLOWER: Yellow.

CHARACTERISTICS: Add this to the list of *Crepis* species that are largely identical to each other. Experts calls this species "polymorphic," meaning that it has a wide natural variability, making it much like other related species.

HABITAT: Desert, strongly alkaline soil.

FORM: Herbaceous flower, typically growing about 12 inches tall.

EDIBLE PART: Leaves.

HARVESTABLE: Spring.

FLAVOR: Mild.

Crepis runcinata

(FIDDLELEAF HAWKSBEARD)

STATES: Arizona, Colorado, Idaho, Montana, Nevada, New Mexico, Utah, Wyoming.

FLOWER: Yellow.

CHARACTERISTICS: This species prefers to live in wet soil, which is not true of most of its cousins, which thrive in the desert.

HABITAT: Desert, strongly alkaline soil.

FORM: Herbaceous flower, typically growing about 12 inches tall.

EDIBLE PART: Leaves.

HARVESTABLE: Spring.

FLAVOR: Mild.

Cucurbita foetidissima

(BUFFALO GOURD)

———

STATES: Arizona, Colorado, Nevada, New Mexico, Utah, Wyoming.

FLOWER: Yellow.

HABITAT: Dry, open, sunny plains.

FORM: Squash plant.

EDIBLE PARTS: Flesh of the fruit, flowers, seeds.

HARVESTABLE: Late summer, autumn.

FLAVOR: Squash.

NOTES: The softball-sized round squash turns from green to yellow when ripe.

The ripe seeds are high in oil and can be pressed for cooking oil. The seeds have been roasted and eaten for centuries, like all squash seeds.

For self-reliant seed saving, in my book *More Forgotten Skills of Self-Sufficiency*, I talk about the importance of growing the different species of squash to prevent garden crossing. Buffalo gourd is one rarely used species that deserves to be more widely grown. I sell buffalo gourd seeds when possible on my website, SeedRenaissance.com, along with seeds from the best and earliest varieties of the other five squash species.

Cycloloma atriplicifolium

(WINGED PIGWEED)

STATES: Arizona, Colorado, Idaho, Montana, Nevada, New Mexico, Utah, Wyoming.

FLOWER: White and green.

HABITAT: Desert, sandy soil.

FORM: Low-growing small shrub.

EDIBLE PART: Seeds.

HARVESTABLE: Autumn.

FLAVOR: Grain.

NOTES: The seeds have an unusual shape, like a fringed button.

Several American Indian tribes ground the seeds to make mush; they would also add the ground seeds to ground corn or wheat to make cakes and breads.

Cymopterus globosus

(GLOBE SPRINGPARSLEY)

———

STATES: Nevada, Utah.

FLOWER: Purple, or purple turning pale pink to white as it grows larger, or purple and white, or rarely pale yellow.

CHARACTERISTICS: This plant often lies low to the ground. Even the flower stems often are low to the ground. It is considered rare, and if you find it, you might want to photograph it instead of harvesting it to eat. One of the reasons it's believed to be rare is because it was so popular among historical peoples that it was harvested almost to extinction, but it has been a few generations since this was true, and it has rebounded slowly, so we know now that it is also simply slow to repopulate.

HABITAT: Desert, mountainsides in rocky or sandy soil.

FORM: Small, ground-hugging herbaceous flower.

EDIBLE PARTS: Leaves, root.

HARVESTABLE: Spring, summer.

FLAVOR: Roots are sweet if picked in early spring before the flowers begin to appear, but at this stage the plants are hard to identify. Roots begin to change to a more parsnip or bitter flavor, or at least a less sweet flavor, once flowering begins, but this can also be affected by drought conditions as the temperature warms.

NOTES: American Indians widely used these roots, stems, and leaves as food, sometimes alone and sometimes adding them to other wild foods.

There are also many other species of *Cymopterus* across the country worth trying, but they are not listed in this book because they don't grow in the Rocky Mountain West.

Cymopterus montanus

(MOUNTAIN SPRINGPARSLEY)

———

STATES: Colorado, New Mexico, Wyoming.

FLOWER: Purple, or purple turning pale pink to white as it grows larger, or purple and white, or rarely pale yellow.

CHARACTERISTICS: Like its cousin on the facing page, this plant often lies low to the ground. Even the flower stems often are low to the ground. This plant grows in a larger area than its cousin but is still considered rare, and if you find it, you might want to photograph it instead of harvesting it to eat. One of the reasons it's believed to be rare is because it was so popular among historical peoples that it was harvested almost to extinction, but it has been a few generations since this was true, and it has rebounded slowly, so we know now that it is also simply slow to repopulate.

HABITAT: Desert, mountainsides in rocky or sandy soil.

FORM: Small, ground-hugging herbaceous flower.

FLOWER: Flowers vary widely by species. Purple turning pale pink to white as it grows larger, or purple and white, or pale yellow.

EDIBLE PARTS: Leaves, root.

HARVESTABLE: Spring, summer.

FLAVOR: Roots are sweet if picked in early spring before the flowers begin to appear, but at this stage, the plants are hard to identify. Roots begin to change to a more parsnip or bitter flavor, or at least a less sweet flavor, once flowering begins, but this can also be affected by drought conditions as the temperature warms.

Cymopterus purpurascens

(GAMOTE)

———

STATES: Arizona, Colorado, Idaho, Nevada, New Mexico, Utah.

FLOWER: Purple, or purple turning pale pink to white as it grows larger, or purple and white, or rarely pale yellow.

CHARACTERISTICS: This plant is somewhat rare and should be harvested sparingly, or not at all if there is not a good-sized natural population in the area where you find it. Sometimes you find wonderfully interesting descriptions of plants in botany, and this one about this species, from the Consortium of Midwest Herbaria, is a real gem: Used historically "for backaches and to settle the stomach after vomiting from swallowing a fly."

HABITAT: Desert, mountainsides in rocky or sandy soil.

FORM: Small, ground-hugging herbaceous flower.

EDIBLE PARTS: Leaves, root.

HARVESTABLE: Spring, summer.

FLAVOR: Roots are sweet if picked in early spring before the flowers begin to appear, but at this stage the plants are hard to identify. Roots begin to change to a more parsnip or bitter flavor, or at least a less sweet flavor, once flowering begins, but this can also be affected by drought conditions as the temperature warms.

Cymopterus purpureus

(PURPLE SPRINGPARSLEY)

STATES: Arizona, Colorado, Nevada, New Mexico, Utah.

FLOWER: Often greenish yellow, sometimes golden yellow, and sometimes turning purple as the flowers age.

CHARACTERISTICS: The stems of this plant are purple, which is how it got the Latin name *purpureus*. The plant is low-growing, as are all *Cymopterus*. This plant is somewhat rare and should be harvested sparingly, or not at all if there is not a good-sized natural population in the area where you find it. Some experts say that all *Cymopterus* species may not be individual species at all and in fact may not even be different than some *Lomatium* species.

HABITAT: Desert, mountainsides in rocky or sandy soil.

FORM: Small, ground-hugging herbaceous flower.

EDIBLE PARTS: Leaves, root.

HARVESTABLE: Spring, summer.

FLAVOR: Roots are sweet if picked in early spring before the flowers begin to appear, but at this stage the plants are hard to identify. Roots begin to change to a more parsnip or bitter flavor, or at least a less sweet flavor, once flowering begins, but this can also be affected by drought conditions as the temperature warms.

SYNONYM: *Aulospermum purpureum.*

Cynoglossum officinale

(HOUNDSTONGUE, GYPSYFLOWER)

STATES: Arizona, Colorado, Idaho, Montana, Nevada, New Mexico, Utah, Wyoming.

FLOWER: Purple and red.

HABITAT: Clay soils in open, sunny spaces, wastelands, roadsides.

FORM: Biennial, herbaceous flower, growing up to 4 feet tall.

EDIBLE PART: Leaves (sparingly).

HARVESTABLE: Summer.

FLAVOR: Bitter.

NOTES: Leaves are used, fresh or dry, to protect stored veggies from animals and to protect gardens from moles, mice, rats, and other critters. This plant is also grown around homes to provide the same natural pest-repellent properties.

Historically the leaves have been eaten, but today we know they are high in alkaloids and even reportedly somewhat narcotic when eaten in large quantities. Some reports even say the plant many be carcinogenic. This plant is also strongly medicinal and has been used medicinally for many years. The flavor is not good, so perhaps it is best to leave this to be a medicinal and pest-control plant.

The seeds are covered in velcro-like hairs that are difficult to get out of clothes, socks, shoes, and pet hair.

Cyperus erythrorhizos

(REDROOT FLATSEDGE)

STATES: Arizona, Colorado, Idaho, Montana, Nevada, New Mexico, Utah, Wyoming.

FLOWER: Green, turning reddish brown with age.

CHARACTERISTICS: The flowers of all *Cyperus* species kind of look like baby bottle brushes.

HABITAT: Open, sunny, disturbed land, roadsides, wastelands.

FORM: Low-growing grass with seed tufts.

EDIBLE PARTS: Leaves, nut-like tuber, seeds.

HARVESTABLE: Summer, autumn

FLAVOR: Seeds have a grain flavor; tubers have a more nutty flavor. Leaves are mild in spring.

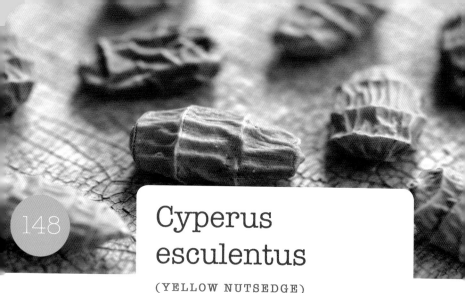

Cyperus esculentus

(YELLOW NUTSEDGE)

STATES: Arizona, Colorado, Idaho, Nevada, New Mexico, Utah.

FLOWER: Green, turning yellow and then brown with age.

CHARACTERISTICS: *Esculentus* is the Latin word for "edible." Prefers moist soil. Flowers in summer, with seeds in late summer or early autumn.

HABITAT: Open, sunny, disturbed land, roadsides, wastelands.

FORM: Low-growing grass with seed tufts.

EDIBLE PARTS: Leaves, nut-like tuber, seeds.

HARVESTABLE: Summer, autumn.

FLAVOR: Seeds have a grain flavor; tubers have a more nutty flavor. Leaves are mild in spring.

Cyperus fendlerianus

(FENDLER'S FLATSEDGE)

———

STATES: Arizona, Colorado, Nevada, New Mexico, Wyoming.

FLOWER: Green, yellow, red, or brown, often turning red or brown with age.

CHARACTERISTICS: *Fendlerianus* is named for Augustus Fendler (1813–1883), a restless free spirit who emigrated to the United States from Germany and became the first botanist to collect specimens in New Mexico. He was known for trying many careers to finance his love of exploration. At one point he decided he needed a solitary life and moved into an abandoned logger's cabin on an island in the Missouri River. The island was home to a flock of wild turkeys, which he easily trapped and ate. Of this time, he wrote about himself in third person: "Removed from the crowd, the hum and strife of men, his pastimes consisted alternately in trapping, hunting, reading, musing and meditating, and on mild and sunny days in paddling up a placid arm of the river, then turning round lean idly back in his canoe, thus floating home again." His leisure did not last long, and he ended up famously collecting and selling specimens of wild New Mexico plants and exploring much of the country. His life was fascinating. You can read his autobiography at Archive.org.

HABITAT: Open, sunny, disturbed land, roadsides, wastelands.

FORM: Low-growing grass with seed tufts.

EDIBLE PARTS: Leaves, nut-like tuber, seeds.

HARVESTABLE: Summer, autumn.

FLAVOR: Seeds have a grain flavor; tubers have a more nutty flavor. Leaves are mild in spring.

Cyperus odoratus

(FRAGRANT FLATSEDGE)

STATES: Arizona, Colorado, Idaho, New Mexico.

FLOWER: Green, turning red then brown.

CHARACTERISTICS: This is a wetland variety that prefers standing water or wet soil and may have fewer nutlet tubers than other varieties. Experts frequently argue about whether the various *Cyperus* species are in fact species or just varieties. Because of this, this particular species has more than a dozen possible synonyms or debated synonyms.

HABITAT: Open, sunny, disturbed land, roadsides, wastelands.

FORM: Low-growing grass with seed tufts.

EDIBLE PARTS: Leaves, nut-like tuber, seeds.

HARVESTABLE: Summer, autumn.

FLAVOR: Seeds have a grain flavor; tubers have a more nutty flavor. Leaves are mild in spring.

In addition to the native varieties listed here, there are many non-native varieties with edible sap that have been widely planted around the Rocky Mountain West as landscape trees.

Cyperus rotundus

(NUT GRASS)

STATE: Arizona.

FLOWER: Green.

CHARACTERISTICS: The Agricultural Extension Service says that a single nutgrass tuber can produce 1,000 new tubers, called "nutlets," in one summer. This is good news if you are looking to raise food—or bad news when this plant gets into a farmer's field.

HABITAT: Open, sunny, disturbed land, roadsides, wastelands.

FORM: Low-growing grass with seed tufts.

EDIBLE PARTS: Leaves, nut-like tuber, seeds.

HARVESTABLE: Summer, autumn.

FLAVOR: Seeds have a grain flavor; tubers have a more nutty flavor. Leaves are mild in spring.

Cyperus schweinitzii

(SCHWEINITZ'S FLATSEDGE)

STATES: Arizona, Colorado, Idaho, Montana, New Mexico, Utah, Wyoming.

FLOWER: Green.

CHARACTERISTICS: *Schweinitzii* is named after Lewis David de Schweinitz (1780–1834), who first classified this species. He is primarily known as an early specialist in mushrooms. Gemeinhaus, the home where he lived, is a museum run by the National Park Service in Bethlehem, Pennsylvania. "The house remained his home until his death in 1834. Lewis David de Schweinitz is significant in the history of science in America as one of the leading botanists and the leading mycologist at the turn of the nineteenth century. He wrote *The Fungi of North Carolina* (1818), containing descriptions of more than 1,000 species, and followed this work with 'A Synopsis of North American Fungi,' published in *Transactions*, the journal of the American Philosophical Society, in 1834. Lewis David de Schweinitz's work in botany and mycology reflected the state of American science of the period, when men who wished to pursue natural history either possessed private means or supported themselves at other professions" (National Park Service data).

HABITAT: Open, sunny, disturbed land, roadsides, wastelands.

FORM: Low-growing grass with seed tufts.

EDIBLE PARTS: Leaves, nut-like tuber, seeds.

HARVESTABLE: Summer, autumn.

FLAVOR: Seeds have a grain flavor; tubers have a more nutty flavor. Leaves are mild in spring.

Cyperus squarrosus

(BEARDED FLATSEDGE)

———

STATES: Arizona, Colorado, Idaho, Montana, Nevada, New Mexico, Utah, Wyoming.

FLOWER: Green.

CHARACTERISTICS: The plant is smaller than most other *Cyperus* species. Nutlet tubers are eaten raw or cooked, as with all *Cyperus* nutlets.

HABITAT: Open, sunny disturbed land, roadsides, wastelands.

FORM: Low-growing grass with seed tufts.

EDIBLE PARTS: Leaves, nut-like tuber, seeds.

HARVESTABLE: Summer, autumn.

FLAVOR: Seeds have a grain flavor; tubers have a more nutty flavor. Leaves are mild in spring.

Daucus carota

(WILD CARROT)

STATES: Arizona, Colorado, Idaho, Montana, Nevada, New Mexico, Utah, Wyoming.

FLOWER: White.

HABITAT: Open, sunny spaces, fields, roadsides, wastelands, gardens, fencelines.

FORM: Slender flower, typically growing 4 feet tall.

EDIBLE PARTS: Root, flower heads (cooked), seeds (used as spice).

HARVESTABLE: Summer.

FLAVOR: Carrot.

NOTE: All modern domesticated carrots come from this genus. This plant is widely used medicinally.

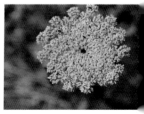

Descurainia incana

(MOUNTAIN TANSY MUSTARD)

———

STATES: Arizona, Colorado, Idaho, Montana, Nevada, New Mexico, Utah, Wyoming.

FLOWER: Yellow.

CHARACTERISTICS: *Descurainia* is named in honor of Francois Descourain (1658–1740), a French pharmacist and associate of Antoine Laurent de Jussieu, who created the modern method of classifying flowering plants.

HABITAT: Disturbed spaces, wastelands, pastures, fields, roadsides, mountainsides.

FORM: Slender, multi-stemmed flower, typically growing about 12 inches tall.

EDIBLE PARTS: Leaves, seeds.

HARVESTABLE: Spring, summer.

FLAVOR: Leaves are bitter. Seeds have a mustardy grain flavor.

NOTES: American Indians widely used the seeds in porridges, cakes, breads, and more.

Descurainia obtusa

(BLUNT TANSY MUSTARD)

STATES: Arizona, Nevada, New Mexico.

FLOWER: Yellow or greenish yellow.

CHARACTERISTICS: Most *Descurainia* can be told apart by just small differences in the spacing or size of their seed pods.

HABITAT: Disturbed spaces, wastelands, pastures, fields, roadsides, mountainsides.

FORM: Slender, multi-stemmed flower, typically growing about 12 inches tall.

EDIBLE PARTS: Leaves, seeds.

HARVESTABLE: Spring, summer.

FLAVOR: Leaves are bitter. Seeds have a mustardy grain flavor.

NOTES: American Indians widely used the seeds in porridges, cakes, breads, and more.

Descurainia pinnata

(WESTERN TANSY MUSTARD)

STATES: Arizona, Colorado, Idaho, Montana, Nevada, New Mexico, Utah, Wyoming.

FLOWER: Yellow, purple, or red.

CHARACTERISTICS: *Descurainia* species are more commonly known as wild mustards. There are also *Brassica* species that look somewhat similar that are also called wild mustards. The Consortium of Midwest Herbaria says that in Native American history, "tansy mustard appears in clan names and migration tales as an important plant."

HABITAT: Disturbed spaces, wastelands, pastures, fields, roadsides, mountainsides.

FORM: Slender, multi-stemmed flower, typically growing about 12 inches tall.

EDIBLE PARTS: Leaves, seeds.

HARVESTABLE: Spring, summer.

FLAVOR: Leaves are bitter. Seeds have a mustardy grain flavor.

NOTES: American Indians widely used the seeds in porridges, cakes, breads, and more.

Descurainia sophia

(FLIXWEED, HERB SOPHIA)

158

STATES: Arizona, Colorado, Idaho, Montana, Nevada, New Mexico, Utah, Wyoming.

FLOWER: Yellow.

CHARACTERISTICS: This plant produces more seeds than other *Descurainia* species and is an important host to some butterfly species. *Sophia* is the Latin word for "wisdom" and was probably given because of the medicinal uses of this plant. A scientific paper from the US National Institutes of Health says this plant has a long history of safe medicinal folk use the world over and yet only two modern clinical trials have been done on it. Those of us who practice herbal medicine in the modern day often feel torn by such recommendations. We only half-heartedly want clinical validation of the medicinal uses that we already know exist from personal experience. We don't want big pharmaceutical companies to come in and try to patent and own the usage of these centuries-old traditional medicines. For information about medicinal herbs, see my book *Forgotten Skills of Backyard Herbal Healing and Family Health*.

HABITAT: Disturbed spaces, wastelands, pastures, fields, roadsides, mountainsides.

FORM: Slender, multi-stemmed flower, typically growing about 12 inches tall.

EDIBLE PARTS: Leaves, seeds.

HARVESTABLE: Spring, summer.

FLAVOR: Leaves are bitter. Seeds have a mustardy grain flavor.

NOTES: American Indians widely used the seeds in porridges, cakes, breads, and more. Flixweed seeds are 25 percent protein.

Digitaria sanguinalis

(HAIRY CRABGRASS)

STATES: Arizona, Colorado, Idaho, Montana, Nevada, New Mexico, Utah, Wyoming.

FLOWER: White.

HABITAT: Clay soils, disturbed spaces, lawns, waste spaces, fields.

FORM: Low-growing multi-stemmed grass that can rise up 12 inches or more when seeds appear.

EDIBLE PART: Seeds, which reportedly make a great pasta flour.

HARVESTABLE: Summer, autumn.

FLAVOR: Grain.

Diospyros virginiana

(AMERICAN PERSIMMON)

———

STATE: Utah.

FLOWER: Greenish yellow.

HABITAT: Tolerates a wide range of soils and moisture levels and is surprisingly drought-tolerant, although it prefers moisture.

FORM: Tree, growing up to 12 feet tall.

EDIBLE PART: Fruit.

HARVESTABLE: Summer, autumn.

FLAVOR: Sweet.

NOTES: How this native tree came to exist in just one Rocky Mountain state is a botanical mystery. It is native on both coasts but so far has not been documented in any state touching Utah, so how did it get from the East Coast, skip some states, land in Utah, skip Nevada, and land in California? We'll probably never know. This tree is not widely found in Utah. The fruits are small, like berries.

Elaeagnus angustifolia

(RUSSIAN OLIVE)

STATES: Arizona, Colorado, Idaho, Montana, Nevada, New Mexico, Utah, Wyoming.

FLOWER: Yellow.

CHARACTERISTICS: Russian olives have thorns and silverberries (on the next page) do not. Both fix nitrogen in the soil.

HABITAT: Usually found near streams, marshes, and other natural water sources.

FORM: Tree growing up to 35 feet tall.

EDIBLE PARTS: Fruit, seeds.

HARVESTABLE: Summer.

FLAVOR: Slightly sweet, but only when fully ripe.

NOTES: These non-natives were originally brought to desert areas because they grow so fast, providing firewood, shade, and food.

Elaeagnus commutata

(SILVERBERRY)

————

STATES: Colorado, Idaho, Montana, Utah, Wyoming.

FLOWER: Yellow.

CHARACTERISTICS: Silverberry trees do not have thorns. This is the best way to tell them apart from Russian olives (on the previous page), which do have thorns. Both fix nitrogen in the soil.

HABITAT: Usually found near streams, marshes, and other natural water sources.

FORM: Tree growing up to 35 feet tall.

EDIBLE PARTS: Fruit, seeds.

HARVESTABLE: Summer.

FLAVOR: Slightly sweet, but only when fully ripe.

NOTES: These non-natives were originally brought to desert areas because they grow so fast, providing firewood, shade, and food.

Eleusine indica

(GOOSEGRASS)

———————

STATES: Arizona, Colorado, Nevada, New Mexico, Utah.

FLOWER: Green.

HABITAT: Wastelands, roadsides, lawns, disturbed areas.

FORM: Low-growing grass, rising up 12–18 inches when bearing seeds.

EDIBLE PARTS: Seeds, leaves, roots.

HARVESTABLE: Spring, summer.

FLAVOR: Seeds have a grain flavor. Leaves can be mild but fibrous. Roots are less useful because they are small and hard to clean.

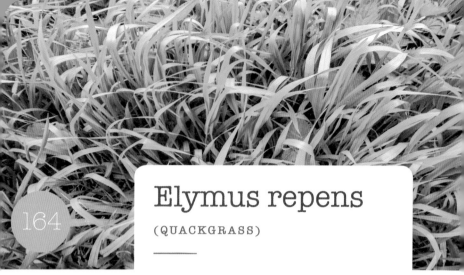

Elymus repens

(QUACKGRASS)

STATES: Arizona, Colorado, Idaho, Montana, Nevada, New Mexico, Utah, Wyoming.

FLOWER: Green.

HABITAT: Pastures, lawns, fields, gardens, roadsides, waste spaces.

FORM: Grass, growing up to 3 feet tall.

EDIBLE PART: Leaves.

HARVESTABLE: Spring, summer.

FLAVOR: Grassy and fibrous.

NOTES: I'm fond of telling people that this plant may have been created by Lucifer himself. It was likely brought to the United States by settlers for use as a pasture grass, but today it invades and destroys gardens, flower beds, and gravel driveways by choking out everything. This plant is the bane of many gardeners because it spreads by rhizome beneath the ground and cannot be killed by any weedkiller; it can be temporarily knocked back, but because it spreads underground, it just grows back in. To think that someone actually brought this plant to the United States on purpose is hard to fathom today. We should find this historical person and make them come back and clean up their mess! If you can't tell already, I hate this plant because of the massive damage it has done. I know families who gave up gardening forever when this invaded their garden plot. Selling the seeds should be illegal, but today the seeds of quackgrass are still sometimes sold in pasture-grass mixes.

Equisetum arvense

(HORSETAIL GRASS)

STATES: Arizona, Colorado, Idaho, Montana, Nevada, New Mexico, Utah, Wyoming.

FLOWER: The flower has a very striking and unusual pagoda-like shape and is green and black.

HABITAT: Grows in water or wet soil.

FORM: Single-stem grass that resembles a dart or spear in spring and a horse's tail, thickly feathery, in summer when its needlelike branches are out. Overall the plant looks and acts like something created by Dr. Seuss.

EDIBLE PARTS: Tubers, newly emerged stems (cooked only, small quantities only).

HARVESTABLE: Spring, summer, autumn.

FLAVOR: Grassy, asparagus-like.

NOTES: This is one of those rare plants that was heavily eaten historically but probably should never be eaten today. Why? Because test after test has shown that *Equisetum* is fantastic at pulling heavy metals out of the soil. Two hundred years ago, this was probably not an issue, but today, air pollution, mining debris, car exhaust, and many other sources lace our soil and water with heavy metals no matter where we live. So instead of eating this plant, we should probably all grow it in our gardens, harvest it, and throw it away, allowing it to clean the soil and take the toxins to the landfill. **This plant should not be composted, because then the heavy metals go right back into the ground.**

While we probably should grow this in our gardens, note that it takes a lot of water, is invasive, and is hard to eradicate. In addition, while this plant has a long history as an edible wild food, modern studies have shown it contains an enzyme that can destroy vitamin B in the body when eaten in large amounts. I use this plant in my homemade toothpaste recipe, which you can find in my book *More Forgotten Skills of Self-Sufficiency*.

Equisetum hyemale

(SCOURINGRUSH HORSETAIL)

———————

STATES: Arizona, Colorado, Idaho, Montana, Nevada, New Mexico, Utah, Wyoming.

FLOWER: The flower has a very striking and unusual pagoda-like shape and is green and black.

CHARACTERISTICS: Historically, this plant was used medicinally for kidneys and constipation; the branches were burned as a disinfectant; it was used as an insecticide for washing hair; and it was used for basketry, mat weaving, and ceremonial medicine, according to the Consortium of Midwest Herbaria. I'm not sure what it means to burn these reeds for disinfectant, but the plants are high in natural silica, so it might mean they used the ash as scrubbing powder for hygiene (but that is just me speculating).

HABITAT: Grows in water or wet soil.

FORM: Single-stem grass that resembles a dart or spear in spring and a horse's tail, thickly feathery, in summer when its needlelike branches are out. Overall the plant looks and acts like something created by Dr. Seuss.

EDIBLE PARTS: Tubers, newly emerged stems (cooked only, small quantities only).

HARVESTABLE: Spring, summer, autumn.

FLAVOR: Grassy, asparagus-like.

NOTES: This is one of those rare plants that was heavily eaten historically but probably should never be eaten today because test after test has shown that *Equisetum* is fantastic at pulling heavy metals out of the soil. Two hundred years ago, this was probably not an issue, but today, air pollution, mining debris, car exhaust, and many other sources lace our soil and water with heavy metals no matter where we live.

Equisetum laevigatum

(SMOOTH HORSETAIL)

STATES: Arizona, Colorado, Idaho, Montana, Nevada, New Mexico, Utah, Wyoming.

FLOWER: The flower has a very striking and unusual pagoda-like shape and is green and black.

CHARACTERISTICS: Historically, several species of horsetail grass were used to treat kidney ailments, which might deserve modern investigation. Native Americans also reportedly used this species to treat poison ivy, among other things.

HABITAT: Grows in water or wet soil.

FORM: Single-stem grass that resembles a dart or spear in spring and a horse's tail, thickly feathery, in summer when its needlelike branches are out. Overall the plant looks and acts like something created by Dr. Seuss.

EDIBLE PARTS: Tubers, newly emerged stems (cooked only, small quantities only).

HARVESTABLE: Spring, summer, autumn.

FLAVOR: Grassy, asparagus-like.

NOTES: This is one of those rare plants that was heavily eaten historically but probably should never be eaten today because test after test has shown that *Equisetum* is fantastic at pulling heavy metals out of the soil. Two hundred years ago, this was probably not an issue, but today, air pollution, mining debris, car exhaust, and many other sources lace our soil and water with heavy metals no matter where we live.

Equisetum pratense

(MEADOW HORSETAIL)

––––––––

STATES: Colorado, Idaho, Montana.

CHARACTERISTICS: Because *Equisetum* species were traditionally used for medicine all over the world, today they are being widely investigated for modern medicinal uses. A search of the the US National Library of Medicine shows these plants are being investigated for anti-inflammatory properties, metabolism health, food uses, chemical uses, poisonous characteristics, and more.

HABITAT: Grows in water or wet soil.

FORM: Single-stem grass that resembles a dart or spear in spring and a horse's tail, thickly feathery, in summer when its needlelike branches are out. Overall the plant looks and acts like something created by Dr. Seuss.

FLOWER: The flower has a very striking and unusual pagoda-like shape and is green and black.

EDIBLE PARTS: Tubers, newly emerged stems (cooked only, small quantities only).

HARVESTABLE: Spring, summer, autumn.

FLAVOR: Grassy, asparagus-like.

NOTES: This is one of those rare plants that was heavily eaten historically but probably should never be eaten today because test after test has shown that *Equisetum* is fantastic at pulling heavy metals out of the soil. Two hundred years ago, this was probably not an issue, but today, air pollution, mining debris, car exhaust, and many other sources lace our soil and water with heavy metals no matter where we live.

Equisetum scirpoides

(DWARF SCOURINGRUSH)

STATES: Idaho, Montana, Wyoming.

FLOWER: The flower has a very striking and unusual pagoda-like shape and is green and black.

CHARACTERISTICS: Interestingly, *Equisetum* species spread not by seeds but by spores, like mushrooms. Occasionally in the mountains I have witnessed this sudden release of *Equisetum* spores, which float up suddenly like smoke. It is at once beautiful and a bit unnerving to behold.

HABITAT: Grows in water or wet soil.

FORM: Single-stem grass that resembles a dart or spear in spring and a horse's tail, thickly feathery, in summer when its needlelike branches are out. Overall the plant looks and acts like something created by Dr. Seuss.

EDIBLE PARTS: Tubers, newly emerged stems (cooked only, small quantities only).

HARVESTABLE: Spring, summer, autumn.

FLAVOR: Grassy, asparagus-like.

NOTES: This is one of those rare plants that was heavily eaten historically but probably should never be eaten today because test after test has shown that *Equisetum* is fantastic at pulling heavy metals out of the soil. Two hundred years ago, this was probably not an issue, but today, air pollution, mining debris, car exhaust, and many other sources lace our soil and water with heavy metals no matter where we live.

Equisetum telmateia

(GIANT HORSETAIL)

STATE: Idaho.

FLOWER: The flower has a very striking and unusual pagoda-like shape and is green and black.

CHARACTERISTICS: This species is somewhat rare in the Rocky Mountain West but more prolific on the West Coast.

HABITAT: Grows in water or wet soil.

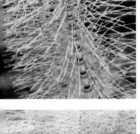

FORM: Single-stem grass that resembles a dart or spear in spring and a horse's tail, thickly feathery, in summer when its needlelike branches are out. Overall the plant looks and acts like something created by Dr. Seuss.

EDIBLE PARTS: Tubers, newly emerged stems (cooked only, small quantities only).

HARVESTABLE: Spring, summer, autumn.

FLAVOR: Grassy, asparagus-like.

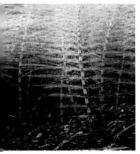

NOTES: This is one of those rare plants that was heavily eaten historically but probably should never be eaten today because test after test has shown that *Equisetum* is fantastic at pulling heavy metals out of the soil. Two hundred years ago, this was probably not an issue, but today, air pollution, mining debris, car exhaust, and many other sources lace our soil and water with heavy metals no matter where we live.

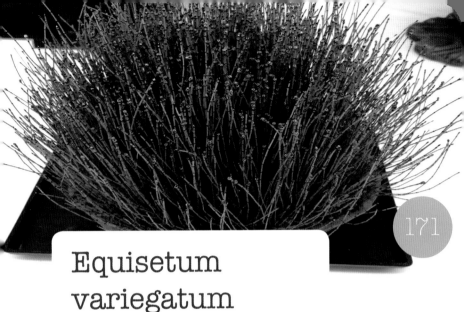

Equisetum variegatum

(VARIEGATED SCOURINGRUSH)

STATES: Colorado, Idaho, Montana, Utah, Wyoming.

FLOWER: The flower has a very striking and unusual pagoda-like shape and is green and black.

CHARACTERISTICS: *Equus* is Latin for "horse," and *saeta* means "bristle," so named because at certain points in its life these unusual species resemble horse tails.

HABITAT: Grows in water or wet soil.

FORM: Single-stem grass that resembles a dart or spear in spring and a horse's tail, thickly feathery, in summer when its needlelike branches are out. Overall the plant looks and acts like something created by Dr. Seuss.

EDIBLE PARTS: Tubers, newly emerged stems (cooked only, small quantities only).

HARVESTABLE: Spring, summer, autumn.

FLAVOR: Grassy, asparagus-like.

NOTES: This is one of those rare plants that was heavily eaten historically but probably should never be eaten today because test after test has shown that *Equisetum* is fantastic at pulling heavy metals out of the soil. Two hundred years ago, this was probably not an issue, but today, air pollution, mining debris, car exhaust, and many other sources lace our soil and water with heavy metals no matter where we live.

Eriogonum alatum

(WINGED BUCKWHEAT)

STATES: Arizona, Colorado, New Mexico, Utah, Wyoming.

FLOWER: Yellow or yellowish green and turning red with age.

HABITAT: Open, sunny desert soil.

FORM: Single-stem flower.

EDIBLE PARTS: Seeds, shoots, leaves, roots.

HARVESTABLE: Spring, summer.

FLAVOR: Mild.

NOTES: This genus was an important food source for many American Indian tribes, who ate it themselves and fed it to their livestock. Some uses were inventive and worth remembering for use today. In his scholarly monograph titled *Native American Food Plants*, Daniel E. Moerman says when they were traveling and thirsty, they drank the juice from the stems of some species. All other parts were also widely eaten fresh or dried or cooked for food. There are dozens of other members of this genus that are edible but not listed here because they don't grow in the Rocky Mountain West or it is unknown if they are edible (even though it is likely that they are).

Eriogonum baileyi

(BAILEY'S BUCKWHEAT)

———————

STATES: Idaho, Nevada, Utah.

FLOWER: Pink, white, or red.

CHARACTERISTICS: The Kawaiisu tribe of California pounded the seeds to a meal and then mixed this with water to make a drink, according to the Consortium of Midwest Herbaria. This reminds me of when I lived in Japan and one of the favorite drinks there was tea made of roasted wheat, which is deliciously earthy.

HABITAT: Open, sunny desert soil.

FORM: Single-stem flower.

EDIBLE PARTS: Seeds, shoots, leaves, roots.

HARVESTABLE: Spring, summer.

FLAVOR: Mild.

Eriogonum cernuum

(NODDING BUCKWHEAT)

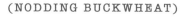

STATES: Arizona, Colorado, Idaho, Montana, Nevada, New Mexico, Utah, Wyoming.

FLOWER: Pink or white, turning red with age.

CHARACTERISTICS: The Navajo tribe not only used the seeds for food but used the plant medicinally too, including to treat ant bites, according to the Consortium of Midwest Herbaria.

HABITAT: Open, sunny desert soil.

FORM: Single-stem flower.

EDIBLE PARTS: Seeds, shoots, leaves, roots.

HARVESTABLE: Spring, summer.

FLAVOR: Mild.

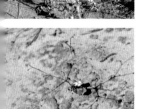

Eriogonum corymbosum

(CRISPLEAF BUCKWHEAT)

STATES: Arizona, Colorado, Nevada, New Mexico, Utah, Wyoming.

FLOWER: Pink, white, or sometimes yellow.

CHARACTERISTICS: This is a host plant for the black and rust-red Mormon metalmark butterfly, which looks almost more like a moth than a butterfly and is one of the most widespread butterfly species of the West.

HABITAT: Open, sunny desert soil.

FORM: Single-stem flower.

EDIBLE PARTS: Seeds, shoots, leaves, roots.

HARVESTABLE: Spring, summer.

FLAVOR: Mild.

Eriogonum davidsonii

(DAVIDSON'S BUCKWHEAT)

———————

STATES: Arizona, Nevada, Utah.

FLOWER: Pink, white, red, and occasionally yellow.

CHARACTERISTICS: *Davidsonii* is in honor of Anstruther Davidson (1860–1932), an immigrant from Scotland who became a medical doctor and then came to California to practice medicine. He did significant botany work in California and Arizona as a hobby, even publishing important books on botany.

HABITAT: Open, sunny desert soil.

FORM: Single-stem flower.

EDIBLE PARTS: Seeds, shoots, leaves, roots.

HARVESTABLE: Spring, summer.

FLAVOR: Mild.

Eriogonum fasciculatum

(CALIFORNIA BUCKWHEAT)

STATES: Arizona, Nevada, Utah.

FLOWER: Pink, white.

CHARACTERISTICS: Native Americans widely used this plant for headaches, which deserves some modern investigation.

HABITAT: Open, sunny desert soil.

FORM: Single-stem flower.

EDIBLE PARTS: Seeds, shoots, leaves, roots.

HARVESTABLE: Spring, summer.

FLAVOR: Mild.

Eriogonum flavum

(ALPINE GOLDEN BUCKWHEAT)

—————

STATES: Colorado, Idaho, Montana, Wyoming.

FLOWER: Yellow.

CHARACTERISTICS: These brightly colored flowers are beautiful enough that they could be used as decorative landscape plants. The more native, drought-tolerant landscaping plants we can find to use in the parched West, the better off our water resources will be.

HABITAT: Open, sunny desert soil.

FORM: Single-stem flower.

EDIBLE PARTS: Seeds, shoots, leaves, roots.

HARVESTABLE: Spring, summer.

FLAVOR: Mild.

Eriogonum hookeri

(HOOKER'S BUCKWHEAT)

———

STATES: Arizona, Colorado, Idaho, Nevada, New Mexico, Utah, Wyoming.

FLOWER: Yellow, reddish yellow, or red.

CHARACTERISTICS: This is a low-growing but widely branching plant that should also be considered for decorative landscaping use in yards because the flowers are stunning, especially the red varieties. And what could be better than a flowering plant you can later use for flour?

HABITAT: Open, sunny desert soil.

FORM: Single-stem flower.

EDIBLE PARTS: Seeds, shoots, leaves, roots.

HARVESTABLE: Spring, summer.

FLAVOR: Mild.

Eriogonum inflatum

(DESERT TRUMPET)

STATES: Arizona, Colorado, Nevada, New Mexico, Utah.

FLOWER: Yellow.

CHARACTERISTICS: Beyond using this plant for food, the hollow stems of this plant were used by the American Indians as drinking straws and pipes, according to the Consortium of Midwest Herbaria.

HABITAT: Open, sunny desert soil.

FORM: Single-stem flower.

EDIBLE PARTS: Seeds, shoots, leaves, roots.

HARVESTABLE: Spring, summer.

FLAVOR: Mild.

Eriogonum longifolium

(LONGLEAF BUCKWHEAT)

STATES: New Mexico.

FLOWER: Yellow or yellowish green and sometimes white.

CHARACTERISTICS: The flowers of Eriogonum species are important food sources for many species of native bees.

HABITAT: Open, sunny desert soil.

FORM: Single-stem flower.

EDIBLE PARTS: Seeds, shoots, leaves, roots.

HARVESTABLE: Spring, summer.

FLAVOR: Mild.

Eriogonum microthecum

(SLENDER BUCKWHEAT)

STATES: Arizona, Colorado, Idaho, Montana, Nevada, New Mexico, Utah, Wyoming.

FLOWER: Yellow, white, cream, pink, or red.

CHARACTERISTICS: This plant provides food for the rare pallid blue butterfly (Euphilotes pallescens), a shimmery metallic-blue creature native to the West which also comes in non-blue varieties.

HABITAT: Open, sunny desert soil.

FORM: Single-stem flower.

EDIBLE PARTS: Seeds, shoots, leaves, roots.

HARVESTABLE: Spring, summer.

FLAVOR: Mild.

Eriogonum nudum

(NAKED BUCKWHEAT)

———————

STATE: Nevada.

FLOWER: Pink, red, white, or yellow.

CHARACTERISTICS: This species is important as a feeding stop for many butterflies, including Bauer's dotted-blue butterfly (Euphilotes baueri) and the gorgon copper (Gaeides gorgon).

HABITAT: Open, sunny desert soil.

FORM: Single-stem flower.

FLOWER: Pink, white.

EDIBLE PARTS: Seeds, shoots, leaves, roots.

HARVESTABLE: Spring, summer.

FLAVOR: Mild.

Eriogonum plumatella

(YUCCA BUCKWHEAT)

———

STATES: Arizona, Nevada.

FLOWER: White or yellow.

CHARACTERISTICS: This is a somewhat rare species, and if you find it, you may want to taste only a few seeds or leaves, especially if there is not a large population in the local area.

HABITAT: Open, sunny desert soil.

FORM: Single-stem flower.

EDIBLE PARTS: Seeds, shoots, leaves, roots.

HARVESTABLE: Spring, summer.

FLAVOR: Mild.

Eriogonum pusillum

(YELLOWTURBANS)

STATES: Arizona, Nevada, Utah.

FLOWER: Yellow when young and then turning red.

CHARACTERISTICS: This plant provides food for two rare desert creatures: the Mojave dotted-blue butterfly (*Euphilotes mojave*) and young desert tortoises (*Gopherus agassizii*). The flowers of this plant can also be a stunning combination of red and yellow at points in the life of the flower, and this plant should be considered for cultivation as a decorative landscaping flower. The common name is yellowturbans for a reason, because that it what the flowers resemble.

HABITAT: Open, sunny desert soil.

FORM: Single-stem flower.

EDIBLE PARTS: Seeds, shoots, leaves, roots.

HARVESTABLE: Spring, summer.

FLAVOR: Mild.

Eriogonum racemosum

(REDROOT BUCKWHEAT)

STATES: Arizona, Colorado, Nevada, New Mexico, Utah.

FLOWER: Pink, white.

CHARACTERISTICS: Often found growing in sand or gravel. This plant provides food for several butterfly species too. The American Indians reportedly used it medicinally for backaches.

HABITAT: Open, sunny desert soil.

FORM: Single-stem flower.

EDIBLE PARTS: Seeds, shoots, leaves, roots.

HARVESTABLE: Spring, summer.

FLAVOR: Mild.

Eriogonum rotundifolium

(ROUNDLEAF BUCKWHEAT)

STATES: Arizona, New Mexico.

FLOWER: Pink or white with green or red ribs on the lower part of the petals.

CHARACTERISTICS: *Eriogonum* is mostly eaten for grain, but Native Americans also ate the shoots (stems). Modern botanists who tried the stems of several species report they are sour in flavor.

HABITAT: Open, sunny desert soil.

FORM: Single-stem flower.

EDIBLE PARTS: Seeds, shoots, leaves, roots.

HARVESTABLE: Spring, summer.

FLAVOR: Mild.

Eriogonum umbellatum

(SULPHUR-FLOWER BUCKWHEAT)

STATES: Arizona, Colorado, Idaho, Montana, Nevada, Utah, Wyoming.

FLOWER: White, yellow, or red.

CHARACTERISTICS: This species was widely used to treat a whole host of ailments by the American Indians, ranging from pain to sores to inflammation of joints and much more. It is also an important source of food for several butterflies, including the Rocky Mountain dotted-blue (*Euphilotes ancilla*).

HABITAT: Open, sunny desert soil.

FORM: Single-stem flower.

EDIBLE PARTS: Seeds, shoots, leaves, roots.

HARVESTABLE: Spring, summer.

FLAVOR: Mild.

Erodium cicutarium

(REDSTEM FILAREE, STORK'S BILL)

STATES: Arizona, Colorado, Idaho, Montana, Nevada, New Mexico, Utah, Wyoming.

FLOWER: Light purple.

HABITAT: Disturbed land, pastures, fields.

FORM: Small annual flower, typically growing about 6 inches tall.

EDIBLE PARTS: Leaves, flowers, roots, stems.

HARVESTABLE: Spring.

FLAVOR: Mild. Leaves taste best before the flower emerges. This plant gets its name from the seed pods which resemble a stork's bill. It is often found in a beautiful mass of flowers in spring.

Fragaria vesca

(WOODLAND, ALPINE, OR WILD STRAWBERRY)

STATES: Arizona, Colorado, Idaho, Montana, New Mexico, Utah, Wyoming.

FLOWER: White.

HABITAT: Mountainsides and forests in dappled light or shade.

FORM: Small multi-stemmed flower.

EDIBLE PARTS: Berries, leaves.

HARVESTABLE: Summer, autumn.

FLAVOR: The berries are a burst of sweetness that beats anything found in stores. The leaves are mild.

NOTES: Probably billions of wild strawberry plants grow in the Rocky Mountains, taking advantage of the cooler temperatures and relatively high humidity in the forests at elevation. The berries rarely get larger than a pea because these plants often grown in shade, but sometimes you get lucky.

Finding ripe strawberries can be a real challenge because many woodland creatures, large and small, also find these berries delicious and begin eating them even before they turn red and ripe. Competition is fierce for the ripe berries, so whenever my wife and I find a berry, it makes our hike extra special.

Ripening times can vary widely depending on elevation, weather patterns, shade, soil alkalinity or acidity, and more. For classes I teach, I take groups into the forests and deserts and suburban pockets to teach them how to identify the best wild berries and where to find them in places they can be legally harvested. You can find information about my various classes, or sign up for my newsletter, at SeedRenaissance.com (enter your email address under "Join the List" in the bottom left corner of the website homepage).

Fragaria virginiana

(VIRGINIA STRAWBERRY)

STATES: Arizona, Colorado, Idaho, Montana, Nevada, New Mexico, Utah, Wyoming.

FLOWER: White.

CHARACTERISTICS: Some sources report that the Native Americans used these berries to treat stomachaches, but this story may immediately sound suspicious to any parent: "Mommy, my stomach hurts; I need to go gather strawberries." Children's tactics probably haven't changed much in centuries. If your kids are driving you crazy on a nice summer day, you probably would be happy to let them go hunt strawberries.

HABITAT: Mountainsides and forests in dappled light or shade.

FORM: Small multi-stemmed flower.

EDIBLE PARTS: Berries, leaves.

HARVESTABLE: Summer, autumn.

FLAVOR: The berries are a burst of sweetness that beats anything found in stores. The leaves are mild.

Gaillardia aristata

(INDIAN BLANKET)

————

STATES: Arizona, Colorado, Idaho, Montana, New Mexico, Utah, Wyoming.

FLOWER: The unique petals, going from yellow to red to black, strongly resemble the Indian blankets that are popular in tourist shops around the West and Southwest.

CHARACTERISTICS: I am always surprised to find these growing in the wild, usually in very dry, sandy conditions. They are sold in stores in the West not only because they are eye-catching but because they have low water requirements. We have grown them for years. There are more flowers which I have noted sporadically in this book that should taken into commercial cultivation because they are also beautiful and drought tolerant, making them perfect yard plants for the hot, dry Western summers.

HABITAT: Alkaline desert soils in open, sunny spaces.

FORM: Flower, typically growing 12 inches tall.

EDIBLE PARTS: Flowers, seeds.

HARVESTABLE: Summer, autumn.

FLAVOR: Mild.

NOTES: The flowers also tend to escape cultivation, and it is not uncommon to find them proliferating in tracts of suburban and rural houses, especially where the soil is alkaline.

Gaillardia pinnatifida

(RED DOME BLANKETFLOWER)

STATES: Arizona, Colorado, Nevada, New Mexico, Utah.

FLOWER: Yellow petals surround a red center dome, per the name.

CHARACTERISTICS: Butterflies love these flowers, so if you like watching butterflies, these plants are a good choice for Western flowerbeds. The flowers themselves can vary widely in form, sometimes having just a few petals and sometimes having many. Sometimes the dome is all red and sometimes it has some black, just to name a few variations.

HABITAT: Alkaline desert soils in open, sunny spaces.

FORM: Flower, typically growing 12 inches tall.

EDIBLE PARTS: Flowers, seeds.

HARVESTABLE: Summer, autumn.

FLAVOR: Mild.

NOTES: Widely grown in the West as landscaping flowers and sold in most plant nurseries. The flowers also tend to escape cultivation, and it is not uncommon to find them proliferating in tracts of suburban and rural houses, especially where the soil is alkaline.

194

Galega officinalis

(GOATSRUE)

STATES: Colorado, Utah.

FLOWER: White, purple.

HABITAT: Moist soil, roadsides.

FORM: Perennial flower, growing up to 3 feet tall.

EDIBLE PARTS: Leaves, rennet.

HARVESTABLE: Late spring, summer.

FLAVOR: Lemony.

NOTES: The leaves of goatsrue are also used as rennet to turn milk into a solid that can be used to make a soft cheese (edible plant #91). For full information about making cheeses with vegetable rennets, see my book *Make Your Own Cheese*. This plant was brought to Utah in the nineteenth century as an agricultural experiment and escaped into the wild.

Galium aparine

(CLEAVERS, GOOSEGRASS)

STATES: Arizona, Colorado, Idaho, Montana, Nevada, New Mexico, Utah, Wyoming.

FLOWER: White.

HABITAT: Mountainsides.

FORM: Herbaceous annual, growing less than a foot tall.

EDIBLE PARTS: Young leaves, seed barbs.

HARVESTABLE: Spring.

FLAVOR: Fresh and mild.

NOTES: For many centuries, the stems of this plant have been woven together and dried for use as a sieve.

This plant is known by dozens of regional names. This plant is also well known to children because the soft, edible seed barbs stick easily to clothing, making them a fun, free throwing toy. This trait is how the plant got it name: *apairo* in Greek means "seize" or "grab" because this plant does that so well.

Gaultheria hispidula

(CREEPING SNOWBERRY)

———

STATE: Idaho.

FLOWER: White.

CHARACTERISTICS: The *Gaultheria* plants in this book are cousins of *Gaultheria procumbens*, which is the plant that is widely used to produce the wintergreen oil in so many products people love for their revitalizing and medically useful fragrance.

BERRIES: White. **Always eat white berries sparingly.**

HABITAT: Moist mountain areas with shade and humidity.

FORM: Low-growing shrub.

EDIBLE PARTS: Leaves and berries.

HARVESTABLE: Summer, autumn.

FLAVOR: Wintergreen.

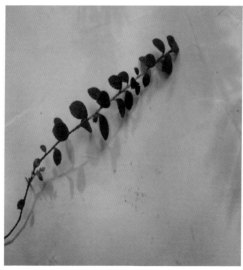

Gaultheria ovatifolia

(WESTERN TEABERRY)

———

STATES: Idaho, Montana.

FLOWER: White.

CHARACTERISTICS: Like all *Gaultheria*, the leaves are thick, leathery, and have a wax-like sheen.

BERRIES: White. **Always eat white berries sparingly.**

HABITAT: Moist mountain areas with shade and humidity.

FORM: Low-growing shrub.

EDIBLE PARTS: Leaves and berries.

HARVESTABLE: Summer, autumn.

FLAVOR: Wintergreen.

Geranium bicknellii

(BICKNELL'S CRANESBILL)

STATES: Colorado, Idaho, Montana, Utah, Wyoming.

FLOWER: Pink, light purple, or white.

CHARACTERISTICS: Like all wild geranium species, this plant is usually found in dappled light or partial shade instead of full sun.

HABITAT: Shady or dappled mountainsides.

FORM: Perennial flower, typically growing up to 3 feet tall.

EDIBLE PARTS: Flowers, leaves.

HARVESTABLE: Spring.

FLAVOR: Mild.

NOTE: The leaves can be sticky and hairy and don't have a texture that make you want to eat them, even though they are edible. The flower petals are the best part of these plants for eating.

Geranium caespitosum

(PINEYWOODS GERANIUM)

STATES: Arizona, Colorado, Nevada, New Mexico, Utah, Wyoming.

FLOWER: Pink, light purple, or white.

CHARACTERISTICS: This plant is a cousin of *Geranium robertianum*, which in the world of medicinal herbs is called "Herb-Robert," which is used by specialists to boost immunity and bring oxygen to cells, especially in cases of chronic sickness.

HABITAT: Shady or dappled mountainsides.

FORM: Perennial flower, typically growing up to 3 feet tall.

EDIBLE PARTS: Flowers, leaves.

HARVESTABLE: Spring.

FLAVOR: Mild.

NOTES: The leaves can be sticky and hairy and don't have a texture that make you want to eat them, even though they are edible. The flower petals are the best part of these plants for eating.

Geranium richardsonii

(RICHARDSON'S GERANIUM, ROCKY MOUNTAIN GERANIUM)

STATES: Arizona, Colorado, Idaho, Montana, Nevada, New Mexico, Utah, Wyoming.

FLOWER: Pink, light purple or white.

CHARACTERISTICS: Like all wild geranium species, the color of the flowers may just be highly variable or may depend on soil nutrients and microclimate.

HABITAT: Shady or dappled mountainsides.

FORM: Perennial flower, typically growing up to 3 feet tall.

EDIBLE PARTS: Flowers, leaves.

HARVESTABLE: Spring.

FLAVOR: Mild.

NOTES: The leaves can be sticky and hairy and don't have a texture that make you want to eat them, even though they are edible. The flower petals are the best part of these plants for eating.

Geranium viscosissimum

(STICKY PURPLE GERANIUM)

STATES: Colorado, Idaho, Montana, Nevada, New Mexico, Utah, Wyoming.

FLOWER: Pink or red, sometimes purple, rarely white.

CHARACTERISTICS: Most if not all wild geraniums have medicinal uses. Another benefit of all wild geraniums is that they are very common, and so in summer, you can find the petals for eating almost anywhere you go in the mountains.

HABITAT: Shady or dappled mountainsides.

FORM: Perennial flower, typically growing up to 3 feet tall.

EDIBLE PARTS: Flowers, leaves.

HARVESTABLE: Spring.

FLAVOR: Mild.

NOTES: The leaves can be sticky and hairy and don't have a texture that make you want to eat them, even though they are edible. The flower petals are the best part of these plants for eating.

Hedysarum alpinum

(ALPINE SWEETVETCH)

STATES: Montana, Wyoming.

FLOWER: Pink, red, or purple, depending on stage and environment.

CHARACTERISTICS: In his scholarly monograph *Native American Food Plants*, Daniel E. Moerman shares this fascinating tidbit about how Arctic peoples found and ate alpine sweetvetch: "Tubers [were] located in mice 'caches' by specially trained dogs and eaten." Dining out of mice nests is probably not going to appeal to many modern stomachs!

HABITAT: Mountainsides.

FORM: Perennial legume with showy flowers.

EDIBLE PART: Root.

HARVESTABLE: Summer.

FLAVOR: Mildly sweet licorice flavor.

Hedysarum boreale

(UTAH SWEETVETCH)

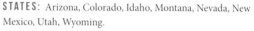

STATES: Arizona, Colorado, Idaho, Montana, Nevada, New Mexico, Utah, Wyoming.

FLOWER: Pink, red, or purple, depending on stage and environment.

CHARACTERISTICS: In 1819, Scottish explorer John Richardson, on an expedition to Canada, began a confusion that exists to this day when he wrote that roots of *Hedysarum boreale* were deliciously sweet and widely eaten by native North American tribes but *Hedysarum mackenziei* was poisonous. In his 1852 memoir of his days as an explorer (available free online on Google Books), he wrote that *Hedysarum mackenziei* "is poisonous and nearly killed an old Indian woman at Fort Simpson who had mistaken it for [*H. boreale*]. Fortunately, it proved emetic; and her stomach having rejected all that she had swallowed, she was restored to health." Problem is, modern research has shown that *H. mackenziei* does not exist—it is actually *H. boreale* and it is now commonly reclassified. This has led to a lot of confusion—is the plant poisonous or great eating? In 2008, researchers in the scientific journal *Ethnobotany Research and Applications* decided to clear up the issue once and for all, conducting extensive research and tests on the plant, which is commonly called wild sweet pea. Their results: "No chemical basis for toxicity could be found." They concluded that the plant is just as edible as *Hedysarum alpinum* but has a smaller root. Some naturalists say *Hedysarum* are entirely edible except for the seeds, which should be avoided. Unfortunately, the internet has done little to clear up the confusion. Bloggers and website owners with no real-world experience simply cut and paste the same old misinformation over and over again. If you are interested in true botanical science, the issues of *Ethnobotany Research and Applications* are available (as of this writing) at http: //journals.sfu.ca/era.

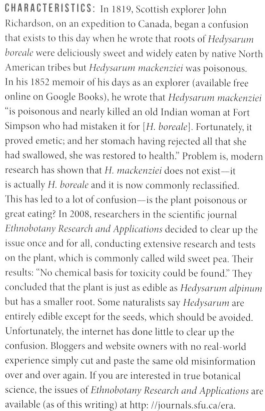

HABITAT: Mountainsides.

FORM: Perennial legume with showy flowers.

EDIBLE PART: Root.

HARVESTABLE: Summer.

FLAVOR: Mildly sweet licorice flavor, or carrot-like when young and tender.

Helianthus annuus

(COMMON SUNFLOWER)

STATES: Arizona, Colorado, Idaho, Montana, Nevada, New Mexico, Utah, Wyoming.

FLOWER: Yellow.

CHARACTERISTICS: The seeds are up to 25 percent protein, so they make a perfect hiking snack, and I eat them a lot. Sunflower oil is cholesterol-free and low in saturated fats.

HABITAT: Roadsides, disturbed lands, desert lands.

FORM: Single-stem tall flower.

EDIBLE PARTS: Seeds—raw, roasted, or sprouted. Immature flower buds—fresh or steamed. Oil from seeds.

HARVESTABLE: Summer.

FLAVOR: The seeds are nutty; the buds are mild, slightly sweet, and resinous.

NOTES: The seeds are easiest to harvest and eat at the moment the petals begin to wilt off the flower head because the hull is soft and can simply be eaten with the nut inside, no shelling necessary.

If you wait until the hull begins to harden, removing the hulls can be difficult. I suggest putting the dried sunflower seeds in a blender and pulsing slightly to crack the hulls or pounding the hulls. Then winnow to separate the seed pieces from hulls. However, this method can still leave little pieces of hull if not done carefully.

Helianthus anomalus

(WESTERN SUNFLOWER)

———————

STATES: Arizona, Nevada, New Mexico, Utah.

FLOWER: Yellow.

CHARACTERISTICS: This is a naturally occurring hybrid that is usually found in sand dunes. This species has a long bloom period, producing flowers for up to seven months a year. Because of this, it is worthy of consideration as a landscaping plant in the arid West, and I will try to make seeds available at SeedRenaissance.com. This plant is somewhat rare, especially in drought years, and if you find it, you may want to photograph it instead of harvesting it. The Xerces Society for Invertebrate Conservation lists this species as critical as food for native bees. The seeds of this species are larger than most wild sunflowers and rich in oil. The leaves are somewhat more leathery than most sunflowers because they are adapted for holding water in areas where water is scarce in summer.

HABITAT: Roadsides, disturbed lands, desert lands.

FORM: Single-stem tall flower.

EDIBLE PARTS: Seeds—raw, roasted, or sprouted. Immature flower buds—fresh or steamed. Oil from seeds.

HARVESTABLE: Summer.

FLAVOR: The seeds are nutty; the buds are mild, slightly sweet, and resinous.

NOTES: The seeds are easiest to harvest and eat at the moment the petals begin to wilt off the flower head because the hull is soft and can simply be eaten with the nut inside, no shelling necessary.

If you wait until the hull begins to harden, removing the hulls can be difficult. I suggest putting the dried sunflower seeds in a blender and pulsing slightly to crack the hulls or pounding the hulls. Then winnow to separate the seed pieces from hulls. However, this method can still leave little pieces of hull if not done carefully.

Helianthus arizonensis

(ARIZONA SUNFLOWER)

STATES: Arizona, New Mexico.

FLOWER: Yellow.

CHARACTERISTICS: Experts agree that some wild sunflowers can be difficult to tell apart, and this is one of those that looks like some other species, including *H. ciliaris*. This species can be perennial.

HABITAT: Roadsides, disturbed lands, desert lands.

FORM: Single-stem tall flower.

FLOWER: Yellow.

EDIBLE PARTS: Seeds—raw, roasted, or sprouted. Immature flower buds—fresh or steamed. Oil from seeds.

HARVESTABLE: Summer.

FLAVOR: The seeds are nutty; the buds are mild, slightly sweet, and resinous.

NOTES: The seeds are easiest to harvest and eat at the moment the petals begin to wilt off the flower head because the hull is soft and can simply be eaten with the nut inside, no shelling necessary.

If you wait until the hull begins to harden, removing the hulls can be difficult. I suggest putting the dried sunflower seeds in a blender and pulsing slightly to crack the hulls or pounding the hulls. Then winnow to separate the seed pieces from hulls. However, this method can still leave little pieces of hull if not done carefully.

Helianthus ciliaris

(TEXAS BLUEWEED)

STATES: Arizona, Colorado, Nevada, New Mexico, Utah.

FLOWER: Yellow, sometimes with large red centers.

CHARACTERISTICS: The stems and leaves have a blueish tint, which is how this plant gets its common name. It spreads underground by rhizome and is perennial but does not produce tubers. Experts agree it can be difficult to tell this species apart from *H. arizonensis.* In Texas, this plant, which can be impossible to get rid of once established, is considered a particularly noxious weed but only in areas with good summer water. This plant does produce seeds, but the germination rate is about 1 percent.

HABITAT: Roadsides, disturbed lands, desert lands.

FORM: Single-stem tall flower.

EDIBLE PARTS: Seeds—raw, roasted, or sprouted. Immature flower buds—fresh or steamed. Oil from seeds.

HARVESTABLE: Summer.

FLAVOR: The seeds are nutty; the buds are mild, slightly sweet, and resinous.

NOTES: The seeds are easiest to harvest and eat at the moment the petals begin to wilt off the flower head because the hull is soft and can simply be eaten with the nut inside, no shelling necessary.

If you wait until the hull begins to harden, removing the hulls can be difficult. I suggest putting the dried sunflower seeds in a blender and pulsing slightly to crack the hulls or pounding the hulls. Then winnow to separate the seed pieces from hulls. However, this method can still leave little pieces of hull if not done carefully.

Helianthus cusickii

(CUSICK'S SUNFLOWER)

———

STATES: Idaho, Nevada.

FLOWER: Yellow.

CHARACTERISTICS: This is one of the species of sunflowers that produces an edible potato-like tuber root. For this reason, it is sometimes called turnip root sunflower. The root is used like a sunchoke.

HABITAT: Roadsides, disturbed lands, desert lands.

FORM: Single-stem tall flower.

EDIBLE PARTS: Seeds—raw, roasted, or sprouted. Roots—raw or cooked. Immature flower buds—fresh or steamed. Oil from seeds.

HARVESTABLE: Summer.

FLAVOR: The seeds are nutty; the buds are mild, slightly sweet, and resinous.

NOTES: The seeds are easiest to harvest and eat at the moment the petals begin to wilt off the flower head because the hull is soft and can simply be eaten with the nut inside, no shelling necessary.

If you wait until the hull begins to harden, removing the hulls can be difficult. I suggest putting the dried sunflower seeds in a blender and pulsing slightly to crack the hulls or pounding the hulls. Then winnow to separate the seed pieces from hulls. However, this method can still leave little pieces of hull if not done carefully.

Helianthus maximiliani

(MAXIMILIAN SUNFLOWER)

———

STATES: Colorado, Idaho, Montana, New Mexico, Wyoming.

FLOWER: Yellow.

CHARACTERISTICS: This species has edible tuber roots, not as many or as large as sunchokes, but they can be plentiful if grown with enough moisture. In recent years, selections of Maximilian sunflowers have begun to be sold nationally as a drought-tolerant landscaping plant with lots of showy flowers. They also make good cut flowers. I will try to make the seeds available at SeedRenaissance. com.

HABITAT: Roadsides, disturbed lands, desert lands.

FORM: Single-stem tall flower.

EDIBLE PARTS: Seeds—raw, roasted, or sprouted. Immature flower buds—fresh or steamed. Oil from seeds.

HARVESTABLE: Summer.

FLAVOR: The seeds are nutty; the buds are mild, slightly sweet, and resinous.

NOTES: The seeds are easiest to harvest and eat at the moment the petals begin to wilt off the flower head because the hull is soft and can simply be eaten with the nut inside, no shelling necessary.

   If you wait until the hull begins to harden, removing the hulls can be difficult. I suggest putting the dried sunflower seeds in a blender and pulsing slightly to crack the hulls or pounding the hulls. Then winnow to separate the seed pieces from hulls. However, this method can still leave little pieces of hull if not done carefully.

Helianthus niveus

(SHOWY SUNFLOWER)

STATES: Arizona, Nevada, New Mexico.

FLOWER: Yellow.

CHARACTERISTICS: This species has been called perhaps the most heat tolerant of all sunflowers by some experts.

HABITAT: Roadsides, disturbed lands, desert lands.

FORM: Single-stem tall flower.

EDIBLE PARTS: Seeds—raw, roasted, or sprouted. Immature flower buds– fresh or steamed. Oil from seeds.

HARVESTABLE: Summer.

FLAVOR: The seeds are nutty; the buds are mild, slightly sweet, and resinous.

NOTES: The seeds are easiest to harvest and eat at the moment the petals begin to wilt off the flower head because the hull is soft and can simply be eaten with the nut inside, no shelling necessary.

If you wait until the hull begins to harden, removing the hulls can be difficult. I suggest putting the dried sunflower seeds in a blender and pulsing slightly to crack the hulls or pounding the hulls. Then winnow to separate the seed pieces from hulls. However, this method can still leave little pieces of hull if not done carefully.

Helianthus nuttallii

(NUTTALL'S SUNFLOWER)

———

STATES: Arizona, Colorado, Idaho, Montana, Nevada, New Mexico, Utah, Wyoming.

FLOWER: Yellow.

CHARACTERISTICS: This can be one of the tallest wild sunflowers, growing 13–15 feet tall in prime conditions. This species often prefers wet soil.

HABITAT: Roadsides, disturbed lands, desert lands.

FORM: Single-stem tall flower.

EDIBLE PARTS: Seeds—raw, roasted, or sprouted. Immature flower buds—fresh or steamed. Oil from seeds.

HARVESTABLE: Summer.

FLAVOR: The seeds are nutty; the buds are mild, slightly sweet, and resinous.

NOTES: The seeds are easiest to harvest and eat at the moment the petals begin to wilt off the flower head because the hull is soft and can simply be eaten with the nut inside, no shelling necessary.

If you wait until the hull begins to harden, removing the hulls can be difficult. I suggest putting the dried sunflower seeds in a blender and pulsing slightly to crack the hulls or pounding the hulls. Then winnow to separate the seed pieces from hulls. However, this method can still leave little pieces of hull if not done carefully.

Helianthus pauciflorus

(STIFF SUNFLOWER)

STATES: Arizona, Colorado, Montana, New Mexico, Wyoming.

FLOWER: Yellow.

CHARACTERISTICS: Here is an interesting tidbit from Illinoiswildflowers.info about *H. pauciflorus*: The roots produce rhizomes, forming dense colonies to shut out other species because the roots exude allelopathic chemicals that inhibit seed germination and growth of young plants. "Because prairie sunflower is somewhat vulnerable to these chemicals itself, the plants in the middle of a colony sometimes die out, creating a 'fairy ring' effect."

HABITAT: Roadsides, disturbed lands, desert lands.

FORM: Single-stem tall flower.

EDIBLE PARTS: Seeds—raw, roasted, or sprouted. Immature flower buds—fresh or steamed. Oil from seeds.

HARVESTABLE: Summer.

FLAVOR: The seeds are nutty; the buds are mild, slightly sweet, and resinous.

NOTES: The seeds are easiest to harvest and eat at the moment the petals begin to wilt off the flower head because the hull is soft and can simply be eaten with the nut inside, no shelling necessary.

    If you wait until the hull begins to harden, removing the hulls can be difficult. I suggest putting the dried sunflower seeds in a blender and pulsing slightly to crack the hulls or pounding the hulls. Then winnow to separate the seed pieces from hulls. However, this method can still leave little pieces of hull if not done carefully.

Helianthus petiolaris

(PRAIRIE SUNFLOWER)

STATES: Arizona, Colorado, Idaho, Montana, Nevada, New Mexico, Utah, Wyoming.

FLOWER: Yellow.

CHARACTERISTICS: Health food stores and some grocery stores have now begun to sell sunflower seed butter, which is like peanut butter but made of ground up sunflower seeds. This is a great use of any of the *Helianthus* species in this book.

HABITAT: Roadsides, disturbed lands, desert lands.

FORM: Single-stem tall flower.

EDIBLE PARTS: Seeds—raw, roasted, or sprouted. Immature flower buds—fresh or steamed. Oil from seeds.

HARVESTABLE: Summer.

FLAVOR: The seeds are nutty; the buds are mild, slightly sweet, and resinous.

NOTES: The seeds are easiest to harvest and eat at the moment the petals begin to wilt off the flower head because the hull is soft and can simply be eaten with the nut inside, no shelling necessary.

   If you wait until the hull begins to harden, removing the hulls can be difficult. I suggest putting the dried sunflower seeds in a blender and pulsing slightly to crack the hulls or pounding the hulls. Then winnow to separate the seed pieces from hulls. However, this method can still leave little pieces of hull if not done carefully.

Helianthus pumilus

(LITTLE SUNFLOWER)

———————

STATES: Colorado, Idaho, Wyoming.

FLOWER: Yellow.

CHARACTERISTICS: This is a naturally dwarf version of a sunflower.

HABITAT: Roadsides, disturbed lands, desert lands.

FORM: Single-stem tall flower.

EDIBLE PARTS: Seeds—raw, roasted, or sprouted. Immature flower buds—fresh or steamed. Oil from seeds.

HARVESTABLE: Summer.

FLAVOR: The seeds are nutty; the buds are mild, slightly sweet, and resinous.

NOTES: The seeds are easiest to harvest and eat at the moment the petals begin to wilt off the flower head because the hull is soft and can simply be eaten with the nut inside, no shelling necessary.

  If you wait until the hull begins to harden, removing the hulls can be difficult. I suggest putting the dried sunflower seeds in a blender and pulsing slightly to crack the hulls or pounding the hulls. Then winnow to separate the seed pieces from hulls. However, this method can still leave little pieces of hull if not done carefully.

Helianthus tuberosus

(SUNCHOKES, JERUSALEM ARTICHOKE)

STATES: Colorado, Idaho, Montana, Utah, Wyoming.

FLOWER: Yellow.

215

CHARACTERISTICS: *Helianthus tuberosus* (sunchoke) is widely grown in self-reliance gardens and backyard food forests, including mine, because it is a variety of sunflower that produces a potato-like root that is excellent when boiled or baked. It is also far healthier than common potatoes because it does not spike the glycemic load when eaten. They are now also being sold in grocery stores, including those local to me. They don't look exactly like potatoes, but when cooked and added to soups, stews, or casseroles, they are almost indistinguishable. I have served them to many people without telling them first what it is, and they all assumed it was potato. If you do grow or buy them to eat, here is a little tip: they don't need to be peeled unless they have an off-color spot. Simply scrub them with a vegetable brush and eat them with the skins on. They can be harvested any time of year, but the ideal time is February and March, making them what used to be called a hunger-gap food (a wild food available when most wild foods are in short supply). The tubers, which are very near the soil surface, spend the winter growing in size and then begin to shrink once the roots send out shoots in spring, so harvesting before the plant is active above ground ensures the best size. The tubers are larger if the plants are moderately fertilized. If you grow them in your garden like I do, it is a good idea to keep them contained because they can be aggressive in places with good water. I sell *Helianthus tuberosus* tubers and live potted plants in season at SeedRenaissance.com.

HABITAT: Roadsides, disturbed lands, desert lands.

FORM: Single-stem tall flower.

EDIBLE PARTS: Seeds—raw, roasted, or sprouted. Immature flower buds—fresh or steamed. Oil from seeds. Potato-like tuber root.

HARVESTABLE: Summer.

FLAVOR: The seeds are nutty; the buds are mild, slightly sweet, and resinous.

NOTES: The seeds are easiest to harvest and eat at the moment the petals begin to wilt off the flower head because the hull is soft and can simply be eaten with the nut inside, no shelling necessary.

   If you wait until the hull begins to harden, removing the hulls can be difficult. I suggest putting the dried sunflower seeds in a blender and pulsing slightly to crack the hulls or pounding the hulls. Then winnow to separate the seed pieces from hulls. However, this method can still leave little pieces of hull if not done carefully.

Heracleum sphondylium montanum

(COW PARSNIP)

216

STATES: Arizona, Colorado, Idaho, Montana, Nevada, New Mexico, Utah, Wyoming.

FLOWER: White.

HABITAT: Mountainsides.

FORM: Multi-stemmed perennial known for its large leaves and large seeds.

EDIBLE PARTS: Root, leaves, flowers.

HARVESTABLE: Spring.

FLAVOR: Bitter in summer; somewhat better in spring, but it is harder to correctly identify this plant in spring, so be careful harvesting at that time.

SYNONYM: *Heracleum maximum.*

Hibiscus trionum

(VENICE MALLOW)

STATES: Arizona, Colorado, Idaho, Montana, New Mexico, Utah, Wyoming.

FLOWER: White petals with a purple base.

HABITAT: Gardens, pasture, disturbed land.

FORM: Branching flower, typically growing 18 inches tall.

EDIBLE PART: Leaves.

HARVESTABLE: Spring, autumn, rarely summer.

FLAVOR: Mild radishy.

NOTES: This plant has an unusually large and showy flower for its size, and a century ago it was grown as a landscaping plant for its beauty.

Hordeum jubatum

(FOXTAIL BARLEY, SQUIRREL-
TAIL GRASS)

———————

STATES: Arizona, Colorado, Idaho, Montana, Nevada, New Mexico, Utah, Wyoming.

FLOWER: Green.

HABITAT: Fields, pastures, meadows, wastelands.

FORM: Single-stem grass, typically growing 18 inches tall.

EDIBLE PART: Seeds—raw, roasted, or ground for flour.

HARVESTABLE: Summer, autumn.

FLAVOR: Grain.

NOTES: This grass often forms colonies when it finds a sunny location that it likes. The seeds are sold by some companies as a landscaping ornamental because of the graceful way the grain moves in a breeze and because landscaping grasses have been popular in recent years.

219

Iliamna rivularis

(MOUNTAIN HOLLYHOCK)

———————

STATES: Colorado, Idaho, Montana, Nevada, Utah, Wyoming.

FLOWER: Pink.

HABITAT: Mountainsides.

FORM: Perennial flower somewhat resembling a hollyhock in shape.

EDIBLE PARTS: Petals, stems.

HARVESTABLE: Summer.

FLAVOR: Sweet, mild.

NOTES: I think this is one of the most beautiful of all the flowers found in the mountains, and that is saying something! These are not actually true hollyhocks, being in the mallow family, but they look so much like hollyhocks that everyone calls them hollyhocks. These should be more widely grown as a landscape plant in the West. Seeds are available at my website, SeedRenaissance.com.

Juglans major

(ARIZONA WALNUT)

STATES: Arizona, New Mexico, Utah.

FLOWER: Green.

CHARACTERISTICS: This tree grows up to 65 feet tall. The walnuts are ripe in midsummer or early autumn, depending on elevation.

HABITAT: Sunny spaces near water.

FORM: Tree.

EDIBLE PART: Nuts.

HARVESTABLE: Autumn.

FLAVOR: Nut.

220

Juglans microcarpa

(LITTLE WALNUT)

———————

STATE: New Mexico.

FLOWER: Green or whitish green.

CHARACTERISTICS: This species grows abou 30 feet tall, making it less than half the size of many walnut trees, which is how it got its common name. This tree is grown in backyards for the nuts and as a shade and landscape tree.

HABITAT: Sunny spaces near water.

FORM: Tree.

EDIBLE PART: Nuts.

HARVESTABLE: Autumn.

FLAVOR: Nut.

Juglans nigra

(BLACK WALNUT)

———

STATES: Colorado, New Mexico, Utah.

FLOWER: Green or yellowish green.

CHARACTERISTICS: This species grows up to 100 feet tall, making it a towering tree.

HABITAT: Sunny spaces near water.

FORM: Tree.

EDIBLE PART: Nuts.

HARVESTABLE: Autumn.

FLAVOR: Nut.

Juglans regia

(ENGLISH WALNUT)

———

STATE: Idaho.

FLOWER: Yellowish green.

CHARACTERISTICS: This tree grows up to 60 feet tall and is one of the most popular cultivated and backyard walnut trees. It is slow to start, like many nut trees, and does not produce a full harvest of nuts for two decades. The walnuts in stores in the United States are from this species partly because of the flavor but also because the shells of this walnut are thinnest and it is easy to get the nuts out. The wood is also long beloved for furniture.

HABITAT: Sunny spaces near water.

FORM: Tree.

EDIBLE PART: Nuts.

HARVESTABLE: Autumn.

FLAVOR: Nut.

Juniperus osteosperma

(JUNIPER TREE)

———

STATES: Arizona, Colorado, Idaho, Montana, Nevada, New Mexico, Utah, Wyoming.

FLOWER: Green.

HABITAT: Desert.

FORM: Tree, typically growing up to 20 feet tall.

EDIBLE PART: Berries—quenches thirst.

HARVESTABLE: Summer.

FLAVOR: Strongly wintergreen.

NOTES: Some people use this as a flavoring (a little goes a long way) for meat sauces (lamb or pork), but I don't like this use because the flavor is too much like wintergreen gum. My favorite use for these berries is to use one to bring water to my mouth when I am at my desert farm, or when hiking or rockhounding in the desert, to quench my thirst. It works very well for this, and the flavor is long lasting and powerful but not unpleasant. Can be bitter if desiccated, so it is better to use the berries when fresh in summer.

225

Kochia scoparia

(KOCHIA)

STATES: Arizona, Colorado, Idaho, Montana, Nevada, New Mexico, Utah, Wyoming.

FLOWER: Green.

HABITAT: Desert, waste spaces, roadsides, ditch banks, disturbed soil.

FORM: Pyramid-shaped herb, growing up to 5 feet tall.

EDIBLE PARTS: Leaves and seeds.

HARVESTABLE: Summer.

FLAVOR: Mild.

NOTES: Seeds are 20 percent protein, 8 percent fat. The pollen is a common allergen. If you suffer from allergies, see the section in this book on stinging nettle (edible plant #417). I am violently allergic to kochia pollen, but nettle has resolved this for me, and I only wish I had known about nettle and allergies years earlier.

Lactuca pulchella

(BLUE LETTUCE)

———————

STATES: Arizona, Colorado, Idaho, Montana, Nevada, New Mexico, Utah, Wyoming.

FLOWER: Blue.

HABITAT: Roadsides, waste spaces, disturbed soil.

FORM: Single-stem flower, typically growing up to 2 feet tall.

EDIBLE PART: Young leaves.

HARVESTABLE: Spring, summer.

FLAVOR: Mild.

NOTES: This plant has a long history of medicinal use. The flowers can be confused with chicory.

SYNONYM: *Mulgedium pulchellum* and *Lactuca tatarica* var. *pulchella*.

Lamium amplexicaule

(HENBIT)

STATES: Arizona, Colorado, Idaho, Montana, Nevada, New Mexico, Utah, Wyoming.

FLOWER: Red, purple.

CHARACTERISTICS: This is one of the mostly widely eaten backyard edibles in the West.

HABITAT: Waste spaces, gardens.

FORM: Low-growing herb unusual for its upright flowers above the foliage.

EDIBLE PARTS: Leaves, flowers.

HARVESTABLE: Spring.

FLAVOR: Herbaceous, ranging from mild to grassy to radishy.

NOTES: These cousins are members of the mint family. They have some resemblance to nettle leaves, but they have no sting.

Lamium purpureum

(PURPLE DEAD NETTLE)

STATES: Colorado, Idaho, Montana, Utah.

FLOWER: Red, purple.

CHARACTERISTICS: Every time I teach students about purple dead nettle (also called red dead nettle), I get the same response: no one wants to eat something with the word "dead" in the name. *Lamium* is from the Greek word for "throat," and *purpureum* means "purple," so the Latin name refers to the purple trumpet flowers. I have never been able to find an explanation for the reason why "dead" is in the name, or for this plant's other name, purple archangel. My only guess about the reason for these names comes from a great two-book set published in 1931 and still in print today (and worth owning) called *A Modern Herbal* by Margaret Grieve, which says that purple dead nettle has been used for centuries to stop bleeding in wounds. This could explain the "dead" reference in the name, and also the reference to archangel. I have never tried using the leaves to stop bleeding, and I have no idea if it works, but I know there are other herbs that do stop bleeding, so I don't doubt the veracity of the claim. It is also possible that "dead" refers to the highly unusual habit this plant has of the leaves turning purple on top as it matures, giving the (incorrect) appearance that the plant is dying from the top down.

At any rate, I've eaten these a lot, and both plants are widely eaten by foragers like me all over the country.

HABITAT: Waste spaces, gardens.

FORM: Low-growing herb unusual for its upright flowers above the foliage.

EDIBLE PARTS: Leaves, flowers.

HARVESTABLE: Spring.

FLAVOR: Herbaceous, ranging from mild to grassy to radishy.

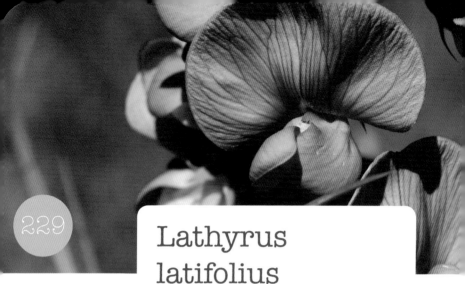

Lathyrus latifolius

(EVERLASTING PEAVINE, WILD SWEET PEA)

STATES: Arizona, Colorado, Idaho, Montana, Nevada, New Mexico, Utah, Wyoming.

FLOWER: Pink, purple.

CHARACTERISTICS: Some sources recommend that **this plant be eaten only in small amounts** because related species contain an acid that causes a neurological disease called "lathyrism." Experts say that there are no known reports regarding this species, just related species, but they still urge caution. I can tell you from personal experience that these peas are delicious when picked fresh on the hiking trail. They are almost as sweet as garden peas, and the pods are great eating too. I try to control myself and eat them only in small amounts, just in case. The flowers are also worthy of the backyard garden because they are huge and beautiful. I sell these seeds at SeedRenaissance.com.

HABITAT: Mountainsides, shady slopes.

FORM: Perennial legume.

EDIBLE PARTS: Peas and pea pod.

HARVESTABLE: Summer.

FLAVOR: Sweet and fresh.

Lepidium latifolium

(PERENNIAL PEPPERWEED)

STATES: Arizona, Colorado, Idaho, Montana, Nevada, New Mexico, Utah, Wyoming.

FLOWER: White.

CHARACTERISTICS: Some people boil these and then soak them overnight to remove the horseradish flavor, making them mild. Some people dry it for later use.

HABITAT: Gardens, disturbed soil, roadsides.

FORM: Small, single-stemmed branching herb known for its shield-like leaves.

EDIBLE PARTS: Leaves of both species, root of *L. latifolium*.

HARVESTABLE: Spring.

FLAVOR: Horseradish.

NOTES: If you like horseradish, you will love this plant. My students either love it or hate it because the flavor is strong and immediate.

231

Lepidium perfoliatum

(CLASPING PEPPERWEED)

———

STATES: Arizona, Colorado, Idaho, Montana, Nevada, New Mexico, Utah, Wyoming.

HABITAT: Gardens, disturbed soil, roadsides.

FORM: Small, single-stemmed branching herb known for its shield-like leaves.

FLOWER: White.

EDIBLE PARTS: Leaves of both species, root of *L. latifolium*.

HARVESTABLE: Spring.

FLAVOR: Horseradish.

NOTES: If you like horseradish, you will love this plant. My students either love it or hate it because the flavor is strong and immediate.

Lolium perenne

(ITALIAN RYEGRASS)

STATES: Arizona, Colorado, Idaho, Montana, Nevada, New Mexico, Utah, Wyoming.

FLOWER: Green.

HABITAT: Disturbed land, roadsides, pastures, waste spaces.

FORM: Perennial multi-stem grass.

EDIBLE PART: Seeds.

HARVESTABLE: Summer, autumn.

FLAVOR: Grain.

NOTES: Since in the 1960s, this grass has been sold and cultivated as lawn turf because it is perennial and withstands mowing well. Today there are dozens of cultivars sold for this purpose.

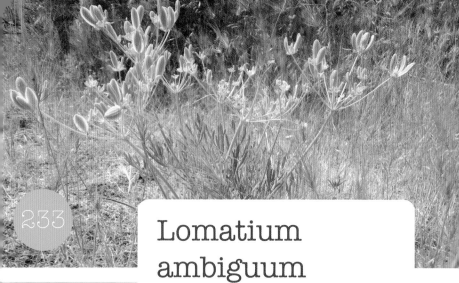

Lomatium ambiguum

(WYETH BISCUITROOT)

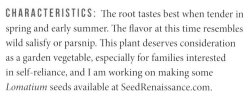

STATES: Idaho, Montana, Utah, Wyoming.

FLOWER: Yellow.

CHARACTERISTICS: The root tastes best when tender in spring and early summer. The flavor at this time resembles wild salisfy or parsnip. This plant deserves consideration as a garden vegetable, especially for families interested in self-reliance, and I am working on making some *Lomatium* seeds available at SeedRenaissance.com.

HABITAT: Rocky soils in desert areas.

FORM: Perennial aromatic herb, typically growing up to 2 feet tall.

EDIBLE PARTS: Root, seeds, flowers, leaves.

HARVESTABLE: Spring, summer, autumn.

FLAVOR: Mild.

NOTES: *Lomatium* species were widely harvested by American Indians, almost to extinction, so they are difficult to find today, but they are not actually extinct. **Harvest sparingly and responsibly.** Some rare butterflies depend on these plants. In addition, these plants flower early and then enter summer dormancy, which contributes to them being hard to locate.

Lomatium canbyi

(CANBY'S BISCUITROOT)

———

STATES: Idaho, Nevada.

FLOWER: White, occasionally pale purple or pale greenish yellow.

CHARACTERISTICS: Flowers in very early spring (March and April). Often found in sagebrush areas.

HABITAT: Rocky soils in desert areas.

FORM: Perennial aromatic herb, typically growing up to 2 feet tall.

EDIBLE PARTS: Root, seeds, flowers, leaves.

HARVESTABLE: Spring, summer, autumn.

FLAVOR: Mild.

NOTES: *Lomatium* species were widely harvested by American Indians, almost to extinction, so they are difficult to find today, but they are not actually extinct. **Harvest sparingly and responsibly.** Some rare butterflies depend on these plants. In addition, these plants flower early and then enter summer dormancy, which contributes to them being hard to locate.

235

Lomatium cous

(COUS BISCUITROOT)

STATES: Idaho, Montana, Nevada, Utah, Wyoming.

FLOWER: Yellow or greenish yellow.

CHARACTERISTICS: Native Americans used this and other *Lomatium* species to make a sort of unleavened bread that was stored for winter eating.

HABITAT: Rocky soils in desert areas.

FORM: Perennial aromatic herb, typically growing up to 2 feet tall.

EDIBLE PARTS: Root, seeds, flowers, leaves.

HARVESTABLE: Spring, summer, autumn.

FLAVOR: Mild.

NOTES: *Lomatium* species were widely harvested by American Indians, almost to extinction, so they are difficult to find today, but they are not actually extinct. **Harvest sparingly and responsibly.** Some rare butterflies depend on these plants. In addition, these plants flower early and then enter summer dormancy, which contributes to them being hard to locate.

Lomatium dissectum

(GIANT BISCUITROOT, FERNLEAF BISCUITROOT)

STATES: Arizona, Colorado, Idaho, Montana, Nevada, New Mexico, Utah, Wyoming.

FLOWER: Yellow, white; red; occasionally purple or blue.

CHARACTERISTICS: In recent years, this plant has taken on legendary status among some practitioners of herbal medicine because of an article published in 1921 in the *Appendix to the Journals of Senate and Assembly of the Thirteenth Session of the Legislature of the State of Nevada*, Volume Two (whew—a mouthful!). A medical doctor name Ernst T. Krebs reported that the "Washoe Indian used a root in the treatment of their sick. . . . It is cut up and a decoction is made by boiling the root in water, skimming off the top and giving large doses of the broth." There was a flu epidemic in the area at the time, and the people who used this treatment did not die. The root was considered rare even then, and is rarer today, but some doctors at the time began scientific trials on the root and found the healing benefits to be true. "It is beyond the experimental stage, as its therapeutic action . . . is established and beyond any doubt. There is probably no therapeutic agent so valuable in the treatment of influenzal pneumonia . . . if started early." As a practitioner of herbal medicine myself, I can tell you from experience that the last bit—"if started early"—is key to success of most herbal medicine. At any rate, today this species is prized for its antiviral potential by some.

HABITAT: Rocky soils in desert areas.

FORM: Perennial aromatic herb, typically growing up to 2 feet tall.

EDIBLE PARTS: Root, seeds, flowers, leaves.

HARVESTABLE: Spring, summer, autumn.

FLAVOR: Mild.

NOTES: These plants flower early and then enter summer dormancy, which contributes to them being hard to locate. There are now commercially available extracts of this plant sold as dietary supplements, all based on Dr. Krebs's 1921 legislative report. The report itself is only two pages long and very interesting to read. In 1921, the species name was *Leptotaenia dissecta*, but today it has been reclassified as *Lomatium dissectum*.

Lomatium foeniculaceum

(DESERT PARSLEY, DESERT BISCUITROOT)

———

STATES: Arizona, Colorado, Idaho, Montana, Nevada, New Mexico, Utah, Wyoming.

FLOWER: Yellow, pale yellow, or white.

CHARACTERISTICS: The leaves have a celery flavor. This species may be the most abundant of all the wild *Lomatium*.

HABITAT: Rocky soils in desert areas.

FORM: Perennial aromatic herb, typically growing up to 2 feet tall.

EDIBLE PARTS: Root, seeds, flowers, leaves.

HARVESTABLE: Spring, summer, autumn.

FLAVOR: Mild.

NOTES: *Lomatium* species were widely harvested by American Indians, almost to extinction, so they are difficult to find today, but they are not actually extinct. **Harvest sparingly and responsibly.** Some rare butterflies depend on these plants. In addition, these plants flower early and then enter summer dormancy, which contributes to them being hard to locate.

Lomatium gormanii

(GORMAN'S BISCUITROOT)

STATE: Idaho.

FLOWER: White with purple anthers, or sometimes the whole flower is pale purple.

CHARACTERISTICS: The leaves of this species are quite a bit less feathery or carrot-like than some other *Lomatium* species.

HABITAT: Rocky soils in desert areas.

FORM: Perennial aromatic herb, typically growing up to 2 feet tall.

EDIBLE PARTS: Root, seeds, flowers, leaves.

HARVESTABLE: Spring, summer, autumn.

FLAVOR: Mild.

NOTES: *Lomatium* species were widely harvested by American Indians, almost to extinction, so they are difficult to find today, but they are not actually extinct. **Harvest sparingly and responsibly.** Some rare butterflies depend on these plants. In addition, these plants flower early and then enter summer dormancy, which contributes to them being hard to locate.

Lomatium grayi

(GRAY'S BISCUITROOT)

STATES: Colorado, Idaho, Nevada, New Mexico, Utah, Wyoming.

FLOWER: Yellow.

CHARACTERISTICS: This is another *Lomatium* species that is prized for its medicinal values, and commercial preparations are sold online. "The first specimen of this plant was collected by Sereno Watson on Antelope Island in the Great Salt Lake in Utah around 1868," according to the Southwest Colorado Wildflowers website, SWColoradoWildflowers.com. (Interesting side note: my relatives were homesteading the island at the time and surely met him—the island is not that big. I imagine they shared a meal.) Watson was a Yale botanist who traveled the West as a botanical explorer in his younger years and later was the director of the Gray Herbarium of Harvard University. He was a monumental presence in North American botany.

HABITAT: Rocky soils in desert areas.

FORM: Perennial aromatic herb, typically growing up to 2 feet tall.

EDIBLE PARTS: Root, seeds, flowers, leaves.

HARVESTABLE: Spring, summer, autumn.

FLAVOR: Mild.

NOTES: *Lomatium* species were widely harvested by American Indians, almost to extinction, so they are difficult to find today, but they are not actually extinct. **Harvest sparingly and responsibly.** Some rare butterflies depend on these plants. In addition, these plants flower early and then enter summer dormancy, which contributes to them being hard to locate.

This plant deserves consideration as a garden vegetable, especially for families interested in self-reliance, and I am working on making seeds available at SeedRenaissance.com.

Lomatium macrocarpum

(BIGSEED BISCUITROOT)

STATES: Colorado, Idaho, Montana, Nevada, Utah, Wyoming.

FLOWER: Yellow, white, occasionally purple or blue. The flower color can change according to age or soil or environment.

CHARACTERISTICS: All *Lomatium* species are often found growing in sagebrush areas and are in bloom roughly at the same time as *Phlox* species, sometimes growing together.

HABITAT: Rocky soils in desert areas.

FORM: Perennial aromatic herb, typically growing up to 2 feet tall.

EDIBLE PARTS: Root, seeds, flowers, leaves.

HARVESTABLE: Spring, summer, autumn.

FLAVOR: Mild.

NOTES: *Lomatium* species were widely harvested by American Indians, almost to extinction, so they are difficult to find today, but they are not actually extinct. **Harvest sparingly and responsibly.** Some rare butterflies depend on these plants. In addition, these plants flower early and then enter summer dormancy, which contributes to them being hard to locate.

Lomatium nudicaule

(PESTLE PARSNIP, BARESTEM BISCUITROOT)

STATES: Idaho, Nevada, Utah.

FLOWER: Yellow.

CHARACTERISTICS: This species has very different leaves than most *Lomatium* species, with an arrow shape.

HABITAT: Rocky soils in desert areas.

FORM: Perennial aromatic herb, typically growing up to 2 feet tall.

EDIBLE PARTS: Root, seeds, flowers, leaves.

HARVESTABLE: Spring, summer, autumn.

FLAVOR: Mild.

NOTES: *Lomatium* species were widely harvested by American Indians, almost to extinction, so they are difficult to find today, but they are not actually extinct. **Harvest sparingly and responsibly.** Some rare butterflies depend on these plants. In addition, these plants flower early and then enter summer dormancy, which contributes to them being hard to locate.

Lomatium
triternatum

(NINELEAF BISCUITROOT)

———

STATES: Idaho, Montana, Nevada, Utah, Wyoming.

FLOWER: Yellow, white, occasionally purple or blue.

CHARACTERISTICS: The leaves of this species somewhat resemble antlers, with long, skinny green leaves that are sparse on the stem, often three to a stem. It makes for an interesting-looking plant, very different from the carrot-like foliage of most *Lomatiums*. The scientific name has been changed numerous times since it was first classified by by Meriwether Lewis on the Lewis and Clark Expedition in Idaho in about 1806. This is not surprising, since it really doesn't look like a "typical" *Lomatium* species. Whether or not it will be reclassified again, only time will tell.

HABITAT: Rocky soils in desert areas.

FORM: Perennial aromatic herb, typically growing up to 2 feet tall.

EDIBLE PARTS: Root, seeds, flowers, leaves.

HARVESTABLE: Spring, summer, autumn.

FLAVOR: Mild.

NOTES: *Lomatium* species were widely harvested by American Indians, almost to extinction, so they are difficult to find today, but they are not actually extinct. **Harvest sparingly and responsibly.** Some rare butterflies depend on these plants. In addition, these plants flower early and then enter summer dormancy, which contributes to them being hard to locate.

242

243

Lonicera involucrata

(TWINBERRY HONEYSUCKLE)

STATES: Arizona, Colorado, Idaho, Montana, Nevada, New Mexico, Utah, Wyoming.

HABITAT: Moist soil, typically near streams or seeps.

FORM: Shrub, growing up to 6 feet tall.

FLOWER: Yellow.

BERRY: Black or dark purple.

EDIBLE PART: Berries.

HARVESTABLE: June, July, August.

FLAVOR: Berries are spicy hot when raw; they are best when boiled and sweetened for juice. For best flavor, the berries should be harvested when soft to the touch, which indicates peak ripeness.

NOTES: I eat these berries a lot—raw, when hiking, because they are so juicy, probably the juiciest berry I know of. The skins of the berries are spicy hot, so I pop the berries in my mouth for the juice and then spit out the skins.

The berries are also valuable because they are available to harvest over most of the summer, especially if you hike at various elevations. Cooking removes most of the spicy flavor of the berries. Pick the ripe berries, bring them home, barely cover with water in a saucepan, and sweeten lightly to taste. I usually sweeten with the stevia herb, or the extract of stevia, but regular table sugar could also be used. Bring to a boil for 1 minute, strain, add ice, and serve.

My personal opinion is that the berries also boost the immune system, but this is based on personal observation. American Indians used various parts of this plant medicinally.

Lonicera utahensis

(UTAH HONEYSUCKLE)

———

STATES: Arizona, Idaho, Montana, New Mexico, Utah, Wyoming.

FLOWER: White or pale yellow.

BERRY: Red or reddish orange. The berries often come in pairs. The flowers are beautiful, as are the berries, and this could easily be an ornamental backyard shrub.

HABITAT: Moist soil, typically near streams or seeps.

FORM: Shrub, growing up to 6 feet tall.

EDIBLE PART: Berries.

HARVESTABLE: June, July, August.

FLAVOR: Berries are spicy hot when raw; they are best when boiled and sweetened for juice. For best flavor, the berries should be harvested when soft to the touch, which indicates peak ripeness.

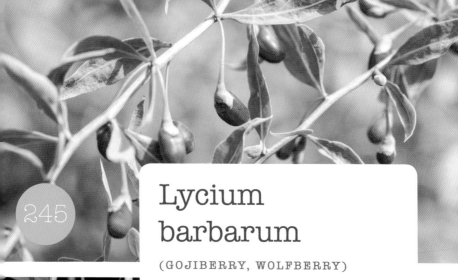

Lycium barbarum

(GOJIBERRY, WOLFBERRY)

————

STATES: Colorado, Idaho, Montana, Nevada, New Mexico, Utah, Wyoming.

FLOWER: Purple.

HABITAT: Moist, open, sunny soil ranging from deserts to mountains.

FORM: Woody perennial.

BERRY: Red.

EDIBLE PART: Berries.

HARVESTABLE: Spring, late summer.

FLAVOR: Sweet.

NOTES: These plants produce two berry crops a year, one in spring and one in early autumn. Occasionally a third crop is possible if there is a long autumn, and the plants also produce a few berries sporadically through summer.

I grow gojiberries in my yard and in my greenhouses and sell the organic plants each spring, and I always thought they were non-native. The first time I found them growing in the wild, I thought it was nice that someone had planted them where they could be harvested by the public. Today, I have found them growing wild in dozens of places ranging from high in the mountains to the deep desert and the suburbs. My guess is that that birds must have spread the seeds from people who were growing these plants in their yards after the plants became trendy "superberries" for a short time a few years ago. Anyone who has grown goji knows that they can be invasive and that they start easily from seed (I grow mine in containers to avoid them becoming a huge hedge). At any rate, however they got spread around the West, I'm always glad to find them and harvest them when hiking or rockhounding.

245

Lythrum salicaria

(PURPLE LOOSESTRIFE, PURPLE LYTHRUM)

STATES: Colorado, Idaho, Montana, Nevada, New Mexico, Utah, Wyoming.

FLOWER: Purple.

HABITAT: Moist soil.

FORM: Multi-stem perennial, showy flower, typically growing up to 3–4 feet tall.

EDIBLE PARTS: Leaves, root.

HARVESTABLE: Summer, autumn.

FLAVOR: Mild to slightly bitter.

NOTES: The name is a misnomer because this is not a true loosestrife. This plant is highly invasive.

Mahonia aquifolium

(OREGON GRAPE)

STATES: Idaho, Montana.

FLOWER: Yellow.

BERRY: Blue.

HABITAT: Mountainsides.

FORM: Woody perennial shrub.

EDIBLE PARTS: Berries, flowers.

HARVESTABLE: Late July, early August.

FLAVOR: Flowers are mild or slightly bitter, depending on microclimate. Berries are somewhat reminiscent of actual grapes, although not as sweet. The flavor also has woody notes and a slight juniper tang. Each berry has a small seed.

NOTES: We grow this evergreen shrub in our yard in several places as an edible landscaping plant. It is widely found in the wild, in the mountains in shady or semi-shady areas. The berries are sweetest when they go soft. The ideal time to harvest the whole cluster is when one or two grapes in the cluster just begin to show signs of wrinkling. The problem with the berries is that the stems have sharp small stickers, **so harvest cautiously or wear leather gloves.** The leaves of the plant are also sharp.

OREGON GRAPE SLUSH

(Makes two servings; may be doubled.)

- 1/4 cup ripe Oregon grape berries
- 1 cup water
- 1 cup ice
- 1/8 teaspoon stevia extract
- 1/2 teaspoon Sweet & Healthy Powdered Sugar Substitute (recipe in *The Stevia Solution*)

1. Rinse berries. Removing tiny stems is not necessary.
2. Add berries and water to blender and mix for 30 seconds, creating a beet-red liquid.
3. Strain into a bowl and discard seeds and pulp.
4. Rinse the blender container and add berry liquid back into blender.
5. Add remaining ingredients and puree until slush is created, about 30 seconds.
6. Serve immediately.

Mahonia fremontii

(FREMONT'S MAHONIA, DESERT HOLLY, DESERT OREGON GRAPE)

STATES: Arizona, Colorado, New Mexico, Utah.

FLOWER: Yellow.

CHARACTERISTICS: This species is commercially sold as a landscape plant because it is evergreen, covered in spring with bright yellow flowers, and long-lived. It is also drought tolerant and easy to care for.

BERRY: Blue.

HABITAT: Mountainsides.

FORM: Woody perennial shrub.

EDIBLE PARTS: Berries, flowers.

HARVESTABLE: Late July, early August.

FLAVOR: Flowers are mild or slightly bitter, depending on microclimate. Berries are somewhat reminiscent of actual grapes, although not as sweet. The flavor also has woody notes and a slight juniper tang. Each berry has a small seed.

Mahonia repens

(CREEPING OREGON GRAPE)

STATES: Arizona, Colorado, Idaho, Montana, Nevada, New Mexico, Utah, Wyoming.

FLOWER: Yellow.

CHARACTERISTICS: This is a smaller, low-growing version of Oregon Grape that is often found in pine forests in the West. This plant is also sold commercially as a landscape addition.

HABITAT: Mountainsides.

FORM: Woody perennial shrub.

BERRY: Blue.

EDIBLE PARTS: Berries, flowers.

HARVESTABLE: Late July, early August.

FLAVOR: Flowers are mild or slightly bitter, depending on microclimate. Berries are somewhat reminiscent of actual grapes, although not as sweet. The flavor also has woody notes and a slight juniper tang. Each berry has a small seed.

Malus coronaria

(SWEET CRAB APPLE)

STATE: Wyoming.

FLOWER: White or pink.

CHARACTERISTICS: The common name comes from the fragrance of the spring flowers, which are sweetly scented. The "sweet" epithet does not apply to the fruit. The crab apples are tart, as is typical of most crab apples.

HABITAT: Streambanks.

FORM: Tree, growing up to 25 feet tall but often shorter.

EDIBLE PART: Fruit.

HARVESTABLE: Summer, autumn.

FLAVOR: Tart.

Malus pumila

(PARADISE APPLE)

STATES: Colorado, Montana, Nevada, New Mexico, Utah, Wyoming.

FLOWER: White or pinkish white.

CHARACTERISTICS: This species is where domesticated apples originated from.

HABITAT: Streambanks.

FORM: Tree, growing between 15 and 20 feet tall.

EDIBLE PART: Fruit.

HARVESTABLE: Summer, autumn.

FLAVOR: Sweet in good conditions and when fully ripe.

Malus sylvestris

(EUROPEAN CRAB APPLE)

STATE: Utah.

FLOWER: White.

CHARACTERISTICS: This species is sometimes planted in apple orchards because it is a good pollinator for many domesticated apples. It is an ancestor of domestic apples.

HABITAT: Streambanks.

FORM: Tree.

EDIBLE PART: Fruit.

HARVESTABLE: Summer, autumn.

FLAVOR: Tart.

Malva neglecta

(COMMON MALLOW)

STATES: Arizona, Colorado, Idaho, Montana, Nevada, New Mexico, Utah, Wyoming.

FLOWER: Pale lavender, white.

HABITAT: Disturbed soils, pastures, gardens, roadsides, slopes.

FORM: Spreading, low-growing herbaceous flower.

EDIBLE PARTS: Leaves, flower, peas.

HARVESTABLE: Spring, summer, autumn.

FLAVOR: Mild and slightly sweet.

NOTES: This is one of the most useful plants in the world. The immature seeds form a flat fruit like a pea, are delicious raw or parboiled, and don't need to be peeled.

The whole plant is mucilaginous, meaning it forms a healthy gelatin-like substance when crushed, blended, or cooked. The cousin of this plant was used to create the original marshmallow, using the mucilage foam, and that plant is called marsh mallow. The foam of common mallow is also used to make homemade marshmallows. I use stevia as the sweetener so they are healthy.

The leaves are great raw or cooked.

The root is a wonderful cheese rennet and is one of the very few plants in the world which produces a rennet that can be used to make hard cheeses instead of just soft cheeses. You can learn to make these simple mallow cheeses in my book *Make Your Own Cheese.*

I grow this plant in my greenhouses in winter because I don't want to be without it, and it is hardy and makes a wonderful winter salad green.

The dried roots can also be used to make homemade liquid soap.

Seeds are available at SeedRenaissance.com.

254

Matricaria discoidea

(PINEAPPLE WEED)

––––––––

STATES: Arizona, Colorado, Idaho, Montana, Nevada, New Mexico, Utah, Wyoming.

FORM: Flowering annual herb, typically less than 12 inches tall.

FLOWER: White, yellow.

HABITAT: Moist disturbed soil, waste places, stream banks.

EDIBLE PART: Flowers.

HARVESTABLE: Summer.

FLAVOR: Has a sweet pineapple-like fragrance if crushed when young, but the flavor, sadly, is often slightly bitter.

Medicago lupulina

(BLACK MEDIC)

————

STATES: Arizona, Colorado, Idaho, Montana, Nevada, New Mexico, Utah, Wyoming.

FLOWER: Yellow.

CHARACTERISTICS: Black medic is often found in lawns and is more drought tolerant than regular grass, making it a good no-mow or seldom-mow lawn alternative. It is soft when stepped on and stays green all summer and autumn.

HABITAT: Roadsides, lawns, pastures, waste spaces.

FORM: Multi-stemmed flowering herb, typically growing up to 2 feet tall.

EDIBLE PARTS: Leaves, seeds.

HARVESTABLE: Summer, autumn.

FLAVOR: Grass.

256

Medicago polymorpha

(CALIFORNIA BURCLOVER)

STATES: Arizona, Idaho, Montana, Nevada, New Mexico, Utah, Wyoming.

FLOWER: Yellow.

CHARACTERISTICS: This plant looks a lot like black medic (on the previous page) but produces burs on the plant.

HABITAT: Roadsides, lawns, pastures, waste spaces.

HARVESTABLE: Summer.

FORM: Multi-stemmed flowering herb, typically growing up to 2 feet tall.

EDIBLE PARTS: Leaves, seeds.

HARVESTABLE: Summer, autumn.

FLAVOR: Grass.

Medicago sativa

(ALFALFA)

STATES: Arizona, Colorado, Idaho, Montana, Nevada, New Mexico, Utah, Wyoming.

FLOWER: Purple.

HABITAT: Roadsides, lawns, pastures, waste spaces.

FORM: Multi-stemmed flowering herb, typically growing up to 2 feet tall.

EDIBLE PARTS: Leaves, seeds.

HARVESTABLE: Summer, autumn.

FLAVOR: Grass.

NOTES: Herbal experts call alfalfa the multivitamin of the herbal world because it is so rich in vitamins, and some people take it every day for this purpose. For information about medicinal herbs, see my book *Forgotten Skills of Backyard Herbal Healing and Family Health*.

Melilotus albus

(WHITE SWEETCLOVER)

STATES: Arizona, Colorado, Idaho, Montana, Nevada, New Mexico, Utah, Wyoming.

FLOWER: White.

CHARACTERISTICS: It's disappointing that *Melilotus* species, named sweetclover, have such a bitter and drying flavor in the mouth, and I wondered aloud about this one day when hiking. My wife said the old-timers called these plants "sweet clover" because cows foddered on them gave sweet milk. The things you learn when you are married!

HABITAT: Roadsides, slopes, waste spaces.

FORM: Single-stem branching herb with spikes of flowers.

EDIBLE PARTS: *M. albus, M. officinalis*—Flowers, seedpods, leaves (not dried). *M. indicas*—Leaves (not dried).

HARVESTABLE: Summer.

FLAVOR: Bitter.

Melilotus indicas

(INDIAN SWEETCLOVER, SOUR
SWEETCLOVER, ANNUAL YELLOW
SWEETCLOVER)

STATES: Arizona, Idaho, Nevada, New Mexico, Utah.

FLOWER: Yellow.

CHARACTERISTICS: The leaves give a sweet smell, and the dried leaves are sometimes used to repel moths and other insects. The beautiful yellow flowers are an important food source for bees. Because this plant also has various traditional medicinal uses, it has been the subject of numerous modern studies showing it may be useful for inflammation and other issues. According to Montana. plant-life.org, "a distilled water obtained from the flowering tops is an effective treatment for conjunctivitis." This plant is nearly identical to *M. officinalis* except that it grows a bit shorter and the flowers are a bit smaller.

HABITAT: Roadsides, slopes, waste spaces.

FORM: Single-stem branching herb with spikes of flowers.

EDIBLE PARTS: *M. albus*, *M. officinalis*—Flowers, seedpods, leaves (not dried). *M. indicas*—Leaves (not dried).

HARVESTABLE: Summer.

FLAVOR: Bitter raw. May be better cooked.

Melilotus officinalis

(YELLOW SWEETCLOVER)

STATES: Arizona, Colorado, Idaho, Montana, Nevada, New Mexico, Utah, Wyoming.

FLOWER: Yellow, white.

CHARACTERISTICS: An important source of food for many pollinators, butterfly and moth caterpillars, and other creatures too. Some experts say this is the same plant as *M. albus* except that albus has white flowers—but as is typical in the world of botany, other experts disagree, and the issue is not likely to ever be resolved.

HABITAT: Roadsides, slopes, waste spaces.

FORM: Single-stem branching herb with spikes of flowers.

EDIBLE PARTS: *M. albus, M. officinalis*—Flowers, seedpods, leaves (not dried). *M. indicas*—Leaves (not dried).

HARVESTABLE: Summer.

FLAVOR: Bitter.

Morus alba

(WHITE MULBERRY)

STATES: Arizona, Colorado, Idaho, Montana, New Mexico, Utah, Wyoming.

FLOWER: Green.

HABITAT: Sunny, open spaces with regular water.

FORM: Tree, growing 50 feet tall.

EDIBLE PARTS: Fruit, leaves.

HARVESTABLE: Summer.

FLAVOR: Sweet and only slightly tart when fully ripe.

NOTES: These trees were introduced to the West and indeed the whole country when settlers attempted to create silkworm industries to manufacture silk. In the West, those efforts survived for a time. Today some of the long-lived trees planted by the pioneers still stand and can often be found in pioneer neighborhoods and early city parks. The berries resemble elongated blackberries.

Nasturtium officinale

(WATERCRESS)

————

STATES: Arizona, Colorado, Idaho, Montana, Nevada, New Mexico, Utah, Wyoming.

FLOWER: White.

HABITAT: Grows in water or wet soil.

FORM: Low-growing, flowering perennial herb.

EDIBLE PARTS: Leaves, seeds.

HARVESTABLE: Summer, autumn, sometimes spring (depending on temperature).

FLAVOR: Hot.

NOTES: When I was growing up, the old-timers still ate watercress sandwiches, which is a lost food that should probably make a comeback. When I was young, the recipe was homemade butter on homemade bread with cress between the slices of bread.

Nuphar polysepala

(SPATTERDOCK, ROCKY
MOUNTAIN POND LILY)

———

STATES: Arizona, Colorado, Idaho, Montana, Nevada, New Mexico, Utah, Wyoming.

FLOWER: Yellow.

HABITAT: Grows in shallow lakes and ponds or at the edges.

FORM: Perennial thick-leaved rhizomatous water plant, typically growing 4 feet tall.

EDIBLE PARTS: Roots, seeds.

HARVESTABLE: Summer.

FLAVOR: The roots have a strong flavor that is not good, but the seeds when roasted have a popcorn flavor; however, it takes a canoe or kayak to harvest them!

NOTES: As with anything being harvested from a waterway, **make sure the water is clean and the vegetable is thoroughly washed before eating.** Don't eat if there are nearby mine tailings, which wash heavy metals into waterways, as the metals are then taken up into plant tissues.

Opuntia polyacantha

(PLAINS PRICKLY PEAR CACTUS)

STATES: Arizona, Colorado, Idaho, Montana, Nevada, New Mexico, Utah, Wyoming.

FLOWER: Yellow with red centers.

CHARACTERISTICS: "The green cactus 'pads' (platyclades) are actually stems that have adapted to survive with very little water. These pads are armed with two kinds of spines; large, smooth, fixed spines and small, hairlike spines called glochids that easily penetrate skin and detach from the plant. Glochids are easily dislodged, difficult to see, and even more difficult to remove. In Mexico and the Southwestern United States, this plant is a vital source of food and drinks that are derived from the juice, fruits, stems, and flowers. Prickly pear fruits and young flower petals are edible. The fruits or 'tunas' are cut in half and seeds removed. They resemble pomegranates in color, taste, and texture, although they have glochids on the outside and must be handled carefully. The tunas can then be eaten raw or used to make jams and jellies. The young petals can be eaten raw or cooked" (US Forest Service data).

HABITAT: Desert.

FORM: Low-growing cactus with pad leaves and thorns.

EDIBLE PARTS: Seeds, fruit, pad **(beware thorns)**.

HARVESTABLE: Any time.

FLAVOR: Fruit is slightly sweet. Pad is mild.

NOTES: There are dozens of species of *Opuntia*, and all are edible. I have many fond memories of *Opuntia*, which I grow in my flower garden thanks to my oldest grandson, Xander, who digs it out of the river gully and brings it to me because he knows I'm fond of this prickly plant.

When I was a youth, my wonderful scoutmaster, Ed Dutson, was intent that we learn American Indian and self-reliance skills. He was an expert in both, and he had a huge influence on my life. He taught us to harvest *Opuntia* and roast it over the campfire, allowing the spines to be burned off by the fire. We then learned to carefully cut open the roasted pad to avoid the hairlike spines under the skin. The flavor is very mild and actually a lot of fun to eat.

Ed Dutson was a giant among men, and I am grateful to him for his devotion to scouting, to helping me earn my Eagle, and for taking us camping once a month, even in winter. We were a handful, and he was patient.

Orogenia linearifolia

(INDIAN POTATO)

————

STATES: Colorado, Idaho, Utah, Wyoming.

FLOWER: White.

HABITAT: Mountain meadows.

FORM: Low-growing flowering perennial that appears quickly after the snow melts.

EDIBLE PART: Root.

HARVESTABLE: Spring, summer, autumn.

FLAVOR: Pleasant and crispy when raw, and not unlike a potato when cooked.

NOTES: Like most of the important tubers that sustained the American Indians, this plant was heavily harvested for centuries and can be difficult to find today. Harvest only sparingly. I am trying to make seeds available at SeedRenaissance.com.

Even though these tubers grow fairly close to the surface, they must be dug up, not pulled up, because the plant separates easily. I have looked in many museums, but I have never seen a tool that I believe they could have used to harvest these easily. I hope that, after death, we get access to an archive of movies allowing us to witness firsthand how previous generations and cultures lived. Fingers crossed!

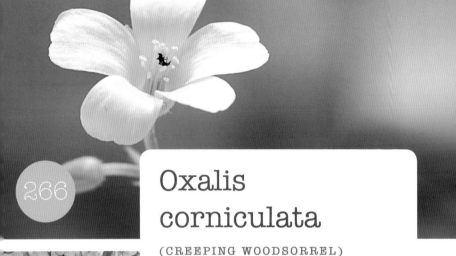

Oxalis corniculata

(CREEPING WOODSORREL)

———

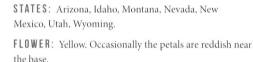

STATES: Arizona, Idaho, Montana, Nevada, New Mexico, Utah, Wyoming.

FLOWER: Yellow. Occasionally the petals are reddish near the base.

CHARACTERISTICS: The leaves and stems can be green or purple or a combination. The leaves fold downward in shade and open up in light. The leaves and petals contain oxalic acid and should be eaten sparingly, but they are delicious. This is a food source for many pollinators, caterpillars, and other creatures, including rabbits and deer.

HABITAT: Shady, moist locations.

FORM: Low-growing flowering herb.

EDIBLE PARTS: Flowers, leaves, roots, seedpods.

HARVESTABLE: Summer, autumn.

FLAVOR: Strong lemon.

Oxalis stricta

(YELLOW WOODSORREL)

STATES: Arizona, Colorado, Idaho, Montana, New Mexico, Wyoming.

FLOWER: Yellow.

CHARACTERISTICS: The leaves and petals contain oxalic acid and should be eaten sparingly, but they are delicious. The leaves fold downward in shade and open up in light. The flowers are what botanists call "diurnal," meaning they open only during the day and close at night. Oxalis planted itself in the earthen walls of one of my geothermal greenhouses, and they grow there year-round, so I often get to snack on them. They are a wonderful treat. Kids love them too, and I always have people taste them on tours of my greenhouses during classes. Woodsorrel is also a possible candidate for no-mow or seldom-mow lawn alternatives. One interesting trait about this plant: it has the unique ability to literally shoot the seeds. The seed pods look like horns.

HABITAT: Shady, moist locations.

FORM: Low-growing flowering herb.

EDIBLE PARTS: Flowers, leaves, roots, seedpods.

HARVESTABLE: Summer, autumn.

FLAVOR: Strong lemon.

Panicum capillare

(WITCHGRASS)

STATES: Arizona, Colorado, Idaho, Montana, Nevada, New Mexico, Utah, Wyoming.

FLOWER: Green.

CHARACTERISTICS: Witchgrass is a beautiful plant that I find fascinating. I always wait before pulling it out of my garden beds because I love the way it looks, but I don't want to leave it long enough to drop too many seeds, causing me weeding problems the next year in my desert-method hugelkultur gardens. Seeds are 10 percent protein, but they are very small.

HABITAT: Disturbed soils, gardens, fields, roadsides.

FORM: Branching, spreading grass.

EDIBLE PART: Seeds.

HARVESTABLE: Late summer, early autumn.

FLAVOR: Grain.

Panicum dichotomiflorum

(FALL PANICUM)

STATES: Arizona, Colorado, Idaho, Montana, Nevada, New Mexico, Utah.

FLOWER: Green.

CHARACTERISTICS: The different panicum species can be difficult to tell apart and are sometimes differentiated only by the size of the seeds or whether they have hairy or hairless stems. This plant, like most panicums, really takes off in the heat of summer and can grow rapidly once it sprouts.

HABITAT: Disturbed soils, gardens, fields, roadsides.

FORM: Branching, spreading grass.

EDIBLE PART: Seeds.

HARVESTABLE: Late summer, early autumn.

FLAVOR: Grain.

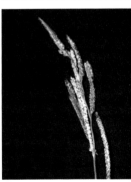

Panicum miliaceum

(WILD PROSO MILLET, BROOM CORN MILLET)

———————

STATES: Arizona, Colorado, Idaho, Montana, Nevada, New Mexico, Utah, Wyoming.

FLOWER: Green.

CHARACTERISTICS: This plant has larger seeds than most panicum species, making the seeds more useful as food. The seeds are shiny and brown in color when ripe. This plant grows wild in my garden, and the youngs plant come up at the same time as the young corn in the garden, which can be very hard to tell apart in the beginning. This is the same species that produces the commercial millet grain, and seeds are usually available at SeedRenaissance. com. This grain has been popular for thousands of years because it tolerates heat and drought and has a mild flavor. According to the US Department of Agriculture, proso millet contains more protein and iron than wheat or rice.

HABITAT: Disturbed soils, gardens, fields, roadsides.

FORM: Branching, spreading grass.

EDIBLE PART: Seeds.

HARVESTABLE: Late summer, early autumn.

FLAVOR: Grain.

Parthenocissus quinquefolia

(VIRGINIA CREEPER)

STATES: Colorado, Utah.

FLOWER: Green, sometimes with pink.

HABITAT: Sunny or shady locations near water, where it is often found climbing trees, shrubs, and even utility poles.

FORM: Climbing vine.

EDIBLE PART: Berries.

HARVESTABLE: Autumn.

FLAVOR: Somewhat bitter. This is not likely to become your favorite berry, even if you use the stevia herb to sweeten it.

NOTES: This vine is widely planted as a landscape plant, and we grow it in our backyard.

Many authors say they are poisonous, and they may be, in large amounts. Some people say the berries leave a tingling sensation in their mouth. Some people have an allergic reaction to the leaves. We know from documentation that the American Indians ate these berries regularly, and they had a far better sense of what was poisonous and what isn't than almost anyone alive today. Their lives depended on knowing what was poisonous every day and every meal!

Pediomelum esculentum

(LARGE INDIAN BREADROOT)

———

STATES: Colorado, Montana, New Mexico, Wyoming.

FLOWER: White.

HABITAT: Prairie.

FORM: A perennial of the pea family with spectacular spikes of flowers.

EDIBLE PART: Root.

HARVESTABLE: Summer, autumn.

FLAVOR: Mild and starchy.

NOTES: American Indians used the roots fresh and dried. These roots were so widely harvested that today they can be difficult to find. Because the roots are so large and useful, this is an important plant for anyone interested in food forests or self-reliance or native foods, and I am working to make seeds available at SeedRenaissance.com.

Perideridia gairdneri

(GARDNER'S YAMPAH)

————

STATES: Colorado, Idaho, Montana, Nevada, Utah, Wyoming.

FLOWER: White.

CHARACTERISTICS: Most *Perideridia* species are lanky plants with stems like bare green sticks and not many leaves. This plant looks like many other plants, some of them poisonous. The roots can look almost like long fingers.

HABITAT: Moist soil.

FORM: Herbaceous flower, growing up to 4 feet tall.

EDIBLE PARTS: Leaves, root.

HARVESTABLE: Spring, summer, autumn.

FLAVOR: Starchy, mild.

SYNONYM: *Carum gairdneri.*

Perideridia lemmonii

(LEMMON'S YAMPAH)

———

STATE: Nevada.

FLOWER: White.

CHARACTERISTICS: The root of this species may be smaller than other *Perideridia* species, and this species is rarer and more difficult to find. All *Perideridia* species can be difficult to tell apart. In addition, this plant looks like many other plants, some of them poisonous. **Never eat any part of any wild plant unless you know with certainty what you are ingesting.**

HABITAT: Moist soil.

FORM: Herbaceous flower, growing up to 4 feet tall.

EDIBLE PARTS: Leaves, root.

HARVESTABLE: Spring, summer, autumn.

FLAVOR: Starchy, mild.

Perideridia parishii

(PARISH'S YAMPAH)

———————

STATES: Arizona, Nevada, New Mexico.

FLOWER: White.

CHARACTERISTICS: Most *Perideridia* species are similar in appearance and can be difficult to tell apart. This and other *Perideridia* species are important food sources for some butterflies. This plant looks like many other plants, some of them poisonous. The ideal time for harvesting the root is in late autumn, after the first frosts and after the plant has begun to die down, which makes correct identification even more problematic.

HABITAT: Moist soil.

FORM: Herbaceous flower, growing up to 4 feet tall.

EDIBLE PARTS: Leaves, root.

HARVESTABLE: Spring, summer, autumn.

FLAVOR: Starchy, mild.

Phlox austromontana

(SOUTHERN MOUNTAIN PHLOX)

STATES: Arizona, Colorado, Idaho, Nevada, New Mexico, Utah.

FLOWER: Often pink, sometimes pale purple or white.

CHARACTERISTICS: This is a low-growing phlox that forms a kind of mat of flowers.

HABITAT: Desert and dry slopes.

FORM: Low-growing perennial flower hugging the ground and covered with early spring flowers.

EDIBLE PART: Flowers.

HARVESTABLE: Spring.

FLAVOR: Mild and slightly sweet.

NOTES: I eat these flower petals a lot when hiking, a great spring treat! These flowers are synonymous with spring and widely sold as landscaping plants for early spring color. These flowers grow wild near my northern Utah home and also all over my central Utah desert farm, bringing welcome color and flavor to the otherwise sparse spring landscape.

Phlox diffusa

(SPREADING PHLOX)

STATES: Arizona, Colorado, Idaho, Montana, Nevada, New Mexico, Utah, Wyoming.

FLOWER: Purple, white, pink, and sometimes even red.

CHARACTERISTICS: Forms a mound or a low mat of flowers. Many *Phlox* species can be difficult to tell apart. If you catch this plant on the right day, it is a mound of flowers which cover all the leaves and is strikingly beautiful, as are all *Phlox*.

HABITAT: Desert and dry slopes.

FORM: Low-growing perennial flower hugging the ground and covered with early spring flowers.

EDIBLE PART: Flowers.

HARVESTABLE: Spring.

FLAVOR: Mild and slightly sweet.

Phlox hoodii

(SPINY PHLOX)

STATES: Arizona, Colorado, Idaho, Montana, Nevada, New Mexico, Utah, Wyoming.

FLOWER: Pink, pale purple, white.

CHARACTERISTICS: Even experts can have trouble telling one *Phlox* species from another, and sometimes argue whether species like *Phlox hoodii* are really separate species or simply varieties of a species. And then some botanists argue that some variations should be considered separate species. Luckily, being able to separate every species and variety of *Phlox* for another is not necessary for enjoying them.

HABITAT: Desert and dry slopes.

FORM: Low-growing perennial flower hugging the ground and covered with early spring flowers.

EDIBLE PART: Flowers.

HARVESTABLE: Spring.

FLAVOR: Mild and slightly sweet.

Phlox longifolia

(LONGLEAF PHLOX)

STATES: Arizona, Colorado, Idaho, Montana, Nevada, New Mexico, Utah, Wyoming.

FLOWER: White or sometimes bright pink.

CHARACTERISTICS: The flowers on this species can be sparse compared to other types that form a mat of flowers. SWColoradowildflowers.com says that botanist Nathaniel Wyeth was the first to collected this plant, probably in 1833 on an expedition. He gave his specimen to Thomas Nuttall, who named and described this plant in 1834.

HABITAT: Desert and dry slopes.

FORM: Low-growing perennial flower hugging the ground and covered with early spring flowers.

EDIBLE PART: Flowers.

HARVESTABLE: Spring.

FLAVOR: Mild and slightly sweet.

NOTES: I eat these flower petals a lot when hiking, a great spring treat! These flowers are synonymous with spring and widely sold as landscaping plants for early spring color. These flowers grow wild near my northern Utah home and also all over my central Utah desert farm, bringing welcome color and flavor to the otherwise sparse spring landscape.

Phlox multiflora

(ROCKY MOUNTAIN PHLOX)

STATES: Colorado, Idaho, Montana, Nevada, New Mexico, Utah, Wyoming.

FLOWER: Often white, sometimes pink, or purple.

CHARACTERISTICS: This species is often found only at high elevations, above 7,000 feet and up to 10,000 feet.

HABITAT: Desert and dry slopes.

FORM: Low-growing perennial flower hugging the ground and covered with early spring flowers.

EDIBLE PART: Flowers.

HARVESTABLE: Spring.

FLAVOR: Mild and slightly sweet.

Phlox paniculata

(COMMON PHLOX)

STATE: Utah.

FLOWER: Pink, pale purple, white.

CHARACTERISTICS: This is the wild *Phlox* species that is widely sold as a perennial landscaping plant, and there are more than 150 varieties in a range of colors sold commercially. This is a great example of how a native flower has been used to create hardy, beautiful garden flowers.

HABITAT: Desert and dry slopes.

FORM: Low-growing perennial flower hugging the ground and covered with early spring flowers.

EDIBLE PART: Flowers.

HARVESTABLE: Spring.

FLAVOR: Mild and slightly sweet.

Phlox stansburyi

(COLD DESERT PHLOX)

STATES: Arizona, Nevada, New Mexico, Utah.

FLOWER: Often pink, sometimes pale purple or white.

CHARACTERISTICS: This is a more upright and relatively taller phlox than most but still only gets about 8 inches tall. It is often found in deserts and blooms early as most phlox do. These plants can turn the desert into a flower garden for about two weeks each year.

HABITAT: Desert and dry slopes.

FORM: Low-growing perennial flower hugging the ground and covered with early spring flowers.

EDIBLE PART: Flowers.

HARVESTABLE: Spring.

FLAVOR: Mild and slightly sweet.

NOTES: I eat these flower petals a lot when hiking, a great spring treat! These flowers are synonymous with spring and widely sold as landscaping plants for early spring color. These flowers grow wild near my northern Utah home and also all over my central Utah desert farm, bringing welcome color and flavor to the otherwise sparse spring landscape.

283

Phlox variabilis

(VARIEGATED PHLOX)

STATES: Colorado, Idaho, Montana, New Mexico, Utah, Wyoming.

FLOWER: Pink or white.

CHARACTERISTICS: This is a fairly rare form of phlox and forms a low-growing mat of flowers in early spring.

HABITAT: Desert and dry slopes.

FORM: Low-growing perennial flower hugging the ground and covered with early spring flowers.

EDIBLE PART: Flowers.

HARVESTABLE: Spring.

FLAVOR: Mild and slightly sweet.

NOTES: I eat these flower petals a lot when hiking, a great spring treat! These flowers are synonymous with spring and widely sold as landscaping plants for early spring color. These flowers grow wild near my northern Utah home and also all over my central Utah desert farm, bringing welcome color and flavor to the otherwise sparse spring landscape.

Phragmites australis

(COMMON REED)

STATES: Arizona, Colorado, Idaho, Montana, Nevada, New Mexico, Utah, Wyoming.

FLOWER: Red.

HABITAT: Grows in water or wet soil.

FORM: Spiky grass growing up to 13 feet high with leaves 2 inches wide and sometimes 2 feet long.

EDIBLE PARTS: Leaves, root, seeds, stem.

HARVESTABLE: Spring, summer, autumn.

FLAVOR: Sweet.

NOTES: As with all edible plants harvested from water, harvest only in locations with clean water and rinse thoroughly before eating. **Don't harvest from areas where mine tailings poison water with heavy metal deposits,** which can be a surprisingly high number of places in the Rocky Mountain West.

285

Physalis acutifolia

(SHARPLEAF GROUNDCHERRY)

STATES: Arizona, New Mexico.

FLOWER: White or pale yellow with a yellow center.

CHARACTERISTICS: The flowers often droop down to face the ground, which is too bad because the flowers are beautiful (this drooping is typical of many *Physalis* species). The flowers of this species can be relatively large compared to other *Physalis* species.

HABITAT: Lawns, gardens, fields, meadows with regular water.

FORM: Flowering perennial, typically growing 1–2 feet tall.

EDIBLE PART: Fruit.

HARVESTABLE: Summer.

FLAVOR: Mild and bland.

NOTES: Historically, these fruits are typically sweetened when eaten or can be added to salsas. Flavor is best when fruits are completely ripe. The berry is covered in a papery shell that dries when the berry is ripe.

Physalis angulata

(CUTLEAF GROUNDCHERRY)

———

STATES: Arizona, Nevada, New Mexico.

FLOWER: White with a pale yellow or pale yellowish-green center.

CHARACTERISTICS: The flowers are fairly small compared to other *Physalis* species.

HABITAT: Lawns, gardens, fields, meadows with regular water.

FORM: Flowering perennial, typically growing 1–2 feet tall.

EDIBLE PART: Fruit.

HARVESTABLE: Summer.

FLAVOR: Mild and bland.

NOTES: Historically, these fruits are typically sweetened when eaten or can be added to salsas. Flavor is best when fruits are completely ripe. The berry is covered in a papery shell that dries when the berry is ripe.

Physalis cinerascens

(SMALLFLOWER GROUNDCHERRY)

STATES: Colorado, New Mexico.

FLOWER: Yellow with a dark center that is black or brown or dark purple.

CHARACTERISTICS: This species has relatively small flowers, thus the common name.

HABITAT: Lawns, gardens, fields, meadows with regular water.

FORM: Flowering perennial, typically growing 1–2 feet tall.

EDIBLE PART: Fruit.

HARVESTABLE: Summer.

FLAVOR: Mild and bland.

NOTES: Historically, these fruits are typically sweetened when eaten or can be added to salsas. Flavor is best when fruits are completely ripe. The berry is covered in a papery shell that dries when the berry is ripe.

Physalis crassifolia

(YELLOW NIGHTSHADE GROUNDCHERRY)

STATES: Arizona, Nevada, Utah.

FLOWER: Yellow or yellowish green.

CHARACTERISTICS: This species can be found in drier areas than most groundcherry species and tolerates drought. This plant is rare and may be endangered in Utah and perhaps in all areas where it is found. If you find this plant, you may want to photograph it instead of harvesting it.

HABITAT: Lawns, gardens, fields, meadows with regular water.

FORM: Flowering perennial, typically growing 1–2 feet tall.

EDIBLE PART: Fruit.

HARVESTABLE: Summer.

FLAVOR: Mild and bland.

NOTES: Historically, these fruits are typically sweetened when eaten or can be added to salsas. Flavor is best when fruits are completely ripe. The berry is covered in a papery shell that dries when the berry is ripe.

Physalis hederifolia

(IVYLEAF GROUNDCHERRY)

———

STATES: Arizona, Colorado, Montana, Nevada, New Mexico, Utah, Wyoming.

FLOWER: Yellow with a darker greenish center.

CHARACTERISTICS: This species is considered critically endangered in Wyoming and may be endangered in other Rocky Mountain states. If you find it, especially in Wyoming, you may want to photograph it instead of harvesting it.

HABITAT: Lawns, gardens, fields, meadows with regular water.

FORM: Flowering perennial, typically growing 1–2 feet tall.

EDIBLE PART: Fruit.

HARVESTABLE: Summer.

FLAVOR: Mild and bland.

NOTES: Historically, these fruits are typically sweetened when eaten or can be added to salsas. Flavor is best when fruits are completely ripe. The berry is covered in a papery shell that dries when the berry is ripe.

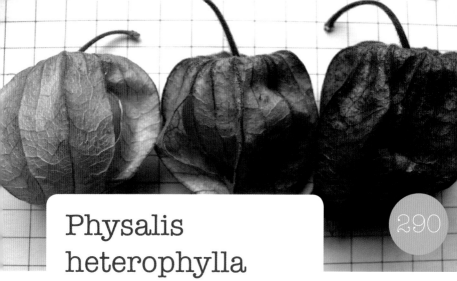

Physalis heterophylla

(CLAMMY GROUNDCHERRY)

STATES: Arizona, Colorado, Idaho, Montana, New Mexico, Utah, Wyoming.

FLOWER: Yellow with a bold dark or black center.

CHARACTERISTICS: This species likes dry soil and is often found in sand or desert areas. This species can have fine white hairs on the leaves and stems and has relatively large leaves.

HABITAT: Lawns, gardens, fields, meadows with regular water.

FORM: Flowering perennial, typically growing 1–2 feet tall.

EDIBLE PART: Fruit.

HARVESTABLE: Summer.

FLAVOR: Mild and bland.

NOTES: Historically, these fruits are typically sweetened when eaten or can be added to salsas. Flavor is best when fruits are completely ripe. The berry is covered in a papery shell that dries when the berry is ripe.

291

Physalis latiphysa

(BROADLEAF GROUNDCHERRY)

———————

STATE: Arizona.

FLOWER: Yellow with a bold dark or black center.

CHARACTERISTICS: This species is very rare and considered critically endangered. It is found only in one state in the nation. If you find this species, you should photograph it and not harvest it.

HABITAT: Lawns, gardens, fields, meadows with regular water.

FORM: Flowering perennial, typically growing 1–2 feet tall.

EDIBLE PART: Fruit.

HARVESTABLE: Summer.

FLAVOR: Mild and bland.

NOTES: Historically, these fruits are typically sweetened when eaten or can be added to salsas. Flavor is best when fruits are completely ripe. The berry is covered in a papery shell that dries when the berry is ripe.

Physalis longifolia

(LONGLEAF GROUNDCHERRY)

STATES: Arizona, Colorado, Idaho, Montana, Nevada, New Mexico, Utah, Wyoming.

FLOWER: Yellow, greenish-yellow, or rarely cream petals, always with a dark center.

CHARACTERISTICS: This species grows in every state in the continental United States. Interestingly, the University of Kansas Native Medicinal Plant Research Program reports that their chemists "have discovered 14 compounds new to science in *Physalis longifolia*. Four of the compounds have shown potent cytotoxity against specific types of cancer."

HABITAT: Lawns, gardens, fields, meadows with regular water.

FORM: Flowering perennial, typically growing 1–2 feet tall.

EDIBLE PART: Fruit.

HARVESTABLE: Summer.

FLAVOR: Mild and bland.

NOTES: Historically, these fruits are typically sweetened when eaten, or can be added to salsas. Flavor is best when fruits are completely ripe. The berry is covered in a papery shell that dries when the berry is ripe.

Physalis philadelphica

(MEXICAN GROUNDCHERRY)

STATES: Arizona, Idaho, New Mexico.

FLOWER: Yellow with a purple center and purple anthers.

CHARACTERISTICS: This species is the tomatillo widely cultivated and sold in stores. Wherever it is found in the wild in the Rocky Mountain West, it has escaped from people's gardens.

HABITAT: Lawns, gardens, fields, meadows with regular water.

FORM: Flowering perennial, typically growing 1–2 feet tall.

EDIBLE PART: Fruit.

HARVESTABLE: Summer.

FLAVOR: Mild and bland.

NOTES: Historically, these fruits are typically sweetened when eaten or can be added to salsas. Flavor is best when fruits are completely ripe. The berry is covered in a papery shell that dries when the berry is ripe.

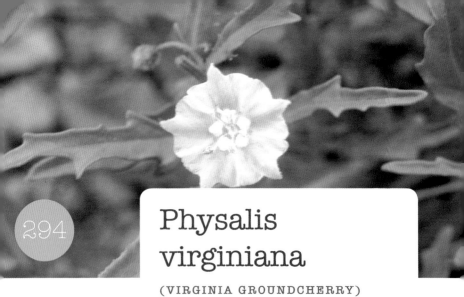

294

Physalis virginiana

(VIRGINIA GROUNDCHERRY)

———

STATES: Colorado, New Mexico, Wyoming.

FLOWER: Yellow with a bold dark center.

CHARACTERISTICS: The ripe fruits are yellow or orange, as are some other physalis species. This species is widely found across the United States.

HABITAT: Lawns, gardens, fields, meadows with regular water.

FORM: Flowering perennial, typically growing 1–2 feet tall.

EDIBLE PART: Fruit.

HARVESTABLE: Summer.

FLAVOR: Mild and bland.

NOTES: Historically, these fruits are typically sweetened when eaten or can be added to salsas. Flavor is best when fruits are completely ripe. The berry is covered in a papery shell that dries when the berry is ripe.

Pinus contorta

(LODGEPOLE PINE)

STATES: Colorado, Idaho, Montana, Nevada, Utah, Wyoming.

FLOWER: Red, brown, or brownish green.

CHARACTERISTICS: Nuts of most of the trees listed here were traditionally eaten whole or pounded into nut butters, which were sometimes mixed with other foods.

The cones that contain the nuts for the *Pinus* species in this book develop for two years before the nuts are ready to harvest. The nuts can sometimes be removed by shaking the cone, but most often the cones must be smashed. Pine nut harvesting is a traditional and popular pastime in the West.

HABITAT: Desert, forest.

FORM: Tree.

EDIBLE PART: Nuts, roasted or raw.

HARVESTABLE: Grass-like.

FLAVOR: Delicious nutty flavor when roasted, somewhat bland when raw.

Pinus edulis

(TWO-NEEDLE PINYON PINE)

———

STATES: Arizona, Colorado, Nevada, New Mexico, Utah, Wyoming.

FLOWER: Red, brown.

CHARACTERISTICS: For all the *Pinus* species in this book, it is easiest to gather the cones with a fruit picker basket, also called an apple picker, or by shaking the limbs of the tree with a stick or lumber with a sheet or blanket below. The nuts can be eaten raw, the cones can be roasted over coals before the nuts are harvested, or the nuts can be oven roasted at home.

HABITAT: Desert, forest.

FORM: Tree.

EDIBLE PART: Nuts, roasted or raw.

HARVESTABLE: Autumn.

FLAVOR: Delicious nutty flavor when roasted, somewhat bland when raw.

Pinus flexilis

(LIMBER PINE)

STATES: Arizona, Colorado, Idaho, Montana, Nevada, New Mexico, Utah, Wyoming.

FLOWER: Red, brown.

CHARACTERISTICS: Many of the forests of pine nut–producing trees are found on Bureau of Land Management land, and harvesting is usually allowed, but permits may be required by some regional offices. As of this writing, Great Basin National Park allows pine nut harvesting by the public only in the autumn, and with the following rules: The nuts may be gathered and removed from the park only for personal non-commercial use. Limit 25 lbs. per household per year or 3 gunnysacks of cones per household per year. No off-road parking or driving. Breaking branches, cutting, pulling, shaking, climbing, or otherwise injuring pines or other plants is illegal. Only free-standing ladders may be used for picking.

HABITAT: Desert, forest.

FORM: Tree.

EDIBLE PART: Nuts, roasted or raw.

FLAVOR: Grass-like.

NOTES: Delicious nutty flavor when roasted, somewhat bland when raw.

Pinus lambertiana

(SUGAR PINE)

STATE: Nevada.

FLOWER: Green.

CHARACTERISTICS: While the nuts of all these trees are edible, sugar pine has something else to offer—sugary sweet sap, which is boiled down to syrup like maple sap. When wounded, the tree extrudes a sweet liquid as well. Both sap and liquid are laxative, so eat in small quantities.

American Indians purposefully wounded the tree to gather the sweet sap as a delicacy and a food sweetener. Nuts of most of the trees listed here were traditionally eaten whole or pounded into nut butters, which were sometimes mixed with other foods.

HABITAT: Desert, forest.

FORM: Tree.

EDIBLE PART: Nuts, roasted or raw.

HARVESTABLE: Autumn.

FLAVOR: Delicious nutty flavor when roasted, somewhat bland when raw.

Pinus monophylla

(SINGLE-LEAF PINYON PINE)

———————

STATES: Arizona, Idaho, Nevada, New Mexico, Utah.

FLOWER: Red, brown.

CHARACTERISTICS: According to Conifers.org, the oldest known living example of this species was born in 1106 AD. This ancient tree was found in Nevada and its location is kept secret for its protection.

HABITAT: Desert, forest.

FORM: Tree.

EDIBLE PART: Nuts, roasted or raw.

HARVESTABLE: Autumn.

FLAVOR: Delicious nutty flavor when roasted, somewhat bland when raw.

Pinus monticola

(WESTERN WHITE PINE)

———

STATES: Idaho, Montana, Nevada, Utah.

FLOWER: Red, brown.

CHARACTERISTICS: This species can grow more than 200 feet tall in the wild. This is the state tree of Idaho and is often used commercially in making matchsticks.

HABITAT: Desert, forest.

FORM: Tree.

EDIBLE PART: Nuts, roasted or raw.

HARVESTABLE: Autumn.

FLAVOR: Delicious nutty flavor when roasted, somewhat bland when raw.

Pinus ponderosa

(PONDEROSA PINE)

STATES: Arizona, Colorado, Idaho, Montana, Nevada, New Mexico, Utah, Wyoming.

FLOWER: Red, brown.

CHARACTERISTICS: Many people don't realize that you can grow pine nut trees in your own backyard in the Rocky Mountain West if you have enough space, and some local nurseries sell pine nut trees. Be aware that it could be eight to ten years after planting before you start getting good nut crops from your trees. Planting two is best for pollination, and if you plant only one, you may never get a good harvest. I recommend putting them on the north side of your property because most of the *Pinus* species listed in this book can grow 60 feet tall or higher, and if you plant them on the south side of your property, they might shade the rest of your yard.

HABITAT: Desert, forest.

FORM: Tree.

EDIBLE PART: Nuts, roasted or raw.

HARVESTABLE: Autumn.

FLAVOR: Delicious nutty flavor when roasted, somewhat bland when raw.

Plantago lanceolata

(NARROWLEAF PLANTAIN)

———

STATES: Arizona, Colorado, Idaho, Montana, Nevada, New Mexico, Utah, Wyoming.

FLOWER: White.

CHARACTERISTICS: Both this species and *P. major* are also widely used medicinally. Broadleaf plantain does not tolerate alkaline soil well and because of this is usually only found at high elevations in the Rocky Mountain West. Narrowleaf plantain tolerates alkaline soil well and is more abundant in the Rocky Mountains for this reason.

HABITAT: Mountainsides, disturbed soil, gardens, roadsides.

FORM: Low-growing perennial flowering herb.

FLOWER: *P. lanceolata* flowers are white. *P. major* flowers are green and red.

EDIBLE PARTS: Leaves, seeds.

HARVESTABLE: Spring, summer, autumn.

FLAVOR: Mild and grassy.

Plantago major

(BROADLEAF PLANTAIN)

STATES: Arizona, Colorado, Idaho, Montana, Nevada, New Mexico, Utah, Wyoming.

FLOWER: Green and red.

CHARACTERISTICS: This species is widely found growing in most of the United States and even in many places around the world, but it is harder to find the Rocky Mountain West because it does not like alkaline soil. Look for it in the acidic soils of the high mountain elevations, especially growing below pine trees.

HABITAT: Mountainsides, disturbed soil, gardens, roadsides.

FORM: Low-growing perennial flowering herb.

EDIBLE PARTS: Leaves, seeds.

HARVESTABLE: Spring, summer.

FLAVOR: Mild and grassy.

Polygonum amphibium

(WILLOW GRASS, WATER KNOTWEED)

———————

STATES: Arizona, Colorado, Idaho, Montana, Nevada, New Mexico, Utah, Wyoming.

FLOWER: Pink.

CHARACTERISTICS: Grows in water. Blooms all summer and can produce a beautiful mass of flowers.

FORM: Herbaceous perennial water plant with floating branches.

HABITAT: Wet mountainside soils along seeps, streams, and lakes.

EDIBLE PARTS: Leaves, seeds.

HARVESTABLE: Spring, summer, autumn.

FLAVOR: Mild.

Polygonum arenastrum

(SMALL-LEAFED KNOTWEED,
OVAL-LEAF KNOTWEED)

———————

STATES: Arizona, Colorado, Idaho, Montana, Nevada, New Mexico, Utah, Wyoming.

FLOWER: White.

FORM: Herbaceous wet-soil annual, sometimes found in dry soils.

HABITAT: Wet mountainside soils along seeps, streams, and lakes.

EDIBLE PARTS: Leaves, seeds.

HARVESTABLE: Spring, summer, autumn.

FLAVOR: Mild.

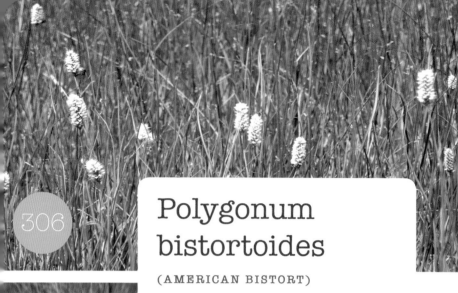

Polygonum bistortoides

(AMERICAN BISTORT)

STATES: Arizona, Colorado, Idaho, Montana, Nevada, New Mexico, Utah, Wyoming.

FLOWER: White.

FORM: Flowering herb, growing up to 2 feet tall.

HABITAT: Wet mountainside soils along seeps, streams, and lakes.

EDIBLE PARTS: Leaves, seeds.

HARVESTABLE: Spring, summer, autumn.

FLAVOR: American bistort leaves are mild, but the root is strongly bitter.

NOTES: Of all the *Polygonum*, I eat bistort the most. The best part of this plant are the leaves, which are tender and mild.

The American Indians ate the tuberous root of American bistort, which is found about 4 inches below ground, and when it is washed and peeled, it is a beautiful pale pink color and appears to be delicious—until you taste it. The flavor is actually strongly bitter. Cooking and boiling reduces the bitterness a little but not enough to make this root worthwhile. Boiling and changing the water several times may help.

The flower of bistort is striking for its beauty. The first time I ever saw the flower in person was at a campground in the High Uintas, and I was enchanted by them. I came home and researched the plants and was pleased to discover it was edible. Today I grow them in my shade garden because I like the flowers so much. For whatever reason, I also like the common name a lot.

FORM: Herbaceous perennial flower.

SYNONYM: *Bistorta bistortoides.*

Polygonum cuspidatum

(JAPANESE KNOTWEED)

STATES: Colorado, Idaho, Montana, Utah.

FLOWER: White or greenish white.

CHARACTERISTICS: Can be aggressive, growing up to 4 inches a day during summer. This plant is also a traditional medicinal plant used around the world. Best eaten when tender in spring.

FORM: Tall herbaceous plant.

HABITAT: Wet mountainside soils along seeps, streams, and lakes.

EDIBLE PARTS: Leaves, seeds, stem.

HARVESTABLE: Spring, summer, autumn.

FLAVOR: Rhubarb.

Polygonum douglasii

(DOUGLAS'S KNOTWEED)

———

STATES: Arizona, Colorado, Idaho, Montana, Nevada, New Mexico, Utah, Wyoming.

FLOWER: White or pinkish.

FORM: Herbaceous grasslike annual.

HABITAT: Wet mountainside soils along seeps, streams, and lakes.

EDIBLE PARTS: Leaves, seeds.

HARVESTABLE: Spring, summer, autumn.

Polygonum lapathifolium

(CURLYTOP KNOTWEED)

————

STATES: Arizona, Colorado, Idaho, Montana, Nevada, New Mexico, Utah, Wyoming.

FLOWER: White changing to pink and red with age.

FORM: Herbaceous wet soil annual.

HABITAT: Wet mountainside soils along seeps, streams, and lakes.

EDIBLE PARTS: Leaves, seeds.

HARVESTABLE: Spring, summer, autumn.

FLAVOR: Mild.

Polygonum persicaria

(SPOTTED LADYSTHUMB)

———

STATES: Arizona, Colorado, Idaho, Montana, Nevada, New Mexico, Utah, Wyoming.

FLOWER: Pink or purple.

CHARACTERISTICS: The leaves are high in pectin and contain about 3 percent sugar.

FORM: Herbaceous wet soil annual.

HABITAT: Wet mountainside soils along seeps, streams, and lakes.

EDIBLE PARTS: Leaves, seeds.

HARVESTABLE: Spring, summer, autumn.

FLAVOR: Mild and somewhat sweet.

Polypogon monspeliensis

(RABBITFOOT POLYPOGON)

STATES: Arizona, Colorado, Idaho, Montana, Nevada, New Mexico, Utah, Wyoming.

HABITAT: Wet mountainside soils along seeps, streams, and lakes.

FLOWER: White, purple.

EDIBLE PARTS: Leaves, seeds.

HARVESTABLE: Spring, summer, autumn.

FLAVOR: Mild.

Portulaca oleracea

(COMMON PURSLANE)

STATES: Arizona, Colorado, Idaho, Montana, Nevada, New Mexico, Utah, Wyoming.

FLOWER: Yellow.

CHARACTERISTICS: The leaves are high in pectin and contain about 3 percent sugar.

HABITAT: Disturbed soils, roadsides, gardens, fields.

FORM: Low-growing, spreading succulent.

EDIBLE PARTS: Leaves, stems, flowers, seeds.

HARVESTABLE: Summer, autumn.

FLAVOR: Lemony, crunchy, and succulent.

NOTES: This is one of the most popular wild edibles wherever it is found growing, and one of my favorites. I like to say it tastes like a crunchy romaine salad with the lemon vinaigrette built right in. The tiny seeds are created in miniature cups on the plant, and are highly windborn, so I weed out hundreds of these plants each year, often eating as I go. Sometimes I eat so many of these plants that I can't stand the thought of eating more for a few days.

Prosopis glandulosa

(WESTERN HONEY MESQUITE)

STATES: Arizona, Colorado, Nevada, New Mexico, Utah.

FLOWER: Yellow.

HABITAT: Desert.

FORM: Tree.

EDIBLE PARTS: Bean pods.

HARVESTABLE: Twice a year, once in spring and once in autumn.

FLAVOR: Unique caramel taste.

NOTES: Beware of mesquite thorns when harvesting the pods. Pods are best harvested off the tree and not off the ground, where they are more likely to develop mold, especially in autumn. Moldy pods should be avoided.

Green pods are boiled to make a caramel-sugary syrup. Dried pods and seed beans are ground and sifted for a naturally sweet pastry flour used for pancakes, pie crust, or crackers. Beans are high in protein.

Wood from these trees is popular for barbecuing.

Mature trees like to have their taproot in the groundwater and are useful for helping locate water in the desert, but their taproots can extend more than 100 feet into the soil.

American Indians heavily harvested these trees and even fought over the rights to harvesting.

Prunus americana

(AMERICAN WILD PLUM)

STATES: Arizona, Colorado, Montana, New Mexico, Utah, Wyoming.

FLOWER: White.

CHARACTERISTICS: Known for naturally peeling bark. Often forms small groves in nature.

HABITAT: Stream banks, slopes near water.

FORM: Shrub or small tree up to 20 feet tall.

EDIBLE PART: Fruit minus the pit.

HARVESTABLE: Summer.

FLAVOR: Sweet.

Prunus andersonii

(DESERT PEACH)

STATE: Nevada.

FLOWER: Pink or pale pink.

CHARACTERISTICS: When growing in wet years, the fruit can be fleshy and somewhat sweet, but in dry years, the fruit can be dry and nothing like a typical peach. Even in wet years, the fruit is going to be somewhat small and not like cultivated peaches. When the peaches are fleshy, they often naturally split to expose the pit inside. The shrubs are beautiful when in full flower and very showy.

HABITAT: Open hills or dry plains.

FORM: Shrub growing up to 6 feet tall.

EDIBLE PART: Fruit minus the pit.

HARVESTABLE: Summer.

FLAVOR: Sweet.

Prunus angustifolia

(CHICKASAW PLUM)

———————

STATES: Colorado, New Mexico.

FLOWER: White.

CHARACTERISTICS: Often forms a natural thicket in the wild because it produces so many suckers from the roots. The fruit are often about the size of cherries and can be tart even when fully ripe.

HABITAT: Stream banks, slopes near water.

FORM: Thorny shrub, typically growing up to 10 feet tall but can be 20 feet tall occasionally.

EDIBLE PART: Fruit minus the pit.

HARVESTABLE: Summer.

FLAVOR: Sweet or tart.

Prunus armeniaca

(APRICOT)

STATES: Colorado, Idaho, Montana, Utah.

FLOWER: White, pink.

CHARACTERISTICS: The fruit is best in areas where this tree gets good water. Wild apricots are about 6 percent sugar.

HABITAT: Stream banks, slopes near water.

FORM: Tree, typically growing up to 15 feet tall.

EDIBLE PART: Fruit minus the pit.

HARVESTABLE: Summer.

FLAVOR: Sweet.

Prunus avium

(SWEET CHERRY)

———

STATES: Idaho, Montana, Utah, Wyoming.

FLOWER: White.

CHARACTERISTICS: Just like cultivated cherries, you have to be fast to harvest these fruits or the birds will get them. This tree is sometimes called a bird cherry because it is so popular among our winged friends. The flowers, like so many of the prunus species, are pleasantly fragrant.

HABITAT: Stream banks, slopes near water.

FORM: Tree, typically growing up to 20 feet tall but sometimes up to 60 feet tall.

EDIBLE PART: Fruit minus the pit.

HARVESTABLE: Summer.

FLAVOR: Sweet.

Prunus besseyi

(WESTERN SANDCHERRY)

STATES: Colorado, Montana, Utah, Wyoming.

FLOWER: White, pink.

CHARACTERISTICS: Some cultivated varieties of this species are available commercially, both as flowering landscape shrubs and fruit trees. The fruits of the wild shrub are very popular with birds, so you may have to act fast if you want to harvest from the wild. The flavor is better if the shrub is near water.

HABITAT: Stream banks, slopes near water.

FORM: Shrub, typically growing up to 6 feet tall.

EDIBLE PART: Fruit minus the pit.

HARVESTABLE: Summer.

FLAVOR: Sweet.

Prunus cerasifera

(CHERRY PLUM)

STATES: Idaho, Montana, Utah.

FLOWER: Pink or pale purple.

CHARACTERISTICS: This tree is known for its purple leaves and is widely sold commercially as a landscaping plant. In the wild, the fruit are best when grown near regular water but do not taste as sweet as cultivated plums.

HABITAT: Stream banks, slopes near water.

FORM: Tree, typically growing up to 15 feet tall.

EDIBLE PART: Fruit minus the pits.

HARVESTABLE: Summer.

FLAVOR: Sweet.

320

Prunus cerasus

(SOUR CHERRY)

STATES: Colorado, Montana, New Mexico, Utah.

FLOWER: White.

CHARACTERISTICS: While the common name gives away the flavor, when found in wet years, the sourness is not bitter and can be pleasant tasting.

HABITAT: Stream banks, slopes near water.

FORM: Tree, typically growing up to 30 feet tall.

EDIBLE PART: Fruit minus the pit.

HARVESTABLE: Summer.

FLAVOR: Tart.

Prunus domestica

(EUROPEAN PLUM)

———

STATES: Idaho, Utah.

FLOWER: White or pale pink.

CHARACTERISTICS: This is one of the parents of cultivated greengage and damson plums that are often sold today for backyard harvesting.

HABITAT: Stream banks, slopes near water.

FORM: Tree, typically growing up to 15 feet tall.

EDIBLE PART: Fruit minus the pit.

HARVESTABLE: Summer.

FLAVOR: Sweet.

Prunus dulcis

(SWEET ALMOND)

STATE: Utah.

FLOWER: White, pink.

CHARACTERISTICS: Do not eat the almonds if they are bitter, as the bitterness may be caused by poisonous natural chemicals.

HABITAT: Stream banks, slopes near water.

FORM: Tree, typically growing up to 15 feet tall.

EDIBLE PARTS: Fruit, seeds.

HARVESTABLE: Summer.

FLAVOR: Sweet.

324

Prunus emarginata

(BITTER CHERRY)

STATES: Arizona, Idaho, Montana, Nevada, New Mexico, Utah, Wyoming.

FLOWER: White.

CHARACTERISTICS: The fruit will have the best flavor in wet years and when fully ripe.

HABITAT: Stream banks, slopes near water.

FORM: Tree, typically growing up to 15 feet tall.

EDIBLE PART: Fruit minus seeds.

HARVESTABLE: Summer.

FLAVOR: Tart or bitter.

Prunus fasciculata

(DESERT ALMOND)

STATES: Arizona, Nevada, Utah.

FLOWER: White, greenish white, or yellowish green.

CHARACTERISTICS: A thorny perennial shrub with lots of branches that often grow in sandy areas or dry slopes or in areas of juniper trees.

HABITAT: Desert or dry slopes.

FORM: Tree, typically growing up to 15 feet tall.

EDIBLE PARTS: Fruit, seeds.

HARVESTABLE: Summer.

FLAVOR: Sweet.

Prunus mahaleb

(MAHALEB CHERRY)

———

STATES: Idaho, Montana, Utah.

FLOWER: White.

CHARACTERISTICS: Grows as a shrub in dry areas or as a tree up to 30 feet tall in areas with regular water. The cherries are red to black when ripe.

HABITAT: Stream banks, slopes near water.

FORM: Shrub or tree, growing up to 30 feet tall.

EDIBLE PART: Fruit minus seeds.

HARVESTABLE: Summer.

FLAVOR: Sweet.

Prunus pensylvanica

(PIN CHERRY)

————

STATES: Colorado, Montana, Wyoming.

FLOWER: White.

CHARACTERISTICS: A shrub in dry areas or a tree where it can access water, growing up to 45 feet tall.

HABITAT: Stream banks, slopes near water. The fruit is juicy and red when fully ripe.

FORM: Shrub or tree.

EDIBLE PART: Fruit minus pit.

HARVESTABLE: Summer.

FLAVOR: Tart.

Prunus persica

(COMMON PEACH)

——————

STATES: Arizona, Idaho, New Mexico, Utah.

FLOWER: Pink, rarely red.

CHARACTERISTICS: This species, native to China and escaped into the wild from cultivation in the West, is the parent of all modern cultivated peaches and nectarines. The wild tree is going to have fruit that is smaller and perhaps less sweet, especially when growing in dry areas. Wild peaches are about 5 percent sugar, compared to about 6 percent for domesticated peaches.

HABITAT: Stream banks, slopes near water.

FORM: Tree, growing up to 30 feet tall.

EDIBLE PART: Fruit minus pits.

HARVESTABLE: Summer.

FLAVOR: Sweet.

Prunus pumila

(SANDCHERRY)

STATES: Colorado, Utah, Montana, Wyoming.

FLOWER: White with yellow-tipped stamens.

CHARACTERISTICS: The cherries are nearly black when ripe and can be nicely fleshy. This shrub typically grows about 3 feet tall in the wild. The species is sold commercially.

HABITAT: Stream banks, slopes near water.

FORM: Shrub, growing up to 9 feet tall, typically smaller.

EDIBLE PART: Fruit minus seeds.

HARVESTABLE: Summer.

FLAVOR: Sweet.

329

Prunus rivularis

(CREEK PLUM)

STATE: Colorado.

FLOWER: White.

CHARACTERISTICS: A shrub that often forms a thicket. The fruit are yellow with a red blush, or fully bright red, or dark red when ripe. They can be sweet and juicy.

HABITAT: Stream banks, slopes near water.

FORM: Shrub, typically growing up to 6 feet tall.

EDIBLE PART: Fruit minus pits.

HARVESTABLE: Summer.

FLAVOR: Sweet.

331

Prunus serotina

(BLACK CHERRY)

STATES: Arizona, New Mexico.

FLOWER: White.

CHARACTERISTICS: The fruit is dark red or almost black when ripe. Often grows in partial shade. The blooms are fragrant.

HABITAT: Stream banks, slopes near water.

FORM: Tree, growing up to 75 feet tall but often much smaller in the wild.

EDIBLE PART: Fruit minus seeds.

HARVESTABLE: Summer.

FLAVOR: Sweet.

Prunus spinosa

(BLACKTHORN)

332

STATE: Idaho.

FLOWER: White.

CHARACTERISTICS: A thorny shrub that forms a thicket and becomes a beautiful mass of white flowers in spring, covering every branch. The fruits, called sloes, are blue or black when ripe and are the size of cherries or smaller. This is the traditional source of wood used to make Irish "shillelaghs," or walking sticks, often using root wood. The wood was coated in butter or lard and placed inside a chimney to be smoke cured, giving the shillelagh a shiny black coat.

HABITAT: Stream banks, slopes near water.

FORM: Shrub, growing up to 20 feet tall but typically shorter.

EDIBLE PART: Fruit minus seeds.

HARVESTABLE: Summer.

FLAVOR: Astringent.

Prunus tomentosa

(NANKING CHERRY)

STATES: Montana, Utah.

FLOWER: White or pale pink.

CHARACTERISTICS: The cherries are bright jewel red when ripe. This species is widely sold as a bush cherry, and we grow several in our backyard for eating.

HABITAT: Stream banks, slopes near water.

FORM: Shrub, typically growing up to 10 feet tall.

EDIBLE PART: Fruit minus pits.

HARVESTABLE: Summer.

FLAVOR: Sweet.

Prunus virginiana

(WESTERN CHOKECHERRY, BLACK CHOKECHERRY)

STATES: Arizona, Colorado, Idaho, Montana, Nevada, New Mexico, Utah, Wyoming.

FLOWER: White.

CHARACTERISTICS: The name chokecherry is a misnomer when the fruits are ripe. The internet passes along the rumor that these fruits taste bad, but they don't—if they are fully ripe. They can be somewhat sweet, and I like them raw and fresh and eat them every chance I get, but the flavor is improved by adding a sweetener when making chokecherry jam. (To make chokecherry jam, see the jam recipe in this book under "golden currant"— edible plant #473—and substitute the fruit for chokecherries.) These cherries are still sought after in the area where we live, and some families gather them each summer for making preserves. These trees are found in the valleys and in the mountains, almost always near water. The fruit is jewel red just before being ripe and dark red or almost black when ripe. One secret for identifying chokecherries: just below most leaves, on the leaf stem, is a little raised bump. Botanists call this a tiny gland on the "petiole."

HABITAT: Stream banks, slopes near water.

FORM: Tree, growing up to 30 feet tall but typically 10 to 15 feet.

EDIBLE PART: Fruit minus pits.

HARVESTABLE: Summer.

FLAVOR: Sweet.

NOTES: For all the species listed here, make sure the fruits are fully ripe for best flavor and sweetness. If *Prunus* fruits are bitter, don't eat them.

Of all the prunus species listed in this book, chokecherries are the easiest to find and the most widely used. In his scholarly monograph titled *Native American Food Plants*, author Daniel E. Moerman says chokecherries had the greatest number of uses by the American Indians of all 1,500 species he studied.

335

Pyrus communis

(COMMON PEAR)

STATES: Idaho, Montana, New Mexico, Utah.

FLOWER: White, rarely pale pink or blushed with pink.

CHARACTERISTICS: This species is the parent of most commercially grown pears. The leafy part of the tree often forms a distinctive pyramidal shape. The leaves turn red and yellow in autumn.

HABITAT: Stream banks, slopes near water.

FORM: Tree, growing up to 30 feet tall.

EDIBLE PART: Fruit.

HARVESTABLE: Summer.

FLAVOR: Sweet.

NOTES: Wild pear fruits can be quite a bit smaller than commercial varieties.

Quercus gambelii

(GAMBEL OAK)

———————

STATES: Arizona, Colorado, Nevada, New Mexico, Utah, Wyoming.

FLOWER: Green.

CHARACTERISTICS: In summer, the small, white, pithy center of the immature acorn can be eaten raw, has a pleasing nutty flavor, and makes a good trail snack. Mature acorns should not be eaten raw. Acorns with worm holes should be discarded. Acorns gathered late in the season or stored too long can go rancid because of the high fat content.

Acorns are an excellent protein source.

Mature, dry acorns are soaked or boiled, the shells are cracked to remove the nut, and the nuts are soaked or boiled again, sometimes several times, to remove the natural tannins. The acorns are boiled until the flavor is mild instead of bitter or astringent. This was a critical winter food for many American Indian tribes, but it is not widely eaten today because of the work required to make the nuts edible.

HABITAT: Dry slopes.

FORM: Deciduous tree, typically growing up to 15 feet tall.

EDIBLE PART: Acorns.

HARVESTABLE: Summer, autumn.

FLAVOR: Nutty.

Raphanus raphanistrum

(WILD RADISH)

———————

STATES: Arizona, Colorado, Idaho, Montana, Nevada.

FLOWER: Cream or pale yellow.

CHARACTERISTICS: The roots don't often form a radish bulb in the wild. Because this species easily hybridizes with garden radishes, the wild forms can be highly variable, especially in the first or second generations after the cross.

HABITAT: Fields, meadows, roadsides, waste places.

FORM: Single-stem flowering annual or biennial, typically growing 2 feet tall.

EDIBLE PARTS: Flowers, leaves, seeds, seedpod, root.

HARVESTABLE: Summer.

FLAVOR: Radish.

Raphanus sativus

(GARDEN RADISH)

STATES: Arizona, Colorado, Idaho, Montana, Nevada, New Mexico, Utah, Wyoming.

FLOWER: Purple, pink, or white.

CHARACTERISTICS: This plant is usually escaped from local gardens and in the long term, the progeny almost always hybridize with wild radishes and revert to wild, which is why the bulbs of garden radishes are not usually found in the wild but only in cultivated gardens. (Garden cultivars always naturalize to their weedy form, unfortunately. You can learn more in my book *Seed Saving: A Beginner's Guide to Heirloom Gardening*.

HABITAT: Fields, meadows, roadsides, waste places.

FORM: Single-stem flowering annual or biennial, typically growing 2 feet tall.

EDIBLE PARTS: Flowers, leaves, seeds, seedpod, root.

HARVESTABLE: Summer.

FLAVOR: Radish.

NOTES: These two species often grow together, and they readily and naturally hybridize.

Rheum rhabarbarum

(GARDEN RHUBARB)

————

STATES: Arizona, Colorado, Idaho, Montana, Nevada, New Mexico, Utah, Wyoming.

FLOWER: White.

CHARACTERISTICS: **Many parts of this plant are actually poisonous, and only the leaf stalks, called "petioles by botanists," should be eaten.** This plant (but not the leaf stalks) is high in oxalic acid, citric acid, and anthraquinone glycosides. The leaf stalks are flavored by malic acid, which is not toxic to humans, and is the reason that strawberry-rhubarb pies exist.

HABITAT: Disturbed soil, escaped from gardens.

FORM: Multi-stem herb.

EDIBLE PART: Leaf stalks.

HARVESTABLE: Summer, autumn.

FLAVOR: Tart.

Rhus glabra
(SMOOTH SUMAC)

STATES: Arizona, Colorado, Idaho, Montana, Nevada, New Mexico, Utah, Wyoming.

FLOWER: White petals; green sepals.

CHARACTERISTICS: The twigs are a pinkish-gray color. This shrub often forms a thicket. The leaves turn bright red in autumn and then fall off. If you break a stem, white milk comes out. This species has a long history of use in traditional medicine to treat many conditions. The fruits are dark red. The velvety fruit is soaked but not boiled to make a lemony drink. Boiling can release toxins, but soaking without boiling is safe. It is also worth noting that poison sumac, which is actually not even a botanical cousin of the *Rhus* genus, does not grow wild in the Rocky Mountain West, according to the US Department of Agriculture.

HABITAT: Mountainsides.

FORM: Shrubby tree, typically growing up to 10 feet tall.

EDIBLE PART: Fruit.

HARVESTABLE: Autumn.

FLAVOR: Lemony.

SUMAC LEMONADE

1. Collect the red ripe fruits and soak them in cold water for 10 or 15 minutes.
2. Do not heat the water and do not make tea.
3. Strain and drink for a refreshing and fast lemon-less lemonade. You can add a sweetener if desired.

The longer you leave the fruits in the water, the darker red the water will be colored, but if you leave them in too long, the flavor can become too strong (and you can dilute with more cold water). This recipe can be made with the fruits of any of the three *Rhus* species in this book.

Rhus trilobata

(THREE-LEAF SUMAC)

STATES: Arizona, Colorado, Idaho, Montana, Nevada, New Mexico, Utah, Wyoming.

FLOWER: Greenish red.

CHARACTERISTICS: The leaves and fruits of this species look almost nothing like the other two *Rhus* species in this book. The plant has an unpleasant smell. The leaves and shape of this shrub almost resemble currant bushes. The fruits are red and look like a cluster of very hairy berries when ripe but are quite small compared to the other two *Rhus* species I've listed. This species sometimes grows low to the ground. The leaves turn yellow or orange red in autumn before dropping.

HABITAT: Mountainsides.

FORM: Shrubby tree, typically growing up to 10 feet tall.

EDIBLE PART: Fruit.

HARVESTABLE: Autumn.

FLAVOR: Lemony.

NOTES: The velvety fruit is soaked but not boiled to make a lemony drink. Boiling can release toxins, but soaking without boiling is safe.

SYNONYM: *Rhus aromatica* var. *trilobata*.

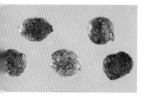

Rhus typhina

(STAGHORN SUMAC)

STATES: Utah.

FLOWER: Greenish red.

CHARACTERISTICS: The fruit is bright red in autumn, not dark red like smooth sumac, but eventually turns dark red in winter. All three *Rhus* species listed in this book are sold commercially as landscape plants. This is the tallest form of sumac in North America. The leaves turn yellow, orange, and red in autumn, which is part of the reason why these are popular landscape plants. Deciduous.

HABITAT: Mountainsides.

FORM: Tree, growing up to 25 feet tall.

EDIBLE PART: Fruit.

HARVESTABLE: Autumn.

FLAVOR: Lemony.

NOTES: The velvety fruit is soaked but not boiled to make a lemony drink. Boiling can release toxins, but soaking without boiling is safe.

Ribes aureum

(GOLDEN CURRANT)

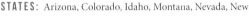

STATES: Arizona, Colorado, Idaho, Montana, Nevada, New Mexico, Utah, Wyoming.

HABITAT: Mountainsides.

FLOWER: White.

FORM: Deciduous shrub, typically growing 2–3 feet tall.

CHARACTERISTICS: The fruit is dark red or almost black when ripe. Often grows in partial shade. The blooms are fragrant.

BERRY: Red, orange, brown, or black, rarely yellow. Smooth.

EDIBLE PARTS: Fruit, flowers, leaves.

HARVESTABLE: Summer.

FLAVOR: Tangy and somewhat sweet.

NOTES: As a general rule, gooseberries are thorny and currants are not. Most if not all of the *Ribes* species are naturally high in pectin and can be made into jam or jelly without added pectin.

CURRANT JAM

- 3 cups rinsed berries with stems removed
- Water
- 3/4 teaspoon powdered stevia extract, 90 percent strength
- 6 tablespoons birch sugar (xylitol)

1. Put berries in a saucepan and add enough water to just cover the berries.
2. Add sweeteners.
3. Bring to a boil and simmer on low heat for 40 minutes, stirring often. Turn off heat.
4. Mash remaining berries. Cool until the liquid stops steaming. Taste and add more sweetener if desired.
5. Freeze or refrigerate.

Traditional sugar can be used as the sweetener instead of the healthy sweeteners. Start with one cup of traditional sugar and add more to taste. To make a jelly instead of a jam, strain out the berry pulp. Stevia is a green herb with naturally sweet leaves I grow in my garden. Extracts are available at health food stores. For more information about healthy sugars, see my book *The Stevia Solution*.

Ribes cereum

(WAX CURRANT)

STATES: Arizona, Colorado, Idaho, Montana, Nevada, New Mexico, Utah, Wyoming.

FLOWER: Green, greenish white, or white, sometimes with a pink blush when white.

CHARACTERISTICS: When I go hiking, I use the leaves of *Ribes cereum* as a kind of lip balm, rubbing the leaves directly on my lips to relieve chapping in the hot summer air. Flowers look like tubes. Thornless.

HABITAT: Mountainsides.

FORM: Deciduous shrub, typically growing 2–3 feet tall.

BERRY: Red.

EDIBLE PARTS: Fruit, flowers, leaves.

HARVESTABLE: Summer.

FLAVOR: Bland or tasteless.

Ribes hudsonianum

(WESTERN BLACK CURRANT)

STATES: Idaho, Montana, Nevada, Utah, Wyoming.

FLOWER: White.

CHARACTERISTICS: Almost always found growing near water or on creek or river banks. Often forms low thickets. Often grows in partial shade. The berries are not very sweet but have a good flavor and can be gathered by the handful when you find a thicket. I have a favorite thicket in the mountains near my house, and this is always a stop when I take groups of students into the mountains to taste wild berries. Excellent for jam or jelly. The plant has a somewhat unpleasant smell. Thornless. These plants are imbued for me with memories of summer berry picking.

HABITAT: Mountainsides.

FORM: Deciduous shrub, growing 2–6 feet tall.

BERRY: Black when ripe. Green and then purple when young.

EDIBLE PARTS: Fruit, flowers, leaves.

HARVESTABLE: Late summer.

FLAVOR: Tangy and slightly sweet. Sometimes nicely sweet if just perfectly ripe.

Ribes inerme

(WHITESTEM GOOSEBERRY)

346

STATES: Arizona, Colorado, Idaho, Montana, Nevada, New Mexico, Utah, Wyoming.

FLOWER: White, pink, whitish pink, or green.

CHARACTERISTICS: Gooseberries have distinctive netted skins on the berries. Ironically, *inerme* means unarmed, as in thornless, but in the Rocky Mountain West, some varieties have thorns.

HABITAT: Mountainsides or near streams.

FORM: Deciduous shrub, growing 5 feet tall.

BERRY: Green, red, purple, or black.

EDIBLE PARTS: Fruit, flowers, leaves.

HARVESTABLE: Summer.

FLAVOR: Tangy and slightly sweet.

Ribes lacustre

(PRICKLY BLACK CURRANT)

STATES: Colorado, Idaho, Montana, Nevada, Utah, Wyoming.

FLOWER: Yellowish green or red.

CHARACTERISTICS: Thorny, as denoted by the common name. May form a thicket or may be single plants.

HABITAT: Mountainsides.

FORM: Deciduous shrub, typically growing 3–6 feet tall.

BERRY: Red but turning black or dark purple when ripe. Berries are sometimes hairy. The berries fall off the stem easily when ripe.

EDIBLE PARTS: Fruit, flowers, leaves

HARVESTABLE: Summer.

FLAVOR: Bland or slightly sweet.

Ribes laxiflorum

(TRAILING BLACK CURRANT)

STATES: Colorado, Idaho, Montana, New Mexico, Utah.

FLOWER: Pink, red, or purple.

CHARACTERISTICS: This *Ribes* species looks like several other *Ribes* species, and the only differences between those species are small botanical ones. This species prefers full sun, while others prefer some shade. The flowers are beautiful and showy.

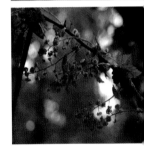

HABITAT: Mountainsides.

FORM: Deciduous shrub, typically growing 2–3 feet tall.

BERRY: Purple or black when ripe.

EDIBLE PARTS: Fruit, flowers, leaves.

HARVESTABLE: Summer.

FLAVOR: Tangy and slightly sweet.

349

Ribes leptanthum

(TRUMPET GOOSEBERRY)

———

STATES: Arizona, Colorado, New Mexico, Utah.

FLOWER: White.

CHARACTERISTICS: Looks similar to *Ribes inerme*. New growth has thorns and older growth loses the thorns.

HABITAT: Mountainsides.

FORM: Deciduous shrub, typically growing 2–3 feet tall.

BERRY: Dark red, purple, or black when ripe.

EDIBLE PARTS: Fruit, flowers, leaves.

HARVESTABLE: Summer.

FLAVOR: Tangy and slightly sweet.

Ribes montigenum

(GOOSEBERRY CURRANT,
MOUNTAIN CURRANT)

STATES: Arizona, Colorado, Idaho, Montana, Nevada, New Mexico, Utah, Wyoming.

FLOWER: Red, pink, or purple.

CHARACTERISTICS: The berries of *Ribes montigenum* are covered in soft, edible hairs, which makes them look unusual, but they have a good flavor, so don't let the hairs stop you from tasting them. And whenever I find these, there are almost always other wild currants or gooseberries growing nearby.

HABITAT: Mountainsides.

FORM: Deciduous shrub, typically growing 2–3 feet tall.

BERRY: Bright red when ripe; may darken with age.

EDIBLE PARTS: Fruit, flowers, leaves.

HARVESTABLE: Summer.

FLAVOR: Tangy and slightly sweet.

Ribes niveum

(SNOW CURRANT)

STATES: Colorado, Idaho, Nevada.

FLOWER: White or pink and have red veins, usually with white sepals, sometimes with greenish or pinkish sepals.

CHARACTERISTICS: This berry is known for being more sour than other currant species. Pick fully ripe for best flavor.

HABITAT: Near water or streams or on moist hillsides.

FORM: Deciduous shrub, typically growing 2–3 feet tall.

BERRY: Blue, purple, or black.

EDIBLE PARTS: Fruit, flowers, leaves.

HARVESTABLE: Summer.

FLAVOR: Tart.

Ribes oxyacanthoides

(CANADIAN GOOSEBERRY)

STATES: Colorado, Idaho, Montana, Nevada, Utah, Wyoming.

FLOWER: White or pink with greenish-white or pinkish-white sepals.

CHARACTERISTICS: Often found growing in forest areas. Berries are 7 percent protein and 10 percent fiber according to the US Forest Service.

HABITAT: Mountainsides.

FORM: Deciduous shrub, typically growing 2–5 feet tall.

BERRY: Red, purple, or black when ripe.

EDIBLE PARTS: Fruit, flowers, leaves.

HARVESTABLE: Summer.

FLAVOR: Tangy and slightly sweet.

Ribes velutinum

(DESERT GOOSEBERRY)

STATES: Arizona, Idaho, Montana, Nevada, Utah.

FLOWER: White or yellowish white.

CHARACTERISTICS: The leaves of this species, like some of the *Ribes* species are thick and leathery.

HABITAT: Mountainsides.

FORM: Deciduous shrub, typically growing 2–6 feet tall.

BERRY: Yellow or greenish yellow, turning red and black when ripe.

EDIBLE PARTS: Fruit, flowers, leaves.

HARVESTABLE: Summer.

FLAVOR: Tangy and slightly sweet.

Ribes viscosissimum

(STICKY CURRANT)

STATES: Arizona, Colorado, Idaho, Montana, Nevada, Utah, Wyoming.

FLOWER: White with white, pink, or purple sepals.

CHARACTERISTICS: This plant has a pleasant fragrance.

HABITAT: Mountainsides.

FORM: Deciduous shrub, typically growing 2–3 feet tall.

BERRY: Blue or black when ripe.

EDIBLE PARTS: Fruit, flowers, leaves.

HARVESTABLE: Summer.

FLAVOR: Tangy and slightly sweet.

Ribes wolfii

(WOLF'S CURRANT)

STATES: Arizona, Colorado, Idaho, New Mexico, Utah.

FLOWER: White, yellowish green, or pink.

CHARACTERISTICS: Prefers moist soil and grows in forests and meadows.

HABITAT: Mountainsides.

FORM: Deciduous shrub, typically growing 2–3 feet tall.

BERRY: Black when ripe.

EDIBLE PARTS: Fruit, flowers, leaves.

HARVESTABLE: Summer.

FLAVOR: Tangy and slightly sweet.

Rosa x harisonii

(HARISON'S YELLOW)

STATE: Utah.

FLOWER: Yellow flowers with double petals.

CHARACTERISTICS: This rose, which we grow in our yard, is known for its stunning display and wonderful fragrance that you just want to drink in. The rosehips are small and black and are not favored for harvesting like red rosehips.

HABITAT: Mountainsides.

FORM: Deciduous shrub, typically growing 5–8 feet tall.

EDIBLE PART: Petals (minus bitter white base).

HARVESTABLE: Summer.

FLAVOR: Slightly sweet.

Rosa canina

(DOG ROSE)

STATES: Idaho, New Mexico, Utah.

FLOWER: White or light pink.

CHARACTERISTICS: This species looks like several other wild rose species, and they differ only by small botanical details. The rosehips are red. Rosehips are the hard berry-like structures left after the flower dies. The red skin of the berry is high in vitamin C, can be used fresh, dried, or tinctured, and is widely sold in health food stores. Only the red skin contains the vitamin.

HABITAT: Mountainsides.

FORM: Deciduous shrub, typically growing 4–9 feet tall.

EDIBLE PARTS: Petals (minus bitter white base), rosehips for tea, seeds (ground up).

HARVESTABLE: Summer, autumn.

FLAVOR: Slightly sweet.

357

Rosa manca

(MANCOS ROSE)

STATES: Colorado, New Mexico, Utah.

FLOWER: Pink.

CHARACTERISTICS: Most botanists classify this as a subspecies of *Rosa woodsii*, but at least for now, the US Department of Agriculture still lists it as separate species, as do several university herbariums. This and almost all wild roses are thorny, and often heavily so, but occasionally only sparsely so. This species is known for being somewhat naturally dwarf.

HABITAT: Mountainsides.

FORM: Deciduous shrub, typically growing 3–5 feet tall.

EDIBLE PARTS: Petals (minus bitter white base), rosehips for tea, seeds (ground up).

HARVESTABLE: Summer, autumn.

FLAVOR: Slightly sweet.

NOTES: Rosehips are the hard berry-like structures left after the flower dies. The red skin of the berry is high in vitamin C, can be used fresh, dried, or tinctured, and is widely sold in health food stores. Only the red skin contains the vitamin.

Rosa nutkana

(NOOTKA ROSE)

STATES: Colorado, Idaho, Montana, Nevada, New Mexico, Utah, Wyoming.

FLOWER: Red, pink, purple-pink, or orange.

CHARACTERISTICS: This species is known for its unusually large flowers. The rosehips are red.

HABITAT: Mountainsides.

FORM: Deciduous shrub, typically growing 5–8 feet tall.

EDIBLE PARTS: Petals (minus bitter white base), rosehips for tea, seeds (ground up).

HARVESTABLE: Summer, autumn.

FLAVOR: Slightly sweet.

359

Rosa rubiginosa

(SWEETBRIAR ROSE)

STATES: Colorado, Idaho, Montana, Utah, Wyoming.

FLOWER: Pink.

CHARACTERISTICS: The rosehips are red or orange. This species is often sold commercially because of its fragrance and the beauty of its blooms.

HABITAT: Mountainsides.

FORM: Deciduous shrub, typically growing 5–8 feet tall.

EDIBLE PARTS: Petals (minus bitter white base), rosehips for tea, seeds (ground up).

HARVESTABLE: Summer, autumn.

FLAVOR: Slightly sweet.

NOTES. Rosehips are the hard berry-like structures left after the flower dies. The red skin of the berry is high in vitamin C, can be used fresh, dried, or tinctured, and is widely sold in health food stores. Only the red skin contains the vitamin.

Rosa woodsii

(WOODS' ROSE, WESTERN WILD ROSE)

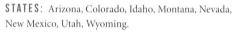

STATES: Arizona, Colorado, Idaho, Montana, Nevada, New Mexico, Utah, Wyoming.

FLOWER: Pink.

CHARACTERISTICS: This species has many subspecies and can be variable. The rosehips are red and can be made into jelly. The roots of this species are used to make a red or pink dye. Prefers moist soil, as do most wild roses. These roses can grow into a thicket if they can access good summer water.

HABITAT: Mountainsides.

FORM: Deciduous shrub, typically growing 5–8 feet tall.

EDIBLE PARTS: Petals (minus bitter white base), rosehips for tea, seeds (ground up).

HARVESTABLE: Summer, autumn.

FLAVOR: Slightly sweet.

NOTES: Rosehips are the hard berry-like structures left after the flower dies. The red skin of the berry is high in vitamin C, can be used fresh, dried, or tinctured, and is widely sold in health food stores. Only the red skin contains the vitamin.

Rubus arcticus

(ARCTIC RASPBERRY)

STATES: Colorado, Montana, Wyoming.

FLOWER: Typically pink, sometimes pale pink, red, or white.

CHARACTERISTICS: A naturally thornless raspberry species. Naturally dwarf.

HABITAT: Mountainsides near water.

FORM: Deciduous shrub, typically growing 1–2 feet tall.

BERRY: Red.

EDIBLE PARTS: Berries, leaves for tea.

HARVESTABLE: Summer.

FLAVOR: Sweet.

WILD BERRY JAM

- 3 cups rinsed berries with stems removed
- Water
- 1/2 teaspoon powdered stevia extract, 90 percent strength
- 4 tablespoons birch sugar (xylitol)

1. Put berries in a saucepan and add enough water to just cover the berries. Add sweeteners.
2. Bring to a boil and simmer on low heat for 25–30 minutes, stirring often. Turn off heat.
3. Mash berries. Cool until the liquid stops steaming. Taste and add more sweetener if desired.
4. Freeze or refrigerate.

Option: Traditional sugar can be used as the sweetener instead of the healthy sweeteners. Start with 1 cup of traditional sugar and add more to taste. To make a jelly instead of a jam, strain out the berry pulp. Stevia is a green herb I grow in my garden with naturally sweet leaves. Extracts are available in health food stores. For more stevia recipes, see my book *The Stevia Solution*.

363

Rubus armeniacus

(HIMALAYAN BLACKBERRY)

STATES: Arizona, Colorado, Idaho, Montana, Nevada, New Mexico, Utah.

FLOWER: White or pale pink.

CHARACTERISTICS: Thorny. Arching stems typical to blackberries.

HABITAT: Mountainsides near water.

FORM: Deciduous shrub, typically reaching 15 feet tall.

BERRY: Red when young; black when ripe.

EDIBLE PARTS: Berries, leaves for tea.

HARVESTABLE: Summer.

FLAVOR: Sweet.

SYNONYM: *Rubus procerus.*

Rubus deliciosus

(DELICIOUS RASPBERRY)

STATES: Colorado, New Mexico, Wyoming.

FLOWER: White.

CHARACTERISTICS: "Delicious raspberry is certainly a lovely deciduous shrub with its bright green leaves and large white flowers. However, it is curiously named for a plant with fruit that tends to be fairly dry, with lots of seeds and little flesh, even if the flavor is nice," according to the US Forest Service. Naturally thornless.

HABITAT: Mountainsides near water.

FORM: Deciduous bush, typically reaching 3–4 feet tall (but can be taller).

BERRY: Red when ripe.

EDIBLE PARTS: Berries, leaves for tea.

HARVESTABLE: Summer.

FLAVOR: Sweet.

Rubus idaeus

(WILD RASPBERRIES)

STATES: Arizona, Colorado, Idaho, Montana, Nevada, New Mexico, Utah, Wyoming.

FLOWER: White.

CHARACTERISTICS: Prefers full sun and not shade. Thorny.

HABITAT: Mountainsides near water.

FORM: Deciduous shrub, typically reaching 3–6 feet tall.

BERRY: Red when ripe.

EDIBLE PARTS: Berries, leaves for tea.

HARVESTABLE: Summer.

FLAVOR: Sweet.

Rubus laciniatus

(CUTLEAF BLACKBERRY)

STATES: Colorado, Idaho, Montana, Wyoming.

FLOWER: Typically pink, sometimes white, sometimes red.

CHARACTERISTICS: Thorny. The leaves are evergreen. Commercial cultivars are sold. The evergreen blackberry, a common garden species, was first cultivated in 1770, according to the US Forest Service.

HABITAT: Moist soil in sunny or partially shaded locations.

FORM: Deciduous shrub, typically reaching 3–4 feet tall.

BERRY: Red when young; black when ripe.

EDIBLE PARTS: Berries, leaves for tea.

HARVESTABLE: Summer.

FLAVOR: Sweet.

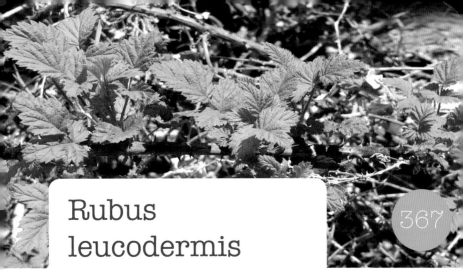

Rubus leucodermis

(WHITEBARK RASPBERRY)

STATES: Arizona, Idaho, Montana, Nevada, New Mexico, Utah.

FLOWER: White.

CHARACTERISTICS: Often grows in forests or forest edges. Thorny. Called whitebark because of a white powder that forms naturally on the canes.

HABITAT: Prefers wet soil.

FORM: Deciduous shrub, typically reaching 3–8 feet tall.

BERRY: Purple or black when ripe, sometimes red.

EDIBLE PARTS: Berries, leaves for tea.

HARVESTABLE: Summer.

FLAVOR: Sweet.

Rubus neomexicanus

(NEW MEXICO RASPBERRY)

STATES: Arizona, Colorado, New Mexico, Utah.

FLOWER: White.

CHARACTERISTICS: Thornless. The fruit are juicy when ripe but dry out soon and don't last long in their best form. This is likely because this raspberry often grows in drier areas, unlike most wild raspberries.

HABITAT: Mountainsides and forests. The berries are quite small.

FORM: Deciduous shrub, typically reaching 3–9 feet tall.

BERRY: Red.

EDIBLE PARTS: Berries, leaves for tea.

HARVESTABLE: Summer.

FLAVOR: Sweet.

NOTE: Some classify *Rubus neomexicanus* as a *Rubus deliciosus* subspecies but the USDA lists them separately.

Rubus nivalis

(SNOW RASPBERRY)

STATE: Idaho.

FLOWER: Pink or red.

CHARACTERISTICS: Thorny. This is another evergreen species of raspberry. The berries are often small.

HABITAT: Prefers moist soil; grows in sunny and shady locations.

FORM: Deciduous shrub, typically reaching 3–4 feet tall.

BERRY: Red when ripe.

EDIBLE PARTS: Berries, leaves for tea.

HARVESTABLE: Summer.

FLAVOR: Sweet.

Rubus occidentalis

(BLACK RASPBERRY)

STATE: Colorado.

FLOWER: White.

CHARACTERISTICS: In nature, one subspecies produces gold berries, which we grow in our yard. They ripen earlier than red raspberries and have a wonderful flavor.

HABITAT: Prefers moist soil.

FORM: Deciduous shrub, typically reaching 3–4 feet tall.

BERRY: Purple or black when ripe. Occasionally yellow when ripe.

EDIBLE PARTS: Berries, leaves for tea.

HARVESTABLE: Summer.

FLAVOR: Sweet.

Rubus parviflorus

(THIMBLEBERRY)

———

STATES: Arizona, Colorado, Idaho, Montana, Nevada, New Mexico, Utah, Wyoming.

FLOWER: White.

CHARACTERISTICS: The berries are wider than raspberries, forming an interesting button shape. The berries are very delicate and best eaten immediately. These are one of my favorite mountain treats and a favorite of students I take into the local mountains for wild berry tasting and identification classes. The leaves of this plant are huge, often reaching 12 inches wide or larger.

HABITAT: Mountainsides near water.

FORM: Deciduous shrub, typically reaching 3–4 feet tall.

BERRY: Red when ripe.

EDIBLE PARTS: Berries, leaves for tea.

HARVESTABLE: Summer.

FLAVOR: Sweet.

371

Rubus pedatus

(STRAWBERRYLEAF RASPBERRY)

———

STATES: Idaho, Montana.

FLOWER: White.

CHARACTERISTICS: This raspberry gets its name from its distinctive leaves which look almost like wild strawberry leaves. This plant is a low-growing, vining, thornless mat. The berries are small.

HABITAT: Mountainsides near water.

FORM: Deciduous shrub, typically reaching 6 inches tall because it trails along the ground.

BERRY: Red when ripe.

EDIBLE PARTS: Berries, leaves for tea.

HARVESTABLE: Summer.

FLAVOR: Sweet.

Rubus pubescens

(DWARF RED BLACKBERRY)

STATES: Colorado, Idaho, Montana, Nevada, Wyoming.

FLOWER: White, rarely pink.

CHARACTERISTICS: Strongly prefers wet soil. This plant often vines along the ground instead of growing erect, which is why it is called dwarf.

HABITAT: Mountainsides near water.

FORM: Deciduous shrub, typically reaching 6–12 inches tall.

BERRY: Red when ripe.

EDIBLE PARTS: Berries, leaves for tea.

HARVESTABLE: Summer.

FLAVOR: Sweet.

Rubus spectabilis

(SALMONBERRY)

STATE: Idaho.

FLOWER: Pink, red, or purple-red.

CHARACTERISTICS: The berries are large and covered in edible hairs. The common name comes from the orange salmon color that the berries often achieve when ripe. This species is sold commercially, as are many of the *Rubus* species with large berries.

HABITAT: Mountainsides near water.

FORM: Deciduous shrub, typically reaching 3–9 feet tall.

BERRY: Salmon colored or red.

EDIBLE PARTS: Berries, leaves for tea.

HARVESTABLE: Summer.

FLAVOR: Sweet.

Rubus ulmifolius

(ELMLEAF BLACKBERRY)

STATE: Nevada.

FLOWER: White or pink.

CHARACTERISTICS: This berry occurs only rarely in the Rocky Mountain West but is more common in California.

HABITAT: Moist soil.

FORM: Deciduous shrub, typically reaching 3–6 feet tall.

BERRY: Black when ripe.

EDIBLE PARTS: Berries, leaves for tea.

HARVESTABLE: Summer.

FLAVOR: Sweet.

375

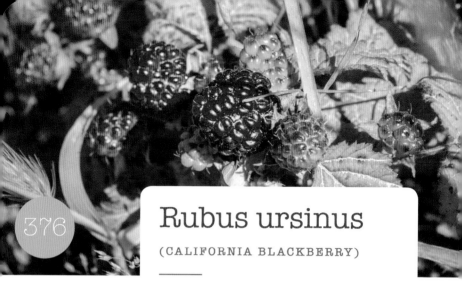

Rubus ursinus

(CALIFORNIA BLACKBERRY)

STATES: Idaho, Montana.

FLOWER: White or pink.

CHARACTERISTICS: The canes are arching and can be very long. This species is sold commercially and is one of the parents of loganberries and boysenberries.

HABITAT: Mountainsides near water.

FORM: Deciduous shrub, typically reaching 5–10 feet tall.

BERRY: Black when ripe.

EDIBLE PARTS: Berries, leaves for tea.

HARVESTABLE: Summer.

FLAVOR: Sweet.

Rumex acetosella

(SHEEP SORREL)

STATES: Arizona, Colorado, Idaho, Montana, Nevada, New Mexico, Utah, Wyoming.

FLOWER: Green.

CHARACTERISTICS: For the best flavor, choose the young leaves of all the *Rumex* species in this book. Most people know dock from the spikes of red seeds that appear in summer.

HABITAT: Roadsides, wastelands, disturbed soils, fields, pastures.

FORM: Multi-stem herb, typically growing up to 3 feet tall.

EDIBLE PARTS: Leaves, root, seeds, stem.

HARVESTABLE: Spring, summer.

FLAVOR: Lemony.

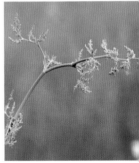

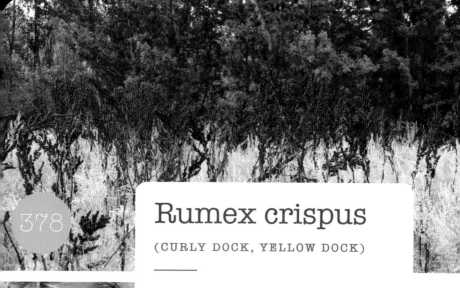

Rumex crispus

(CURLY DOCK, YELLOW DOCK)

STATES: Arizona, Colorado, Idaho, Montana, Nevada, New Mexico, Utah, Wyoming.

FLOWER: Green.

CHARACTERISTICS: Curly dock is widely eaten as a wild forage food and is valued for adding to green smoothies for its lemony flavor. In later summer, dock leaves are particularly attacked by grasshoppers, which eat big holes in the leaves, but they continue to put out smaller leaves all summer, which are great for eating fresh.

HABITAT: Roadsides, wastelands, disturbed soils, fields, pastures.

FORM: Multi-stem herb, typically growing up to 3 feet tall.

EDIBLE PARTS: Leaves, root, seeds, stem.

HARVESTABLE: Spring, summer.

FLAVOR: Lemony.

Rumex obtusifolius

(BROADLEAF DOCK)

STATES: Arizona, Colorado, Idaho, Montana, New Mexico, Utah.

FLOWER: Green.

CHARACTERISTICS: All *Rumex* species in this book are known for their long leaves, which is where this plant gets its common name.

HABITAT: Roadsides, wastelands, disturbed soils, fields, pastures.

FORM: Multi-stem herb, typically growing up to 3 feet tall.

EDIBLE PARTS: Leaves, root, seeds, stem.

HARVESTABLE: Spring, summer.

FLAVOR: Lemony.

Rumex occidentalis

(WESTERN DOCK)

STATES: Arizona, Colorado, Idaho, Montana, Nevada, New Mexico, Utah, Wyoming.

FLOWER: Green.

CHARACTERISTICS: *Rumex* species can be difficult to tell apart, with some being different only by small botanical details.

HABITAT: Roadsides, wastelands, disturbed soils, fields, pastures.

FORM: Multi-stem herb, typically growing up to 3 feet tall.

EDIBLE PARTS: Leaves, root, seeds, stem.

HARVESTABLE: Spring, summer.

FLAVOR: Lemony.

Sagittaria cuneata

(WAPATO, ARUMLEAF
ARROWHEAD)

———————

STATES: Arizona, Colorado, Idaho, Montana, Nevada, New Mexico, Utah, Wyoming.

FLOWER: Green.

CHARACTERISTICS: Harvest only from clean and unpolluted water, rinsing thoroughly before eating.

HABITAT: Grows in water or wet soil.

FORM: Aquatic herb that typically grows 2 feet tall.

EDIBLE PART: Tuber.

HARVESTABLE: Spring, summer, autumn.

FLAVOR: Starchy and slightly nutty.

Salsola tragus

(RUSSIAN THISTLE)

STATES: Arizona, Colorado, Idaho, Montana, Nevada, New Mexico, Utah, Wyoming.

FLOWER: White, pink.

CHARACTERISTICS: Since thistles are so invasive, especially in disturbed soils, we might as well seek them out in spring to eat them as our revenge for being such a pest plant. Because they are so spiny, avoid this plant except in its young stages.

HABITAT: Desert.

FORM: Annual tumbleweed, typically growing 2–3 feet tall and 2–3 feet wide.

EDIBLE PARTS: Young leaves, young shoots, young stems, seeds.

HARVESTABLE: Spring.

FLAVOR: Mild and slightly salty. *Salsola* means "salty."

382

Sambucus nigra

(BLUE ELDERBERRY)

STATES: Arizona, Colorado, Idaho, Montana, Nevada, New Mexico, Utah, Wyoming.

FLOWER: White.

CHARACTERISTICS: Mature bushes are often covered in berries in late summer or early autumn, and competition to get the berries can be fierce because so many people like to harvest them. Go early. For your best bet, find bushes when hiking that are not right next to popular roads and trails because the plants that are most easily accessed are always the first harvested by the public. The berries are widely used medicinally and are one of the most important native medicinal plants of the Rocky Mountain West. I air-dry the berries so I can use them in winter to stave off colds and flu. Medicinal extracts of elderberry are sold in pharmacies and grocery stores nationwide. For identification, it is helpful to know that the leaves are toothed, pinnate, and lanceolate. Branches are dotted with raised lenticels (pores).

HABITAT: Mountainsides.

FORM: Deciduous shrubby tree, growing up to 20 feet tall.

EDIBLE PARTS: Ripe berries, flowers.

HARVESTABLE: Autumn.

FLAVOR: Slightly sweet.

ELDERBERRY SYRUP

- 3 cups fresh blue elderberries, rinsed and stems removed
- Water
- 3/4 teaspoon stevia powder extract, 90 percent strength
- 1/2 cup birch sugar (xylitol)

1. Remove the largest stems. Tiny stems do not need to be removed, since stems and pulp will be removed later.
2. Put berries in a saucepan and add enough water to just cover the berries.
3. Bring to a boil and then simmer on low until water is reduced by half, approximately 30–40 minutes, stirring frequently. The berries will turn colors as they heat up, changing from blue to black to red and finally to purple.
4. Turn off heat and strain or sieve berries from liquid. Discard pulp.
5. Cool the liquid until it stops steaming and then refrigerate. The liquid will slowly thicken in the fridge, becoming syrup after about 24 hours.

Use on pancakes or vanilla ice cream or add 1 teaspoon to a cup of water for a delicious drink. You can substitute the stevia and birch sugar in this recipe with 1 cup of regular white refined sugar if desired. Add a little more or less sweetener as desired.

Sambucus racemosa

(RED ELDERBERRY)

STATES: Arizona, Colorado, Idaho, Montana, Nevada, New Mexico, Utah, Wyoming.

HABITAT: Mountainsides.

FORM: Bush, typically growing 2–4 feet tall, sometimes up to 6 feet.

FLOWER: White.

CHARACTERISTICS: Red elderberry is generally a much shorter plant than the blue species. Some sources still argue that red elderberries are poisonous. I'm not sure where this rumor comes from. The berries have been widely eaten for centuries. I eat them by the handful when hiking and have never had a problem. There have been some isolated reports that the berries may cause upset stomach for some people. This has not been my experience. The leaves and stems are considered poisonous, but I'm not sure why anyone would be eating those anyway. Red elderberries are a much shorter plant than blue elderberries.

EDIBLE PARTS: Ripe berries, flowers.

HARVESTABLE: Autumn.

FLAVOR: Slightly sweet.

Sambucus racemosa *var.* melanocarpa

(BLACK ELDERBERRY)

STATES: Arizona, Colorado, Idaho, Montana, Nevada, New Mexico, Utah, Wyoming.

FLOWER: White.

CHARACTERISTICS: Black elderberry is generally a much shorter plant than the blue species. Some sources still argue that black elderberries are poisonous. There have been some isolated reports that the berries may cause upset stomach for some people. The leaves and stems are considered poisonous, but I'm not sure why anyone would be eating those anyway. Some experts list this as a subspecies of *S. racemosa* instead of being its own species. Others disagree.

HABITAT: Mountainsides.

FORM: Bush, typically growing 2–4 feet tall, sometimes up to 6 feet.

EDIBLE PARTS: Ripe berries, flowers.

HARVESTABLE: Autumn.

FLAVOR: Slightly sweet.

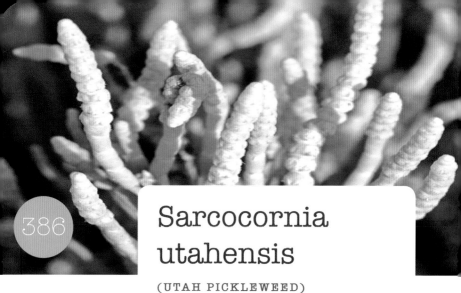

Sarcocornia utahensis

(UTAH PICKLEWEED)

STATES: Arizona, New Mexico, Utah.

HABITAT: Desert alkaline soil.

FORM: Perennial, low-growing, woody-stemmed herb growing in clumps.

FLOWER: Green, yellow, red.

CHARACTERISTICS: This is an interesting treat in the deep desert. When I'm rockhounding far from civilization on hot summer days, this salty, crunchy plant is not only fun to eat but seems to boost my electrolytes and energy with its natural salts. If your vehicle was broken down in the desert and you were in need of water (and electrolytes to save your life), this would be the plant to turn to. The leaves contain water even on the hottest days in the driest summer conditions. Don't confuse this plant with mature horsetail grass in its feathery stage. If you do an online search for Utah pickleweed, you will find that some amateurs have posted photos of horsetail grass, believing it to be pickleweed, and they can look similar at first glance. Horsetail grass is known to pick up heavy metals from the soil and can be toxic to eat in areas of polluted soil, and it tastes nothing like pickleweed, so it is important not to confuse the two if harvesting in the wild. Pickleweed can remove salt from soils and has a relatively high salt content for a wild edible.

EDIBLE PART: Leaves.

HARVESTABLE: Summer.

FLAVOR: Crunchy, slightly salty, and not unlike pickles.

Secale cereale

(CEREAL RYE)

————

STATES: Arizona, Colorado, Idaho, Montana, Nevada, New Mexico, Utah, Wyoming.

FLOWER: Green.

HABITAT: Roadsides, fields, dry wastelands.

FORM: Single-stemmed grass, typically growing up to 4 feet tall.

EDIBLE PART: Grain.

HARVESTABLE: Summer.

FLAVOR: Grain.

NOTES: This is perhaps the single most important wild edible in the West. The pioneers are believed to have brought it here from Europe because is so easily self-seeds. This important foodstuff helped sustain the pioneers and has since sustained itself, a sort of latent food security surrounding us on a massive scale. Everyone has seen it, but few recognize its value or history.

Today, cereal rye grows rampantly across hundreds of thousands of acres around the West, providing an important food supply for birds and critters, but there is also plenty for humans who want to harvest it. There is enough wild rye growing in the West to provide critical winter food stores for probably the entire population—if it were harvested. Like all grains, rye must be harvested in July or it begins to disappear, knocked to the ground by winds and taken by birds. The seeds then plant themselves in early spring, pressed to the ground and covered in their own cozy blanket of straw, laid flat by the winter snows.

Rye can be used on its own for bread or mixed with wheat or other grains. At our house, we harvest this grain from the wild every year by hand. Keep in mind that cereal rye, like all wild edibles, must be legally harvested, with permission if on lands you don't own. Or you can harvest on many public lands, like Bureau of Land Management lands, often with no permission necessary. If you are not sure, call your local BLM office or US Forest Service office to ask about harvesting by hand for personal use.

Setaria pumila

(YELLOW FOXTAIL)

STATES: Arizona, Colorado, Idaho, Montana, Nevada, New Mexico, Utah, Wyoming.

FLOWER: Green.

HABITAT: Disturbed soil, fields, meadows.

FORM: Annual bunch grass, growing up to 3 feet tall.

EDIBLE PART: Seeds.

HARVESTABLE: Summer.

FLAVOR: Grain.

Shepherdia argentea

(SILVER BUFFALOBERRY)

———

STATES: Arizona, Colorado, Idaho, Montana, Nevada, New Mexico, Utah, Wyoming.

FLOWER: Greenish white or yellowish white.

CHARACTERISTICS: These berries were widely eaten by many Native American tribes, who used them fresh and dried and often sweetened them to eat as a treat but also added them into mush or porridge as a flavoring.

HABITAT: Mountainsides.

EDIBLE PART: Berries.

FORM: Deciduous, perennial, nitrogen-fixing shrub, typically growing from 3 to 10 feet tall, depending on sunlight and water resources.

BERRY: Red.

HARVESTABLE: Summer.

FLAVOR: Spicy. The flavor can be bitter until after the first frosts, and even then, the berries benefit from cooking.

Shepherdia canadensis

(RUSSET BUFFALOBERRY)

STATES: Arizona, Colorado, Idaho, Montana, Nevada, New Mexico, Utah, Wyoming.

FLOWER: Greenish yellow.

CHARACTERISTICS: Like some other wild berries, you have to navigate thorns if you are going to get to these. These berries also make a mild foamy soap, especially if picked before fully ripe. This foam was sometimes sweetened and eaten as a type of ice cream treat by some American Indian tribes, according to Daniel E. Moerman in *Native American Food Plants*.

EDIBLE PART: Berries.

HABITAT: Mountainsides.

FORM: Deciduous, perennial, nitrogen-fixing shrub, typically growing from 3 to 10 feet tall, depending on sunlight and water resources.

BERRY: Red.

HARVESTABLE: Summer.

FLAVOR: The flavor can be bitter until after the first frosts, and even then, the berries benefit from cooking.

Sisymbrium irio

(LONDON ROCKET)

STATES: Arizona, Colorado, New Mexico, Utah.

FLOWER: Yellow.

CHARACTERISTICS: The seed pods of this plant are long and thin and form from the lowest flowers first, meaning the young seed pods often stick up above the flowers above them. (This is also a characteristic of some wild mustards listed in this book.)

HABITAT: Disturbed soils, fields, pastures, roadsides.

FORM: Annual mustard, typically growing up to 3 feet tall when in flower.

EDIBLE PARTS: Flowers, leaves, seeds.

HARVESTABLE: Late spring, summer.

FLAVOR: Horseradish.

Sonchus arvensis

(SOWTHISTLE)

STATES: Colorado, Idaho, Montana, Nevada, New Mexico, Utah, Wyoming.

FLOWER: Yellow.

HABITAT: Disturbed soils, roadsides, wastelands.

FORM: Perennial that grows 2–4 feet tall.

EDIBLE PART: Young, tender leaves.

HARVESTABLE: Summer.

FLAVOR: Mild. If the flavor of the greens is bitter, you have waited until they are too old to pick them. **Do not ingest milky white sap from any part of the plant.**

Sonchus asper

(SPINY SOWTHISTLE)

393

STATES: Arizona, Colorado, Idaho, Montana, Nevada, New Mexico, Utah, Wyoming.

HABITAT: Disturbed soils, roadsides, wastelands.

FORM: Annual plant, growing 1–3 feet tall depending on moisture and sun.

FLOWER: Yellow.

EDIBLE PART: Young, tender leaves.

HARVESTABLE: Summer.

FLAVOR: Mild. If the flavor of the greens is bitter, you have waited until they are too old to pick them. **Do not ingest milky white sap from any part of the plant.**

394

Sonchus oleraceus

(COMMON SOWTHISTLE)

———

STATES: Arizona, Colorado, Idaho, Montana, Nevada, New Mexico, Utah, Wyoming.

HABITAT: Disturbed soils, roadsides, wastelands.

FORM: Annual plant that grows 2–4 feet tall.

FLOWER: Yellow.

CHARACTERISTICS: All *Sonchus* species prefer disturbed soils and are often found at roadsides and in fields.

EDIBLE PART: Young, tender leaves.

HARVESTABLE: Summer.

FLAVOR: Mild. If the flavor of the greens is bitter, you have waited until they are too old to pick them. **Do not ingest milky white sap from any part of the plant.**

NOTES: If you raise rabbits, you can feed *Sonchus* species to them since they are also fond of eating these plants.

Sorghum bicolor

(WILD GRAIN SORGHUM)

STATES: Arizona, Colorado, Idaho, Montana, Nevada, New Mexico, Utah, Wyoming.

FLOWER: Green.

CHARACTERISTICS: There are many commercial cultivars of this species, and they all easily naturally cross with this wild plant, which can make the wild plant variable. Sorghum grows fairly easily in dry conditions, tolerates alkaline soil, and is an important grain for anyone looking for wild sources that can be used to make flour. The grains are 4 percent protein and 2 percent fiber according to Purdue University data. I sell garden sorghum seeds at SeedRenaissance.com.

HABITAT: Disturbed soils, roadsides, fields.

FORM: Perennial grass, typically growing about 3 feet tall.

EDIBLE PART: Seeds can be used cooked or ground for flour.

HARVESTABLE: Late summer.

FLAVOR: Grain.

NOTES: This plant spreads by rhizome and also by seeds, which disperse easily. In many parts of the world, farmers consider this plant to be invasive and aggressive.

Sorghum halepense

(JOHNSONGRASS)

STATES: Arizona, Colorado, Idaho, Montana, Nevada, New Mexico, Utah, Wyoming.

FLOWER: Green.

CHARACTERISTICS: The grain is 13 percent protein according to the US Forest Service: "In the United States, Johnsongrass was introduced in South Carolina from Turkey around 1830. William Johnson, whom the plant is named after, established Johnsongrass along the Alabama River in the 1840s as a forage species, and Johnsongrass spread rapidly across the South. Johnson grass is now widely escaped from cultivation in much of the United States."

HABITAT: Disturbed soils, roadsides, fields.

FORM: Perennial grass, typically growing about 3 feet tall.

EDIBLE PART: Seeds can be used cooked or ground for flour.

HARVESTABLE: Late summer.

FLAVOR: Grain.

NOTES: This plant spreads by rhizome and also by seeds, which disperse easily. In many parts of the world, farmers consider this plant to be invasive and aggressive.

Sporobolus flexuosus

(MESA DROPSEED)

STATES: Arizona, Colorado, Montana, Nevada, New Mexico, Utah.

FLOWER: Greenish tan.

CHARACTERISTICS: The seeds are 5 to 8 percent protein according to the US Department of Agriculture.

HABITAT: Desert.

FORM: Tufted perennial, typically growing up to 3 feet tall.

EDIBLE PART: Seeds.

HARVESTABLE: Summer, autumn.

FLAVOR: Grain.

NOTES: This plant is called dropseed because once the seeds are dry, even a breeze can scatter them to the sandy or rocky soil below.

Stellaria media

(CHICKWEED)

STATES: Arizona, Colorado, Idaho, Montana, Nevada, New Mexico, Utah, Wyoming.

FLOWER: White.

CHARACTERISTICS: This plant can be invasive. However, I have allowed it to naturalize in one of my greenhouses so I can eat it during the winter and early spring, because where I live in the desert, this plant grows wild only in the high mountains. I have even been criticized for selling the seeds for these plants on my website, SeedRenaissance.com, because they are so invasive in some places in the world, but if I didn't plant them from seed, I wouldn't have them to eat.

HABITAT: Moist, shady mountainside locations.

FORM: Low-growing flowering herb.

EDIBLE PARTS: Leaves and seeds, raw or cooked. The seeds are 18 percent protein and 6 percent fat.

HARVESTABLE: Summer.

FLAVOR: Mild.

Streptopus amplexifolius

399

(WILD CUCUMBER, CLASPLEAF
TWISTEDSTALK)

———————

STATES: Arizona, Colorado, Idaho, Montana, New
Mexico, Utah, Wyoming.

FLOWER: Greenish white.

CHARACTERISTICS: "The flowers give rise to a single
elliptic yellow or red berry, which is edible. Wayne
Phillips, retired Forest Service ecologist, author, and noted
Lewis and Clark impersonator, reports that the green
shoots are also edible and taste like cucumber when eaten
raw. Populations tend to be small and the species can be
mistaken for the poisonous *Veratrum*, so perhaps twisted
stalk is better left unsampled for others to observe rather
than taste," according to the US Forest Service.

BERRIES: Red.

HABITAT: Moist mountainside locations, typically in
shade.

FORM: Low-growing perennial herb.

EDIBLE PARTS: Fruit, leaves, root.

HARVESTABLE: Summer.

FLAVOR: Cucumber.

Streptopus streptopoides

(SMALL TWISTEDSTALK)

STATE: Idaho.

FLOWER: White or greenish white when young.

CHARACTERISTICS: This can be mistaken for several poisonous *Veratrum* species, some of which also produce red berries. Never eat any wild edible of any kind unless you know with certainty what you are ingesting.

BERRIES: Red.

HABITAT: Moist mountainside locations, typically in shade.

FORM: Low-growing perennial herb.

EDIBLE PARTS: Fruit, leaves, root.

HARVESTABLE: Summer.

FLAVOR: Cucumber.

Symphoricarpos albus

(SNOWBERRY, WAXBERRY)

STATES: Colorado, Idaho, Montana, New Mexico, Utah, Wyoming.

FLOWER: Typically pinkish white; sometimes all white or all pink.

CHARACTERISTICS: Typically produces flowers in June.

HABITAT: Mountainsides.

FORM: Shrubs, typically growing 2–3 feet tall.

EDIBLE PART: There is considerable debate about whether these berries are edible or poisonous. I eat them only infrequently and in small amounts. (I've never had a problem with them.) Most experts agree that white berries should generally be avoided, and anyway, they don't have a good flavor. These berries occur prolifically in many canyons, in both shady and sunny areas. Once you know how to recognize them   will often find them when hiking or camping   ountains.

HARVESTABLE: Summer, autumn.

FLAVOR: Bitter.

Symphoricarpos occidentalis

(WESTERN SNOWBERRY)

STATES: Colorado, Idaho, Montana, New Mexico, Utah, Wyoming.

FLOWER: Typically pinkish white; sometimes all white or all pink.

CHARACTERISTICS: There are only small botanical differences between this species and *Symphoricarpos albus*.

HABITAT: Mountainsides.

FORM: Shrubs, typically growing 2–3 feet tall.

EDIBLE PART: There is considerable debate about whether these berries are edible or poisonous. I eat them only infrequently and in small amounts. (I've never had a problem with them.) Most experts agree that white berries should generally be avoided, and anyway, they don't have a good flavor. These berries occur prolifically in many canyons, in both shady and sunny areas. Once you know how to recognize them, you will often find them when hiking or camping in the mountains.

HARVESTABLE: Summer, autumn.

FLAVOR: Bitter.

Syringa vulgaris

(COMMON LILAC)

STATES: Colorado, New Mexico, Utah.

FLOWER: Lilac, of course!

CHARACTERISTICS: Unfortunately, and surprisingly, the flavor is awful—bitter. Eating them is almost disconcerting because they smell so great as you put them in your mouth. They are better as a garnish than a food.

HABITAT: Open, sunny spaces near water.

FORM: Tall deciduous shrub.

EDIBLE PART: Flowers.

HARVESTABLE: Spring.

FLAVOR: Bitter.

Taraxacum officinale

(COMMON DANDELION)

STATES: Arizona, Colorado, Idaho, Montana, Nevada, New Mexico, Utah, Wyoming.

FLOWER: Yellow.

CHARACTERISTICS: When anyone becomes interested in wild edibles, it seems they invariably and quickly get pointed to this weedy lawn invader, probably because it is easily recognizable and easily found. Let me just say this: if dandelion is among the first wild edibles you taste, stick with us—there are much better wild edibles available. Don't give up just because this was the first wild food you dared to try! It's not bad as far as flavor, but it doesn't deserve to be the poster child of wild edibles. Yet somehow it is. My favorite ways to eat this plant are using the leaves to make homemade green pasta noodles (you can find a recipe on my blog at CalebWarnock.blogspot.com), or the rinsed white crowns in ravioli, made with homemade fresh ground whole wheat pasta dough. It's also good for green smoothies and has many medicinal uses too. The toasted roots are used to make homemade root beer.

HABITAT: Lawns, gardens, roadsides, waste spaces, meadows, pastures, mountainsides.

FORM: Flowering herb.

EDIBLE PARTS: Flowers, leaves, root, crowns.

HARVESTABLE: Spring, summer, autumn—even the dead of winter in my greenhouses.

FLAVOR: Mild.

Thlaspi arvense

(FIELD PENNYCRESS)

STATES: Arizona, Colorado, Idaho, Montana, Nevada, New Mexico, Utah, Wyoming.

FLOWER: White.

CHARACTERISTICS: Known for its coin-like seeds, which give this plant its name.

HABITAT: Disturbed soils, roadsides, pastures, fields.

FORM: Annual branching, flowering herb, typically growing 2 feet tall.

EDIBLE PARTS: Young leaves, seeds.

HARVESTABLE: Spring.

FLAVOR: Bitter when raw, but cooking makes the leaves milder.

Tragopogon dubius

(YELLOW SALSIFY)

STATES: Arizona, Colorado, Idaho, Montana, Nevada, New Mexico, Utah, Wyoming.

HABITAT: Fields, disturbed soils, pastures, gardens.

FORM: Biennial single-stemmed flowering herb.

FLOWER: Yellow.

CHARACTERISTICS: I love these plants and eat them often. I grow these in my greenhouse because the plants are so useful and tasty, and I can get larger roots for harvesting in the spring when I grow them indoors. The wild plants sometimes have stunted roots because of heavy clay soil, but not always. Root flavor can also be affected by how much water the wild plants get.

The early flower buds, while they are small, have a sweet resin on them, and eating them is a treat, but they are fibrous as they get closer to opening the flower petals.

EDIBLE PARTS: Root, leaves, flower buds.

HARVESTABLE: Spring, summer.

Tragopogon pratensis

(GOAT'S BEARD, MEADOW SALSIFY)

———

STATES: Arizona, Colorado, Idaho, Montana, Nevada, New Mexico, Utah, Wyoming.

HABITAT: Fields, disturbed soils, pastures, gardens.

FORM: Biennial single-stemmed flowering herb.

FLOWER: Yellow.

CHARACTERISTICS: Goat's beard refers to the hairs on the seeds. The roots are somewhat like skinny parsnips. Root flavor can also be affected by how much water the wild plants get. The early flower buds, while they are small, have a sweet resin on them, and eating them is a treat, but they are fibrous as they get closer to opening the flower petals.

EDIBLE PARTS: Root, leaves, flower buds.

HARVESTABLE: Spring, summer.

FLAVOR: The flower buds are slightly sweet with a sticky resin that I love.

Trifolium cyathiferum

(CUP CLOVER)

———

STATES: Idaho, Montana, Nevada, Utah.

FLOWER: Greenish white with reddish-brown tips.

CHARACTERISTICS: This species is somewhat rare, and there are reports that it has been slowly getting rarer. It prefers moist soil.

HABITAT: Lawns, roadsides, waste spaces, pastures.

FORM: Low-growing leafy herb.

EDIBLE PARTS: Flowers, leaves, roots.

HARVESTABLE: Spring, summer, autumn.

FLAVOR: Mild.

Trifolium microcephalum

409

(SMALLHEAD CLOVER)

———

STATES: Arizona, Idaho, Montana, Nevada.

FLOWER: Greenish white with reddish-brown tips.

CHARACTERISTICS: This species is somewhat rare, and there are reports that it has been slowly getting rarer. It prefers moist soil.

HABITAT: Lawns, roadsides, waste spaces, pastures.

FORM: Low-growing leafy herb.

EDIBLE PARTS: Flowers, leaves, roots.

HARVESTABLE: Spring, summer, autumn.

FLAVOR: Mild.

410

Trifolium pratense

(RED CLOVER)

————

STATES: Arizona, Colorado, Idaho, Montana, Nevada, New Mexico, Utah, Wyoming.

FLOWER: Red, rarely white.

CHARACTERISTICS: Many species of butterflies rely on this plant as a food source.

HABITAT: Lawns, roadsides, waste spaces, pastures.

FORM: Perennial spreading leafy herb.

EDIBLE PARTS: Flowers, leaves, roots.

HARVESTABLE: Spring, summer, autumn.

FLAVOR: Mild.

Trifolium repens

(WHITE CLOVER, DUTCH CLOVER)

STATES: Arizona, Colorado, Idaho, Montana, Nevada, New Mexico, Utah, Wyoming.

FLOWER: White, rarely pale pink.

CHARACTERISTICS: *Trifolium* is the Latin for "three-leafed," and this is the three-leaf clover.

HABITAT: Lawns, roadsides, waste spaces, pastures.

FORM: Herbaceous perennial.

EDIBLE PARTS: Flowers, leaves, roots.

HARVESTABLE: Spring, summer, autumn.

FLAVOR: Mild.

412

Trifolium variegatum

(WHITETIP CLOVER)

STATES: Arizona, Idaho, Montana, Nevada, Utah, Wyoming.

FLOWER: Pink, purple, or red with white tips.

CHARACTERISTICS: This species can be highly variable in flower color, which is why it has the Latin name *Variegatum*, meaning various or changing. The flowers are very showy and unusual.

HABITAT: Lawns, roadsides, waste spaces, pastures.

FORM: Perennial spreading leafy herb.

EDIBLE PARTS: Flowers, leaves, roots.

HARVESTABLE: Spring, summer, autumn.

FLAVOR: Mild.

Trifolium wormskioldii

(COW CLOVER)

STATES: Arizona, Colorado, Idaho, Montana, Nevada, New Mexico, Utah, Wyoming.

FLOWER: White, red, pink, or purple, or sometimes white with a blush or dots of red, pink, or purple.

CHARACTERISTICS: The flowers are smaller than most *Trifolium* species.

HABITAT: Lawns, roadsides, waste spaces, pastures.

FORM: Perennial leafy and low-growing herb.

EDIBLE PARTS: Flowers, leaves, roots.

HARVESTABLE: Spring, summer, autumn.

FLAVOR: Mild.

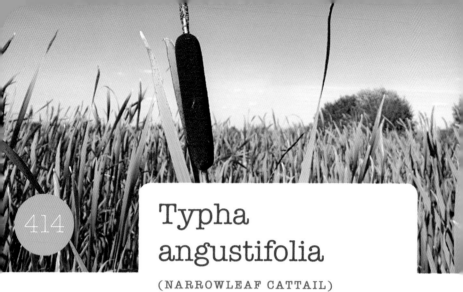

414

Typha angustifolia

(NARROWLEAF CATTAIL)

———

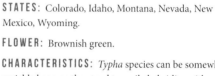

STATES: Colorado, Idaho, Montana, Nevada, New Mexico, Wyoming.

FLOWER: Brownish green.

CHARACTERISTICS: *Typha* species can be somewhat variable because they tend to easily hybridize with related species, and the species can vary only by small botanical details.

HABITAT: Grows in water or wet soil.

FORM: Tall single-stem grass, typically growing 6–10 feet tall.

EDIBLE PARTS: Flowers, leaves, pollen, root, seeds, stem.

HARVESTABLE: Spring, summer, autumn.

FLAVOR: Where to begin? The inner stems of cattails should be sold in grocery stores because they are unbelievably delicious—crunchy, fresh, mildly sweet. They are one of my all-time favorite wild foods. **The only caution is that you want to make sure you get them clean, because they are often growing in standing water.** Make sure the water is clean, and be sure to rinse them carefully. They taste best in spring.

Typha glauca

(HYBRID CATTAIL)

STATES: Colorado, Montana, Utah, Wyoming.

FLOWER: Brownish green.

HABITAT: Grows in water or wet soil.

FORM: Tall single-stem grass, typically growing 6–10 feet tall.

CHARACTERISTICS: Both the settlers and the American Indians ground the dried pollen and seeds as flour and mixed them with wheat flour to make any number of baked goods, especially in times when wheat flour was scarce or expensive. I do this too. The roots were also used fresh and dried and, when dried, were often ground for flour.

EDIBLE PARTS: Flowers, leaves, pollen, root, seeds, stem.

HARVESTABLE: Spring, summer, autumn.

FLAVOR: Inner stems are crunchy, fresh, and mildly sweet. The pollen of all *Typha* species is best mixed with other grains.

Typha latifolia

(BROADLEAF CATTAIL)

STATES: Arizona, Colorado, Idaho, Montana, Nevada, New Mexico, Utah, Wyoming.

HABITAT: Grows in water or wet soil.

FORM: Tall single-stem grass, typically growing 6–10 feet tall.

FLOWER: Brownish green.

CHARACTERISTICS: One stem provides a huge amount to eat. According to Purdue University, the roots of *Typha* species are about 8 percent protein and 1 percent sugar. The leaves are 7–12 percent protein, and the pollen is 19 percent protein. Studies have shown that *Typha* species may accumulate heavy metals when grown in contaminated soil and water, so harvest all *Typha* species only in clean areas.

The pollen fluff is the best tinder for starting flint and steel fires. It sparks easily and quickly and is easy to store for this purpose. It's a lot of fun to practice flint and steel sparking with.

EDIBLE PARTS: Flowers, leaves, pollen, root, seeds, stem.

HARVESTABLE: Spring, summer, autumn.

416

Urtica dioica

(STINGING NETTLE)

STATES: Arizona, Colorado, Idaho, Montana, Nevada, New Mexico, Utah, Wyoming.

FLOWER: Greenish to greenish tan.

HABITAT: Shady moist soils on mountainsides and slopes.

FORM: Tall, single-stem, branching flower.

EDIBLE PART: Leaves.

HARVESTABLE: Spring, summer, autumn.

FLAVOR: Mild.

NOTES: Yes, I know: you have questions. Eat stinging nettle? Yes. This plant has changed my life. It is a strong natural antihistamine that controls my allergies and asthma far better than anything from the pharmacy. I grow stinging nettle in my gardens and my four greenhouses because I need it as medicine, and I eat it on almost every hike I go on, wherever I am in the world.

The needles of the plant are located on the main stem and the leaf stems. To harvest a leaf, I pinch off the leaf just above the leaf stem without touching the stem. Some large leaves also have a few needles on the main leaf vein, so I fold the leaves before eating. For centuries, people have stung themselves on purpose, because the "sting" takes away arthritis pain instantly. I have autoimmune arthritis, and I control it when it hurts by purposefully stinging myself. I have stung myself so many times with nettle that I no longer have a reaction at all.

The cure for nettle is nettle. If you get stung, *don't* itch or scratch. Once you irritate the skin, the swelling and itching will be much more difficult to get rid of. But if you don't touch your skin, you can eat one or two leaves and all the sting, swelling, and scratching will be gone in three to four minutes.

Stinging nettle is also a widely sold and widely used medicinally, so you can still use it to control your allergies even if you don't want to harvest it wild. You can also grow it yourself. I sell the seeds at SeedRenaissance.com.

Everyone in our family uses this. Recently, while working in the garden, an inch-long red beetle of some kind bit my forearm, and it immediately started to sting and swell. I was near my greenhouse and helped myself to three nettle leaves. In two minutes, the sting and swelling was gone. The bite mark remained visible for days but never bothered me again.

I tell you all this to give you courage. Both the settlers and the American Indians ate nettle as a common vegetable because it is so high in protein. A 2015 study in the scientific journal *Food Science & Nutrition* showed the leaves of this species to be 34 percent protein and 10 percent fiber—containing more protein and fiber than wheat or barley flour!

If I had to pick only one wild plant to harvest the rest of my life, stinging nettle would be my choice, without question or hesitation!

Vaccinium cespitosum

(DWARF BILBERRY)

———————

STATES: Colorado, Idaho, Montana, Nevada, New Mexico, Utah, Wyoming.

FLOWER: Pink, whitish pink, or red.

CHARACTERISTICS: The flowers are waxy and bell-shaped. The berries look and taste like blueberries. Summer drought and late spring frosts can dramatically reduce the number of berries that appear, but they are never prolific. Because of this, they are like Saskatoon serviceberries—they are generally eaten on the spot instead of gathered for home use.

EDIBLE PART: Berries.

BERRIES: Blue when ripe.

HABITAT: Shady understory plant, usually found in forests where it is moist and temperatures are cooler.

FORM: Perennial shrub.

HARVESTABLE: Summer, autumn.

FLAVOR: Sweet when fully ripe; some have tartness.

Vaccinium geminiflorum

(MEXICAN BLUEBERRY)

STATE: Arizona.

FLOWER: White or pink, rarely reddish pink.

CHARACTERISTICS: Low-growing, rarely getting more than a foot tall. These berries look and taste like common blueberries.

EDIBLE PART: Berries.

BERRY: Blue.

HABITAT: Shady understory plant, usually found in forests where it is moist and temperatures are cooler.

FORM: Perennial shrub.

HARVESTABLE: Summer, autumn.

FLAVOR: Sweet when fully ripe; some have tartness.

SYNONYM: *Vaccinium caespitosum.*

Vaccinium membranaceum

(THINLEAF HUCKLEBERRY)

STATES: Arizona, Colorado, Idaho, Montana, Utah, Wyoming.

FLOWER: White, pink, or occasionally brownish red.

CHARACTERISTICS: This is the huckleberry plant that is famous in the West and has given rise to huckleberry jam, milkshakes, and chocolates that fill tourist shops around Yellowstone National Park and many other areas. And why not? Huckleberries are delicious. Even the American Indians gathered them widely for fresh eating and dried them to flavor food in winter.

EDIBLE PART: Berries.

BERRIES: Black or dark purple, occasionally red.

HABITAT: Shady understory plant usually found in forests where it is moist and temperatures are cooler.

FORM: Perennial shrub.

HARVESTABLE: Summer, autumn.

FLAVOR: Sweet when fully ripe; some have tartness.

Vaccinium myrtillus

(WHORTLEBERRY)

STATES: Arizona, Colorado, Idaho, Montana, Nevada, New Mexico, Utah, Wyoming.

FLOWER: White, pink.

CHARACTERISTICS: This species, like most *Vaccinium* species, grow low to the ground. This species typically gets no taller than 18 inches high. The US Forest Service says "fruit of whortleberry is juicy, edible, and has a nutlike flavor. Berries are eaten fresh or gathered for use in jams and jellies. Fruit may be used in pie filling; however, collecting enough of the small berries can be difficult. Leaves of whortleberry have been used to make tea. Both fruit and leaves are reported to have some medicinal value. *Vaccinium* berries were traditionally an important food source for many native peoples."

EDIBLE PART: Berries.

BERRY: Blue or bluish black when ripe.

HABITAT: Shady understory plant, usually found in forests where it is moist and temperatures are cooler.

FORM: Perennial shrub.

HARVESTABLE: Summer, autumn.

FLAVOR: Sweet when fully ripe; some have tartness.

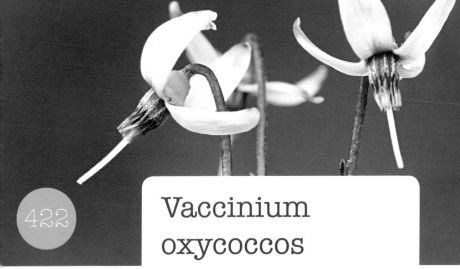

Vaccinium oxycoccos

(SMALL CRANBERRY, BOG CRANBERRY)

STATE: Idaho.

FLOWER: White, pink, or dark pink.

CHARACTERISTICS: Prefers areas of high groundwater, thus the common name bog cranberry. "Bog cranberry fruits have good flavor and are often used to make jams and jellies. However, they are seldom abundant enough to be gathered in large quantities. Native Americans used the berries, twigs, and bark for medicinal purposes," according to the US Forest Service.

EDIBLE PART: Berries.

BERRIES: Dark red when ripe.

HABITAT: Shady understory plant, usually found in forests where it is moist and temperatures are cooler.

FORM: Perennial shrub.

HARVESTABLE: Summer, autumn.

FLAVOR: Sweet when fully ripe; some have tartness.

Vaccinium scoparium

(GROUSE WHORTLEBERRY)

STATES: Colorado, Idaho, Montana, Nevada, New Mexico, Utah, Wyoming.

FLOWER: Pink.

CHARACTERISTICS: The berries are eaten fresh, cooked, or made into jam and wine and were an important traditional food for many Native American peoples, according to the US Forest Service. They also used the leaves to make beverages. The fruit is sweet and high in energy value and vitamin C.

EDIBLE PART: Berries.

BERRY: Blue or bluish purple.

HABITAT: Shady understory plant, usually found in forests where it is moist and temperatures are cooler.

FORM: Perennial shrub.

HARVESTABLE: Summer, autumn.

FLAVOR: Sweet when fully ripe; some have tartness.

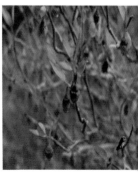

Vaccinium uliginosum

(BOG BLUEBERRY)

———

STATES: Idaho, Montana, Nevada, Utah, Wyoming.

FLOWER: White or pink.

CHARACTERISTICS: The berries of this species "are rich in vitamin C, high in energy content, and low in fat. Bog blueberries are edible and have good flavor. The berries are often picked in large quantities and used in jams, jellies, and pies. They are the most popular fruit of Native Americans in the Fort Yukon region. Fresh or dried leaves can be used for tea," according to the US Forest Service.

EDIBLE PART: Berries.

BERRIES: Blue when ripe.

HABITAT: Shady understory plant, usually found in forests where it is moist and temperatures are cooler.

FORM: Perennial shrub.

HARVESTABLE: Summer, autumn.

FLAVOR: Sweet when fully ripe; some have tartness.

Veronica biloba

(TWOLOBE SPEEDWELL)

STATES: Colorado, Idaho, Montana, Nevada, Utah, Wyoming.

FLOWER: Blue and white pattern.

CHARACTERISTICS: These pretty little spring flowers bloom on the floor of my greenhouse in early March and have an acceptable mild flavor. The plant can colonize an entire area.

HABITAT: Gardens, pastures, disturbed land.

FORM: Low-growing flower.

EDIBLE PARTS: Leaves, flowers.

HARVESTABLE: Spring.

FLAVOR: Grassy.

SYNONYM: *Veronica agrestis.*

Viola adunca

(HOOKEDSPUR VIOLET)

STATES: Arizona, Colorado, Idaho, Montana, Nevada, New Mexico, Utah, Wyoming.

FLOWER: Purple or blue with white centers, or sometimes reversed.

CHARACTERISTICS: Some flowers on these plants never open but still produce seeds by self-pollinating. Botanists call such flowers "cleistogamous."

HABITAT: Gardens, mountainsides, meadows.

FORM: Low-growing, showy flower.

EDIBLE PARTS: Young leaves, flower buds, flower.

HARVESTABLE: Spring.

FLAVOR: Mild. Flowers are slightly sweet.

Viola canadensis

(CANADIAN WHITE VIOLET)

STATES: Arizona, Colorado, Idaho, Montana, New Mexico, Utah, Wyoming.

FLOWER: White with a yellow center and purple veins on the lower part of the petal toward the center.

CHARACTERISTICS: These flowers are an important source of nectar for many pollinators.

HABITAT: Gardens, mountainsides, meadows.

FORM: Low-growing, showy flower.

EDIBLE PARTS: Young leaves, flower buds, flower.

HARVESTABLE: Spring.

FLAVOR: Mild. Flowers are slightly sweet.

Viola odorata

(SWEET VIOLET)

STATES: Arizona, Colorado, Idaho, Montana, Utah.

FLOWER: Purplish blue.

CHARACTERISTICS: This species is sold commercially for its showy and colorful blooms and fragrance. The flowers are sometimes candied and are a favorite edible flower for adding to early summer salads.

HABITAT: Gardens, mountainsides, meadows.

FORM: Low-growing, showy flower.

EDIBLE PARTS: Young leaves, flower buds, flower.

HARVESTABLE: Spring.

FLAVOR: Mild. Flowers are slightly sweet.

Viola palustris

(MARSH VIOLET)

STATES: Arizona, Colorado, Idaho, Montana, Nevada, Utah, Wyoming.

FLOWER: White, pink, or lilac.

CHARACTERISTICS: The flowers are perennial, and some cultivars are sold commercially.

HABITAT: Gardens, mountainsides, meadows in moist soil.

FORM: Low-growing, showy flower.

EDIBLE PARTS: Young leaves, flower buds, flower.

HARVESTABLE: Spring.

FLAVOR: Mild. Flowers are slightly sweet.

Viola tricolor

(JOHNNY JUMPUP)

STATES: Utah, Wyoming.

FLOWER: Purple, yellow, and white in patches.

CHARACTERISTICS: This flower is a long-time favorite for spring color. Thomas Jefferson recorded sowing seeds of this flower at his boyhood home on April 2, 1767, according to Monticello.org. This flower was even mentioned by Shakespeare in his plays.

HABITAT: Gardens, mountainsides, meadows.

FORM: Low-growing, showy flower.

EDIBLE PARTS: Young leaves, flower buds, flower.

HARVESTABLE: Spring.

FLAVOR: Mild. Flowers are slightly sweet.

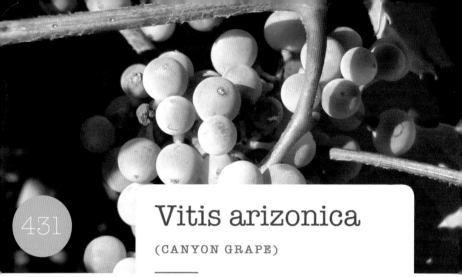

Vitis arizonica

(CANYON GRAPE)

431

STATES: Arizona, Nevada, New Mexico, Utah.

FLOWER: White.

CHARACTERISTICS: The berries can be bitter in low water years. Just like backyard grapes (of which these are a cousin), the berries are best when eaten fully ripe on the vine. Wild grape plants can be difficult to find. According to the Consortium of Midwest Herbaria, the grapes were historically given as a courtship gifts by Navajo Indians.

EDIBLE PARTS: Berries, leaves.

BERRIES: Black or dark purple.

HABITAT: Mountain canyons near water.

FORM: Perennial vine.

HARVESTABLE: Summer.

FLAVOR: Grape.

Vitis labrusca

(FOX GRAPE)

———

STATE: Utah.

FLOWER: Greenish white.

CHARACTERISTICS: This species is the parent of the Concord grapes that are famous for their juice and flavor and other commercial cultivars too. Even in the wild, these berries are juicier than other wild grapes.

EDIBLE PARTS: Berries, leaves.

BERRIES: Dark red or black.

HABITAT: Mountain canyons near water.

FORM: Perennial vine.

HARVESTABLE: Summer.

FLAVOR: Grape.

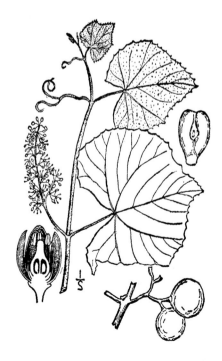

432

Vitis monticola

(SWEET MOUNTAIN GRAPE)

STATE: New Mexico.

FLOWER: White.

CHARACTERISTICS: The rootstocks of this wild species are sometimes used when grafting commercial varieties to make them tolerant of drought and alkaline soil.

EDIBLE PARTS: Berries, leaves.

BERRIES: Black or dark purple when ripe, and sometimes red.

HABITAT: Mountain canyons near water.

FORM: Perennial vine.

HARVESTABLE: Summer.

FLAVOR: Grape.

433

Vitis riparia

(RIVERBANK GRAPE)

STATES: Colorado, Montana, Wyoming.

HABITAT: Mountain canyons near water.

FORM: Perennial vine.

FLOWER: Yellowish green.

CHARACTERISTICS: Prefers to grow near water, thus its common name. These grapes are naturally sweet and juicy.

EDIBLE PARTS: Berries, leaves.

BERRIES: Purple or black when ripe.

HARVESTABLE: Summer.

FLAVOR: Grape.

Vitis vinifera

(WINE GRAPE)

STATES: Idaho, Utah.

HABITAT: Mountain canyons near water.

FORM: Perennial vine.

FLOWER: Greenish white.

CHARACTERISTICS: These have escaped out of cultivation after being imported from Europe. This species is the parent of many famous white wine grape cultivars and some red wine grape cultivars. This species does not vine out as far as other species.

EDIBLE PARTS: Berries, leaves.

BERRIES: Green or blushed pink; may also be found as red, purple, or black.

HARVESTABLE: Summer.

FLAVOR: Grape.

Ziziphus obtusifolia

(LOTEBUSH)

STATES: Arizona, Nevada, New Mexico, Utah.

FLOWER: White or pale green with yellowish-green sepals.

CHARACTERISTICS: Thorny. The berry-like fruits are typically covered with a white, waxy powder coating, like grapes. The fruits look somewhat like a date. Native Americans used the roots as a source of natural soap.

EDIBLE PART: Elongated, berry-like fruits.

FRUIT: Blue, purple, or black.

HABITAT: Desert.

FORM: Deciduous shrub, typically 6–12 feet tall.

HARVESTABLE: Summer.

FLAVOR: Sweet and sour.

437

Ziziphus zizyphus

(COMMON JUJUBE, INDIAN JUJUBE)

STATES: Arizona, Utah.

FLOWER: White or yellowish green.

HABITAT: Desert.

FORM: Deciduous shrub, typically 6–12 feet tall.

CHARACTERISTICS: For fun, just try saying the name out loud. It sounds like something made up by Dr. Seuss in his children's books. While this fruit is beloved in other parts of the world, it has never taken off in popularity in the United States, perhaps because of the serious thorns sported by this shrub.

EDIBLE PART: Elongated, berry-like fruits.

FRUIT: Can be picked when red and crisp and has a flavor and texture somewhat like an apple at this stage. Can also be picked when brown and wrinkled, when they look and taste like dates.

HARVESTABLE: Summer.

FLAVOR: Sweet and sour.

PART TWO:

POISONS, USEFUL LISTS, AND Q&A

POISONS

- *Actaea pachypoda* (pokeweed): some people say healthy adults may eat up to ten berries. Others say no.
- *Bromus catharticus*: poisonous grass
- *Bromus purgans*: poisonous grass
- *Bryonia alba* (white bryony): berries and all parts poisonous
- *Chamaesyce*, all species (asthma plant): poisonous
- *Datura inoxia* (sacred datura): poisonous
- *Datura stramonium* (jimsonweed): poisonous
- *Eragrostis megastachya* (stinkgrass): poisonous grass
- *Holcus lanatus* (common velvetgrass): poisonous grass
- *Iris missouriensis* (Rocky Mountain iris): poisonous
- *Lolium temulentum* (poison darnel): poisonous grass
- *Ranunculus acris* (buttercup): poisonous
- *Rhamnus cathartica* (common buckthorn): berries are purgative
- *Senecio jacobaea* (tansy ragwort): poisonous, all parts
- *Senecio vulgaris* (common groundsel): poisonous, all parts
- *Solanum dulcamara* (bittersweet nightshade): poisonous
- *Veratrum californicum* (California false-hellebore): poisonous
- *Zigadenus paniculatus* (foothill death camas): poisonous, all parts

LISTS: BY FOOD TYPE

IMPORTANT FOR FOOD VALUE (HIGH IN PROTEIN OR WIDELY AND EASILY AVAILABLE)

- *Amaranthus* species (amaranth)
- *Amelanchier* species (serviceberry)
- *Arctium* species (burdock)
- *Asclepias* species (milkweed)
- *Bistorta bistortoides* (American bistort)
- *Calochortus* species (mariposa lilies)
- *Camelina* species (gold of pleasure grain)
- *Capsella bursa-pastoris* (shepherd's purse)
- *Chenopodium album* (lambsquarters, wild spinach)
- *Chenopodium berlandieri* (goosefoot, netseed lambsquarters)
- *Crepis* species (hawksbeard)
- *Cucurbita foetidissima* (buffalo gourd)
- *Cymopterus* species (springparsley)
- *Cyperus* species (sedges)
- *Eriogonum* species (buckwheat)
- *Erodium cicutarium* (redstem filaree, stork's bill)
- *Geranium* species (mountain geraniums)
- *Helianthus* species (sunflowers)
- *Kochia scoparia* (kochia)
- *Lamium* species (greens)
- *Lomatium* species (biscuitroot)
- *Malva neglecta* (common mallow)
- *Medicago lupulina* (black medic)
- *Medicago sativa* (alfalfa)
- *Panicum* species (panicum grains)

- *Phlox* species (phlox)
- *Phragmites australis* (common reed)
- *Pinus* species (pinenut)
- *Plantago lanceolata* (narrowleaf plantain)
- *Portulaca oleracea* (common purslane)
- *Prunus virginiana* (western chokecherry, black chokecherry)
- *Quercus gambelii* (Gambel oak)
- *Ribes aureum* (golden currant)
- *Ribes hudsonianum* (western black currant)
- *Rumex* species (docks)
- *Sambucus* species (elderberries)
- *Secale cereale* (cereal rye)
- *Sorghum bicolor* (wild grain sorghum)
- *Sorghum halepense* (Johnsongrass)
- *Stellaria media* (chickweed)
- *Taraxacum officinale* (common dandelion)
- *Tragopogon* species (salsify)
- *Typha* species (cattails)
- *Urtica dioica* (stinging nettle)

WILD EDIBLES I EAT MOST

- *Aquilegia coerulea* (Rocky Mountain columbine)
- *Aquilegia formosa* (Western columbine)
- *Arctium lappa* (greater burdock)
- *Arctium minus* (lesser burdock)
- *Bistorta bistortoides* (American bistort)
- *Chamerion angustifolium* (fireweed)
- *Chenopodium album* (lambsquarters, wild spinach)
- *Descurainia sophia* (flixweed)
- *Erodium cicutarium* (redstem filaree, stork's bill)
- *Geranium bicknellii* (Bicknell's cranesbill)
- *Geranium richardsonii* (Richardson's geranium, Rocky Mountain geranium)
- *Helianthus annuus* (common sunflower)
- *Helianthus anomalus* (western sunflower)
- *Helianthus petiolaris* (prairie sunflower)
- *Helianthus tuberosus* (sunchokes, Jerusalem artichoke)
- *Hibiscus trionum* (venice mallow)
- *Kochia scoparia* (kochia)
- *Lamium amplexicaule* (henbit)
- *Lamium purpureum* (purple dead nettle)
- *Lathyrus latifolius* (everlasting peavine, wild sweet pea)
- *Lonicera involucrata* (twinberry honeysuckle)
- *Lonicera utahensis* (Utah honeysuckle)
- *Lycium barbarum* (gojiberry, wolfberry)
- *Mahonia aquifolium* (Oregon grape)
- *Mahonia fremontii* (Fremont's mahonia)
- *Mahonia repens* (creeping Oregon grape)
- *Malva neglecta* (common mallow)
- *Medicago lupulina* (black medic)
- *Medicago sativa* (alfalfa)
- *Melilotus officinalis* (yellow sweetclover)
- *Oxalis stricta* (yellow woodsorrel)
- *Phlox austromontana* (southern mountain phlox)
- *Phlox diffusa* (spreading phlox)
- *Phlox hoodii* (spiny phlox)
- *Phlox longifolia* (longleaf phlox)

- *Phlox multiflora* (Rocky Mountain phlox)
- *Phlox paniculata* (common phlox)
- *Phlox stansburyi* (cold desert phlox)
- *Phlox variabilis* (variegated phlox)
- *Pinus monophylla* (single-leaf pinyon pine)
- *Plantago lanceolata* (narrowleaf plantain)
- *Portulaca oleracea* (common purslane)
- *Prunus virginiana* (western chokecherry, black chokecherry)
- *Quercus gambelii* (Gambel oak)
- *Ribes hudsonianum* (western black currant)
- *Rumex crispus* (curly dock, yellow dock)
- *Rumex obtusifolius* (broadleaf dock)
- *Rumex occidentalis* (western dock)
- *Sambucus nigra* (blue elderberry)
- *Sambucus racemosa* (red elderberry)
- *Sambucus racemosa* var. *melanocarpa* (black elderberry)
- *Secale cereale* (cereal rye)
- *Stellaria media* (chickweed)
- *Syringa vulgaris* (common lilac)
- *Taraxacum officinale* (common dandelion)
- *Tragopogon dubius* (yellow salsify)
- *Tragopogon pratensis* (goat's beard, meadow salsify)
- *Typha angustifolia* (narrowleaf cattail)
- *Urtica dioica* (stinging nettle)

FRUITS & BERRIES

- *Amelanchier alnifolia* (Saskatoon serviceberry)
- *Amelanchier pumila* (dwarf serviceberry)
- *Amelanchier utahensis* (Utah serviceberry)
- *Berberis fendleri* (Colorado barberry)
- *Celtis laevigata* (southern hackberry, sugarberry)
- *Celtis occidentalis* (common hackberry)
- *Celtis reticulata* (netleaf hackberry)
- *Cornus canadensis* (creeping dogwood)
- *Cornus sericea* (western dogwood)
- *Cornus unalaschkensis* (bunchberry)
- *Crataegus chrysocarpa* (red haw tree)
- *Crataegus douglasii* (black hawthorn)
- *Crataegus erythropoda* (cerro hawthorn)
- *Crataegus monogyna* (hawthorn)
- *Crataegus rivularis* (river hawthorn)
- *Crataegus saligna* (willow hawthorn)
- *Crataegus succulenta* (fleshy hawthorn) fruit
- *Cucurbita foetidissima* (buffalo gourd)
- *Diospyros virginiana* (American persimmon)
- *Elaeagnus angustifolia* (Russian olive)
- *Elaeagnus commutata* (silverberry)
- *Fragaria vesca* (woodland, alpine, or wild strawberry)
- *Fragaria virginiana* (Virginia strawberry)
- *Gaultheria hispidula* (creeping snowberry)
- *Gaultheria humifusa* (alpine spicy wintergreen)
- *Gaultheria ovatifolia* (western teaberry)
- *Juniperus osteosperma* (juniper tree)
- *Lonicera involucrata* (twinberry honeysuckle)
- *Lonicera utahensis* (Utah honeysuckle)
- *Lycium barbarum* (gojiberry, wolfberry)
- *Mahonia aquifolium* (Oregon grape)
- *Mahonia fremontii* (Fremont's mahonia)
- *Mahonia repens* (creeping Oregon grape)

- *Malus coronaria* (sweet crab apple)
- *Malus pumila* (paradise apple)
- *Malus sylvestris* (European crab apple)
- *Morus alba* (white mulberry)
- *Parthenocissus quinquefolia* (Virginia creeper)
- *Physalis acutifolia* (sharpleaf groundcherry)
- *Physalis angulata* (cutleaf groundcherry)
- *Physalis caudella* (southwestern groundcherry)
- *Physalis cinerascens* (smallflower groundcherry)
- *Physalis crassifolia* (yellow nightshade groundcherry)
- *Physalis grisea* (strawberry-tomato)
- *Physalis hederifolia* (ivyleaf groundcherry)
- *Physalis heterophylla* (clammy groundcherry)
- *Physalis latiphysa* (broadleaf groundcherry)
- *Physalis longifolia* (longleaf groundcherry)
- *Physalis philadelphica* (Mexican groundcherry)
- *Physalis pubescens* (husk tomato)
- *Physalis virginiana* (Virginia groundcherry)
- *Prosopis glandulosa* (western honey mesquite)
- *Prunus americana* (American wild plum)
- *Prunus andersonii* (desert peach)
- *Prunus angustifolia* (Chickasaw plum)
- *Prunus armeniaca* (apricot)
- *Prunus avium* (sweet cherry)
- *Prunus besseyi* (western sandcherry)
- *Prunus cerasifera* (cherry plum)
- *Prunus cerasus* (sour cherry)
- *Prunus domestica* (European plum)
- *Prunus emarginata* (bitter cherry)
- *Prunus gracilis* (Oklahoma plum)
- *Prunus mahaleb* (mahaleb cherry)
- *Prunus pensylvanica* (pin cherry)
- *Prunus persica* (common peach)
- *Prunus pumila* (sandcherry)
- *Prunus rivularis* (creek plum)
- *Prunus serotina* (black cherry)
- *Prunus spinosa* (blackthorn)
- *Prunus tomentosa* (Nanking cherry)
- *Prunus virginiana* (western chokecherry, black chokecherry)
- *Pyrus communis* (common pear)
- *Rhus glabra* (smooth sumac)
- *Rhus typhina* (staghorn sumac)
- *Ribes aureum* (golden currant)
- *Ribes cereum* (wax currant)
- *Ribes hudsonianum* (western black currant)
- *Ribes inerme* (whitestem gooseberry)
- *Ribes lacustre* (prickly black currant)
- *Ribes laxiflorum* (trailing black currant)
- *Ribes leptanthum* (trumpet gooseberry)
- *Ribes montigenum* (gooseberry currant, mountain currant)
- *Ribes niveum* (snow currant)
- *Ribes oxyacanthoides* (Canadian gooseberry)
- *Ribes velutinum* (desert gooseberry)
- *Ribes viscosissimum* (sticky currant)
- *Ribes wolfii* (wolf's currant)
- *Rubus arcticus* (Arctic raspberry)
- *Rubus arizonensis* (Arizona dewberry)
- *Rubus armeniacus* (Himalayan blackberry)
- *Rubus deliciosus* (delicious raspberry)
- *Rubus idaeus* (wild raspberry)
- *Rubus laciniatus* (cutleaf blackberry)
- *Rubus leucodermis* (whitebark raspberry)
- *Rubus neomexicanus* (New Mexico raspberry)
- *Rubus nivalis* (snow raspberry)
- *Rubus occidentalis* (black raspberry)
- *Rubus parviflorus* (thimbleberry)

- *Rubus pedatus* (strawberryleaf raspberry)
- *Rubus pubescens* (dwarf red blackberry)
- *Rubus spectabilis* (salmonberry) berries, flowers, young stems
- *Rubus ulmifolius* (elmleaf blackberry)
- *Rubus ursinus* (California blackberry)
- *Rumex acetosella* (sheep sorrel)
- *Rumex crispus* (curly dock, yellow dock)
- *Rumex obtusifolius* (broadleaf dock)
- *Rumex occidentalis* (western dock)
- *Sambucus nigra* (blue elderberry)
- *Sambucus racemosa* (red elderberry)
- *Sambucus racemosa* var. *melanocarpa* (black elderberry)
- *Shepherdia argentea* (silver buffaloberry)
- *Shepherdia canadensis* (russet buffaloberry)
- *Streptopus amplexifolius* (wild cucumber, claspleaf twistedstalk)
- *Symphoricarpos albus* (snowberry, waxberry)
- *Symphoricarpos occidentalis* (western snowberry)
- *Vaccinium cespitosum* (dwarf bilberry)
- *Vaccinium geminiflorum* (Mexican blueberry)
- *Vaccinium membranaceum* (thinleaf huckleberry)
- *Vaccinium myrtillus* (whortleberry)
- *Vaccinium oxycoccos* (small cranberry)
- *Vaccinium scoparium* (grouse whortleberry)
- *Vaccinium uliginosum* (bog blueberry)
- *Vitis acerifolia* (mapleleaf grape)
- *Vitis arizonica* (canyon grape)
- *Vitis labrusca* (fox grape)
- *Vitis monticola* (sweet mountain grape)
- *Vitis riparia* (riverbank grape)
- *Vitis vinifera* (wine grape)
- *Ziziphus obtusifolia* (lotebush)
- *Ziziphus zizyphus* (common jujube)

GRAINS

- *Aegilops cylindrica* (jointed goatgrass)
- *Amaranthus albus* (tumble pigweed)
- *Amaranthus blitoides* (mat amaranth, prostrate pigweed)
- *Amaranthus blitum* (slender amaranth)
- *Amaranthus palmeri* (Palmer amaranth)
- *Amaranthus retroflexus* (redroot pigweed, redroot amaranth)
- *Avena barbata* (slender oat) seeds
- *Avena fatua* (wild oat) seeds
- *Avena sativa* (common oat) seeds
- *Brassica juncea* (brown mustard)
- *Brassica napus* (rape mustard)
- *Brassica nigra* (black mustard)
- *Brassica rapa* (field mustard)
- *Bromus breviaristatus* (mountain brome)
- *Bromus carinatus* (California brome)
- *Bromus diandrus* (ripgut brome)
- *Bromus japonicus* (Japanese brome, field brome)
- *Bromus marginatus* (mountain brome)
- *Bromus secalinus* (cheat, rye brome)
- *Bromus tectorum* (downy brome, cheat grass)
- *Camelina microcarpa* (lesser gold of pleasure)
- *Camelina sativa* (gold of pleasure)
- *Cyperus erythrorhizos* (redroot flatsedge)
- *Cyperus esculentus* (yellow nutsedge)
- *Cyperus fendlerianus* (Fendler's flatsedge)
- *Cyperus odoratus* (fragrant flatsedge)
- *Cyperus rotundus* (nut grass)

- *Cyperus schweinitzii* (Schweinitz's flatsedge)
- *Cyperus squarrosus* (bearded flatsedge)
- *Descurainia sophia* (flixweed, herb sophia)
- *Digitaria sanguinalis* (hairy crabgrass)
- *Eriogonum alatum* (winged buckwheat)
- *Eriogonum baileyi* (Bailey's buckwheat)
- *Eriogonum cernuum* (nodding buckwheat)
- *Eriogonum corymbosum* (crispleaf buckwheat)
- *Eriogonum davidsonii* (Davidson's buckwheat)
- *Eriogonum fasciculatum* (California buckwheat)
- *Eriogonum flavum* (alpine golden buckwheat)
- *Eriogonum hookeri* (Hooker's buckwheat)
- *Eriogonum inflatum* (desert trumpet)
- *Eriogonum longifolium* (longleaf buckwheat)
- *Eriogonum microthecum* (slender buckwheat)
- *Eriogonum nudum* (naked buckwheat)
- *Eriogonum plumatella* (yucca buckwheat)
- *Eriogonum pusillum* (yellowturbans)
- *Eriogonum racemosum* (redroot buckwheat)
- *Eriogonum rotundifolium* (roundleaf buckwheat)
- *Eriogonum umbellatum* (sulphur-flower buckwheat)
- *Hordeum jubatum* (foxtail barley, squirrel-tail grass)
- *Lolium perenne* (Italian ryegrass)
- *Panicum capillare* (witchgrass)
- *Panicum dichotomiflorum* (fall panicum)
- *Panicum miliaceum* (wild proso millet)
- *Secale cereale* (cereal rye)
- *Setaria pumila* (yellow foxtail)
- *Sorghum bicolor* (wild grain sorghum)
- *Sorghum halepense* (Johnsongrass)
- *Sporobolus flexuosus* (mesa dropseed)

ROOTS, BULBS & TUBERS

- *Allium acuminatum* (Hooker's onion)
- *Allium bispectrum* (twincrest onion)
- *Allium brevistyium* (shortstyle onion)
- *Allium macropetalum* (largeflower wild onion)
- *Allium textile* (textile onion)
- *Anthriscus sylvestris* (wild chervil, cow parsley)
- *Arctium lappa* (greater burdock)
- *Arctium minus* (lesser burdock)
- *Balsamorhiza hookeri* (Hooker's balsamroot)
- *Balsamorhiza incana* (hoary balsamroot)
- *Balsamorhiza sagittata* (arrowleaf balsamroot)
- *Bistorta bistortoides* (American bistort)
- *Callirhoe involucrata* (buffalo rose, winecup poppy mallow)
- *Calochortus nuttallii* (sego lily)
- *Calypso bulbosa* (fairy slipper)
- *Carum gairdneri* (squaw root)
- *Cichorium intybus* (chicory)
- *Cymopterus globosus* (globe springparsley)
- *Cymopterus purpurascens* (gamote)
- *Cymopterus purpureus* (purple springparsley)
- *Cyperus erythrorhizos* (redroot flatsedge)
- *Cyperus esculentus* (yellow nutsedge)

- *Cyperus fendlerianus* (Fendler's flatsedge)
- *Cyperus odoratus* (fragrant flatsedge)
- *Cyperus rotundus* (nut grass)
- *Cyperus schweinitzii* (Schweinitz's flatsedge)
- *Cyperus squarrosus* (bearded flatsedge)
- *Daucus carota* (wild carrot)
- *Heracleum sphondylium montanum* (cow parsnip)
- *Lomatium ambiguum* (Wyeth biscuitroot)
- *Lomatium canbyi* (Canby's biscuitroot)
- *Lomatium cous* (cous biscuitroot)
- *Lomatium gormanii* (Gorman's biscuitroot)
- *Lomatium grayi* (Gray's biscuitroot)
- *Lomatium macrocarpum* (bigseed biscuitroot)

- *Lomatium nudicaule* (pestle parsnip, barestem biscuitroot)
- *Lomatium triternatum* (nineleaf biscuitroot)
- *Orogenia linearifolia* (Indian potato)
- *Raphanus raphanistrum* (wild radish)
- *Raphanus sativus* (garden radish)
- *Rumex crispus* (curly dock, yellow dock)
- *Rumex obtusifolius* (broadleaf dock)
- *Rumex occidentalis* (western dock)
- *Sagittaria cuneata* (wapato, arumleaf arrowhead)
- *Taraxacum officinale* (common dandelion)
- *Tragopogon dubius* (yellow salsify)
- *Tragopogon pratensis* (goat's beard, meadow salsify)
- *Typha angustifolia* (narrowleaf cattail)
- *Typha glauca* (hybrid cattail)
- *Typha latifolia* (broadleaf cattail)

NUTS

- *Corylus cornuta* (beaked hazelnut)
- *Juglans major* (Arizona walnut)
- *Juglans microcarpa* (little walnut)
- *Juglans nigra* (black walnut)
- *Juglans regia* (English walnut)
- *Pinus contorta* (lodgepole pine)
- *Pinus edulis* (two-needle pinyon pine)
- *Pinus flexilis* (limber pine)
- *Pinus lambertiana* (sugar pine)

- *Pinus monophylla* (single-leaf pinyon pine)
- *Pinus monticola* (western white pine)
- *Pinus ponderosa* (ponderosa pine)
- *Prosopis glandulosa* (western honey mesquite)
- *Prunus dulcis* (sweet almond) seed
- *Prunus fasciculata* (desert almond)
- *Quercus gambelii* (Gambel oak)

LISTS: BY FORM

TREES, SHRUBS & BUSHES

- *Acer glabrum* (Rocky Mountain maple)
- *Acer negundo* (box elder maple)

- *Amelanchier alnifolia* (Saskatoon serviceberry)
- *Amelanchier pumila* (dwarf serviceberry)

- *Amelanchier utahensis* (Utah serviceberry)
- *Artemisia frigida* (fringed sagebrush)
- *Artemisia tridentata* (big sagebrush)
- *Berberis fendleri* (Colorado barberry)
- *Celtis laevigata* (southern hackberry, sugarberry)
- *Celtis occidentalis* (common hackberry)
- *Celtis reticulata* (netleaf hackberry)
- *Chrysothamnus nauseosus* (rubber rabbitbrush)
- *Chrysothamnus viscidiflorus* (douglas rabbitbrush)
- *Cornus canadensis* (creeping dogwood)
- *Cornus sericea* (western dogwood)
- *Cornus unalaschkensis* (bunchberry)
- *Corylus cornuta* (beaked hazelnut)
- *Crataegus chrysocarpa* (red haw tree)
- *Crataegus douglasii* (black hawthorn)
- *Crataegus erythropoda* (cerro hawthorn)
- *Crataegus monogyna* (hawthorn)
- *Crataegus rivularis* (river hawthorn)
- *Crataegus saligna* (willow hawthorn)
- *Crataegus succulenta* (fleshy hawthorn) fruit
- *Diospyros virginiana* (American persimmon)
- *Elaeagnus angustifolia* (Russian olive)
- *Elaeagnus commutata* (silverberry)
- *Gaultheria hispidula* (creeping snowberry)
- *Gaultheria humifusa* (alpine spicy wintergreen)
- *Gaultheria ovatifolia* (western teaberry)
- *Juglans major* (Arizona walnut)
- *Juglans microcarpa* (little walnut)
- *Juglans nigra* (black walnut)
- *Juglans regia* (English walnut)
- *Juniperus osteosperma* (juniper tree)
- *Lonicera involucrata* (twinberry honeysuckle)
- *Lonicera utahensis* (Utah honeysuckle)
- *Lycium barbarum* (gojiberry, wolfberry)
- *Mahonia aquifolium* (Oregon grape)
- *Mahonia fremontii* (Fremont's mahonia)
- *Mahonia repens* (creeping Oregon grape)
- *Malus coronaria* (sweet crab apple)
- *Malus pumila* (paradise apple)
- *Malus sylvestris* (European crab apple)
- *Morus alba* (white mulberry)
- *Pinus contorta* (lodgepole pine)
- *Pinus edulis* (two-needle pinyon pine)
- *Pinus flexilis* (limber pine)
- *Pinus lambertiana* (sugar pine)
- *Pinus monophylla* (single-leaf pinyon pine)
- *Pinus monticola* (western white pine)
- *Pinus ponderosa* (ponderosa pine)
- *Prosopis glandulosa* (western honey mesquite)
- *Prunus americana* (American wild plum)
- *Prunus andersonii* (desert peach)
- *Prunus angustifolia* (Chickasaw plum)
- *Prunus armeniaca* (apricot)
- *Prunus avium* (sweet cherry)
- *Prunus besseyi* (western sandcherry)
- *Prunus cerasifera* (cherry plum)
- *Prunus cerasus* (sour cherry)
- *Prunus domestica* (European plum)
- *Prunus dulcis* (sweet almond) seed
- *Prunus emarginata* (bitter cherry)
- *Prunus fasciculata* (desert almond)
- *Prunus gracilis* (Oklahoma plum)
- *Prunus mahaleb* (mahaleb cherry)
- *Prunus pensylvanica* (pin cherry)
- *Prunus persica* (common peach)
- *Prunus pumila* (sandcherry)
- *Prunus rivularis* (creek plum)
- *Prunus serotina* (black cherry)
- *Prunus spinosa* (blackthorn)

- *Prunus tomentosa* (Nanking cherry)
- *Prunus virginiana* (western chokecherry, black chokecherry)
- *Pyrus communis* (common pear)
- *Quercus gambelii* (Gambel oak)
- *Rhus glabra* (smooth sumac)
- *Rhus trilobata* (three-leaf sumac)
- *Rhus typhina* (staghorn sumac)
- *Ribes aureum* (golden currant)
- *Ribes cereum* (wax currant)
- *Ribes hudsonianum* (western black currant)
- *Ribes inerme* (whitestem gooseberry)
- *Ribes lacustre* (prickly black currant)
- *Ribes laxiflorum* (trailing black currant)
- *Ribes leptanthum* (trumpet gooseberry)
- *Ribes montigenum* (gooseberry currant, mountain currant)
- *Ribes niveum* (snow currant)
- *Ribes oxyacanthoides* (Canadian gooseberry)
- *Ribes velutinum* (desert gooseberry)
- *Ribes viscosissimum* (sticky currant)
- *Ribes wolfii* (wolf's currant)
- *Rosa × harisonii* (Harison's yellow)
- *Rosa canina* (dog rose)
- *Rosa manca* (Mancos rose)
- *Rosa nutkana* (Nootka rose)
- *Rosa rubiginosa* (sweetbriar rose)
- *Rosa woodsii* (western wild rose)
- *Rubus arcticus* (Arctic raspberry)
- *Rubus arizonensis* (Arizona dewberry)
- *Rubus armeniacus* (Himalayan blackberry)
- *Rubus deliciosus* (delicious raspberry)
- *Rubus idaeus* (wild raspberries)
- *Rubus laciniatus* (cutleaf blackberry)
- *Rubus leucodermis* (whitebark raspberry)
- *Rubus neomexicanus* (New Mexico raspberry)
- *Rubus nivalis* (snow raspberry)
- *Rubus occidentalis* (black raspberry)
- *Rubus parviflorus* (thimbleberry)
- *Rubus pedatus* (strawberryleaf raspberry)
- *Rubus pubescens* (dwarf red blackberry)
- *Rubus spectabilis* (salmonberry)
- *Rubus ulmifolius* (elmleaf blackberry)
- *Rubus ursinus* (California blackberry)
- *Sambucus nigra* (blue elderberry)
- *Sambucus racemosa* (red elderberry)
- *Sambucus racemosa* var. *melanocarpa* (black elderberry)
- *Shepherdia argentea* (silver buffaloberry)
- *Shepherdia canadensis* (russet buffaloberry)
- *Symphoricarpos albus* (snowberry, waxberry)
- *Symphoricarpos occidentalis* (western snowberry)
- *Syringa vulgaris* (common lilac)
- *Vaccinium cespitosum* (dwarf bilberry)
- *Vaccinium geminiflorum* (Mexican blueberry)
- *Vaccinium membranaceum* (thinleaf huckleberry)
- *Vaccinium myrtillus* (whortleberry)
- *Vaccinium oxycoccos* (small cranberry)
- *Vaccinium scoparium* (grouse whortleberry)
- *Vaccinium uliginosum* (bog blueberry)
- *Ziziphus obtusifolia* (lotebush)
- *Ziziphus zizyphus* (common jujube)

FLOWERS: BICOLOR OR VARIOUSLY COLORED

- *Allium macropetalum* (largeflower wild onion)
- *Allium textile* (textile onion)
- *Antirrhinum majus* (snapdragon)

- *Aquilegia coerulea* (Rocky Mountain columbine)
- *Aquilegia formosa* (western columbine)
- *Asclepias asperula* (spider milkweed)
- *Asclepias involucrata* (dwarf milkweed)
- *Calochortus elegans* (elegant mariposa lily)
- *Calochortus eurycarpus* (white mariposa lily)
- *Calochortus gunnisonii* (Gunnison's mariposa lily)
- *Calochortus invenustus* (plain mariposa lily)
- *Calochortus leichtlinii* (smokey mariposa lily)
- *Calochortus macrocarpus* (sagebrush mariposa lily)
- *Calochortus nitidus* (broadfruit mariposa lily)
- *Calochortus nuttallii* (sego lily)
- *Calochortus panamintensis* (Panamint Mountain mariposa lily)
- *Calochortus striatus* (alkali mariposa lily)
- *Calystegia sepium* (hedge bindweed)
- *Centaurea jacea* (brown knapweed)
- *Chorispora tenella* (blue mustard)
- *Cymopterus globosus* (globe springparsley)
- *Cymopterus purpurascens* (gamote)
- *Cymopterus purpureus* (purple springparsley)
- *Cymopterus montanus* (mountain springparsley)
- *Equisetum arvense* (horsetail grass)
- *Equisetum laevigatum* (smooth horsetail)
- *Equisetum hyemale* (scouringrush horsetail)
- *Equisetum pratense* (meadow horsetail)
- *Equisetum scirpoides* (dwarf scouringrush)
- *Equisetum telmateia* (giant horsetail)
- *Equisetum variegatum* (variegated scouringrush)
- *Eriogonum alatum* (winged buckwheat)
- *Eriogonum baileyi* (Bailey's buckwheat)
- *Eriogonum cernuum* (nodding buckwheat)
- *Eriogonum corymbosum* (crispleaf buckwheat)
- *Eriogonum davidsonii* (Davidson's buckwheat)
- *Eriogonum fasciculatum* (California buckwheat)
- *Eriogonum flavum* (alpine golden buckwheat)
- *Eriogonum hookeri* (Hooker's buckwheat)
- *Eriogonum inflatum* (desert trumpet)
- *Eriogonum longifolium* (longleaf buckwheat)
- *Eriogonum microthecum* (slender buckwheat)
- *Eriogonum nudum* (naked buckwheat)
- *Eriogonum plumatella* (yucca buckwheat)
- *Eriogonum pusillum* (yellowturbans)
- *Eriogonum racemosum* (redroot buckwheat)
- *Eriogonum rotundifolium* (roundleaf buckwheat)
- *Eriogonum umbellatum* (sulphur-flower buckwheat)
- *Galega officinalis* (goatsrue)
- *Gaillardia aristata* (Indian blanket)
- *Gaillardia pinnatifida* (red dome blanketflower)
- *Hibiscus trionum* (venice mallow)
- *Lomatium dissectum* (giant biscuitroot, fernleaf biscuitroot)
- *Opuntia polyacantha* (plains prickly pear cactus)
- *Parthenocissus quinquefolia* (Virginia creeper)
- *Phlox austromontana* (southern mountain phlox)

- *Phlox diffusa* (spreading phlox)
- *Phlox hoodii* (spiny phlox)
- *Phlox longifolia* (longleaf phlox)
- *Phlox multiflora* (Rocky Mountain phlox)
- *Phlox paniculata* (common phlox)
- *Phlox stansburyi* (cold desert phlox)
- *Phlox variabilis* (variegated phlox)
- *Physalis acutifolia* (sharpleaf groundcherry)
- *Physalis angulata* (cutleaf groundcherry)
- *Physalis caudella* (southwestern groundcherry)
- *Physalis cinerascens* (smallflower groundcherry)
- *Physalis crassifolia* (yellow nightshade groundcherry)
- *Physalis grisea* (strawberry-tomato)
- *Physalis hederifolia* (ivyleaf groundcherry)
- *Physalis heterophylla* (clammy groundcherry)
- *Physalis latiphysa* (broadleaf groundcherry)
- *Physalis longifolia* (longleaf groundcherry)
- *Physalis philadelphica* (Mexican groundcherry)
- *Physalis pubescens* (husk tomato)
- *Physalis virginiana* (Virginia groundcherry)
- *Plantago major* (broadleaf plantain)
- *Polygonum arenastrum* (small-leafed knotweed, oval-leaf knotweed)
- *Polygonum cuspidatum* (Japanese knotweed)
- *Polygonum lapathifolium* (curlytop knotweed)
- *Polygonum persicaria* (spotted ladysthumb)
- *Prunus persica* (common peach)
- *Rhus glabra* (smooth sumac)
- *Rhus trilobata* (three-leaf sumac)
- *Rhus typhina* (staghorn sumac)
- *Ribes montigenum* (gooseberry currant, mountain currant)
- *Salsola tragus* (Russian thistle)
- *Viola adunca* (hookedspur violet)
- *Viola canadensis* (Canadian white violet)
- *Viola odorata* (sweet violet)
- *Viola palustris* (marsh violet)
- *Viola tricolor* (johnny jumpup)

FLOWERS: BLUE

- *Aquilegia coerulea* (Rocky Mountain columbine)
- *Centaurea cyanus* (garden cornflower)
- *Centaurea jacea* (brown knapweed)
- *Chorispora tenella* (blue mustard)
- *Cichorium intybus* (chicory)
- *Lactuca pulchella* (blue lettuce)
- *Veronica biloba* (twolobe speedwell)

FLOWERS: GREEN

- *Amaranthus albus* (tumble pigweed)
- *Amaranthus blitoides* (mat amaranth, prostrate pigweed)
- *Amaranthus blitum* (slender amaranth)
- *Amaranthus palmeri* (Palmer amaranth)
- *Amaranthus retroflexus* (redroot pigweed, redroot amaranth)
- *Asclepias asperula* (spider milkweed)
- *Asclepias erosa* (desert milkweed)
- *Asclepias subverticillata* (horsetail milkweed)

- *Asclepias viridiflora* (green comet milkweed)
- *Avena barbata* (slender oat)
- *Avena fatua* (wild oat)
- *Avena sativa* (common oat)
- *Bromus breviaristatus* (mountain brome)
- *Bromus carinatus* (California brome)
- *Bromus diandrus* (ripgut brome)
- *Bromus japonicus* (Japanese brome, field brome)
- *Bromus marginatus* (mountain brome)
- *Bromus secalinus* (cheat, rye brome)
- *Bromus tectorum* (downy brome, cheat grass)
- *Celtis laevigata* (southern hackberry, sugarberry)
- *Celtis occidentalis* (common hackberry)
- *Celtis reticulata* (netleaf hackberry)
- *Cenchrus longispinus* (longspine sandbur)
- *Chenopodium album* (lambsquarters, wild spinach)
- *Chenopodium berlandieri* (goosefoot, netseed lambsquarters)
- *Chenopodium murale* (nettleleaf goosefoot)
- *Cyperus erythrorhizos* (redroot flatsedge)
- *Cyperus esculentus* (yellow nutsedge)
- *Cyperus fendlerianus* (Fendler's flatsedge)
- *Cyperus odoratus* (Fragrant flatsedge)
- *Cyperus rotundus* (nut grass)
- *Cyperus schweinitzii* (Schweinitz's flatsedge)
- *Cyperus squarrosus* (bearded flatsedge)
- *Eleusine indica* (goosegrass)
- *Elymus repens* (quackgrass)
- *Hordeum jubatum* (foxtail barley, squirrel-tail grass)
- *Juniperus osteosperma* (juniper tree)
- *Kochia scoparia* (kochia)
- *Lolium perenne* (Italian ryegrass)
- *Morus alba* (white mulberry)
- *Panicum capillare* (witchgrass)
- *Panicum dichotomiflorum* (fall panicum)
- *Panicum miliaceum* (wild proso millet)
- *Polypogon monspeliensis* (rabbitfoot polypogon)
- *Quercus gambelii* (Gambel oak)
- *Rumex acetosella* (sheep sorrel)
- *Rumex crispus* (curly dock, yellow dock)
- *Rumex obtusifolius* (broadleaf dock)
- *Rumex occidentalis* (western dock)
- *Sarcocornia utahensis* (Utah pickleweed)
- *Secale cereale* (cereal rye)
- *Setaria pumila* (yellow foxtail)
- *Sorghum bicolor* (wild grain sorghum)
- *Sorghum halepense* (Johnsongrass)
- *Sporobolus flexuosus* (mesa dropseed)
- *Urtica dioica* (stinging nettle)
- *Vitis acerifolia* (mapleleaf grape)
- *Vitis arizonica* (canyon grape)
- *Vitis labrusca* (fox grape)
- *Vitis monticola* (sweet mountain grape)
- *Vitis riparia* (riverbank grape)
- *Vitis vinifera* (wine grape)

FLOWERS: RED, PURPLE, PINK, BROWN

- *Achillea millefolium* (western yarrow)
- *Agastache urticifolia* (horsemint, nettleleaf giant hyssop)
- *Allium acuminatum* (Hooker's onion)
- *Allium bispectrum* (twincrest onion)
- *Allium brevistyium* (shortstyle onion)
- *Aquilegia formosa* (western columbine)
- *Arctium lappa* (greater burdock, gobo)
- *Arctium minus* (lesser burdock)
- *Asclepias cordifolia* (heartleaf milkweed)

- *Asclepias fascicularis* (Mexican whorled milkweed)
- *Asclepias incarnata* (swamp milkweed)
- *Asclepias speciosa* (showy milkweed)
- *Asclepias syriaca* (common milkweed)
- *Calandrinia ciliata* (redmaids)
- *Callirhoe involucrata* (buffalo rose, winecup poppy mallow)
- *Calochortus flexuosus* (winding mariposa lily)
- *Calochortus kennedyi* (desert mariposa lily)
- *Calypso bulbosa* (fairy slipper)
- *Campanula rapunculoides* (creeping bellflower)
- *Carduus nutans* (musk thistle)
- *Castilleja angustifolia* (northwestern Indian paintbrush)
- *Castilleja applegatei Fernald* (wavyleaf Indian paintbrush)
- *Castilleja aquariensis* (Indian paintbrush)
- *Castilleja hispida* (harsh Indian paintbrush)
- *Castilleja linariifolia* (Wyoming Indian paintbrush)
- *Castilleja lineata* (marshmeadow Indian paintbrush)
- *Castilleja miniata* (giant red Indian paintbrush)
- *Castilleja sessiliflora* (downy paintedcup)
- *Chamerion angustifolium* (fireweed)
- *Chamerion latifolium* (dwarf fireweed)
- *Cirsium arvense* (Canada thistle)
- *Cirsium ochrocentrum* (yellowspine thistle)
- *Cirsium vulgare* (common thistle, bull thistle)
- *Cleome serrulata* (Rocky Mountain bee plant)
- *Cynoglossum officinale* (houndstongue, gypsyflower)
- *Erodium cicutarium* (redstem filaree, stork's bill)
- *Geranium bicknellii* (Bicknell's cranesbill)
- *Geranium caespitosum* (pineywoods geranium)
- *Geranium richardsonii* (Richardson's geranium, Rocky Mountain geranium)
- *Geranium viscosissimum* (sticky purple geranium)
- *Hedysarum alpinum* (alpine sweetvetch)
- *Hedysarum boreale* (Utah sweetvetch)
- *Iliamna rivularis* (mountain hollyhock)
- *Juglans major* (Arizona walnut)
- *Juglans microcarpa* (little walnut)
- *Juglans nigra* (black walnut)
- *Juglans regia* (English walnut)
- *Lamium amplexicaule* (henbit)
- *Lamium purpureum* (purple dead nettle)
- *Lathyrus latifolius* (everlasting peavine, wild sweet pea)
- *Lycium barbarum* (gojiberry, wolfberry)
- *Lythrum salicaria* (purple loosestrife, purple lythrum)
- *Malva neglecta* (common mallow)
- *Medicago sativa* (alfalfa)
- *Phragmites australis* (common reed)
- *Pinus contorta* (lodgepole pine)
- *Pinus edulis* (two-needle pinyon pine)
- *Pinus flexilis* (limber pine)
- *Pinus lambertiana* (sugar pine)
- *Pinus monophylla* (single-leaf pinyon pine)
- *Pinus monticola* (western white pine)
- *Pinus ponderosa* (ponderosa pine)
- *Polygonum amphibium* (willow grass, water knotweed)
- *Prunus andersonii* (desert peach)
- *Prunus cerasifera* (cherry plum)
- *Ribes cereum* (wax currant)
- *Ribes lacustre* (prickly black currant)
- *Ribes laxiflorum* (trailing black currant)

- *Rosa canina* (dog rose)
- *Rosa manca* (Mancos rose)
- *Rosa nutkana* (Nootka rose)
- *Rosa rubiginosa* (sweetbriar rose)
- *Rosa woodsii* (western wild rose)
- *Rubus arcticus* (Arctic raspberry)
- *Rubus nivalis* (snow raspberry)
- *Rubus spectabilis* (salmonberry)
- *Rubus ulmifolius* (elmleaf blackberry)
- *Syringa vulgaris* (common lilac)
- *Trifolium microcephalum* (smallhead clover)
- *Trifolium pratense* (red clover)
- *Trifolium variegatum* (whitetip clover)
- *Trifolium wormskioldii* (cow clover)
- *Typha angustifolia* (narrowleaf cattail)
- *Typha glauca* (hybrid cattail)
- *Typha latifolia* (broadleaf cattail)
- *Vaccinium cespitosum* (dwarf bilberry)
- *Vaccinium geminiflorum* (Mexican blueberry)
- *Vaccinium oxycoccos* (small cranberry)
- *Vaccinium scoparium* (grouse whortleberry)
- *Vaccinium uliginosum* (bog blueberry)

FLOWERS: WHITE

- *Achillea millefolium* (western yarrow)
- *Amelanchier alnifolia* (Saskatoon serviceberry)
- *Amelanchier pumila* (dwarf serviceberry)
- *Amelanchier utahensis* (Utah serviceberry)
- *Anthriscus caucalis* (bur chervil)
- *Anthriscus sylvestris* (wild chervil, cow parsley)
- *Asclepias fascicularis* (Mexican whorled milkweed)
- *Asclepias subverticillata* (horsetail milkweed)
- *Asclepias verticillata* (whorled milkweed)
- *Calochortus ambiguus* (doubting mariposa lily)
- *Calochortus apiculatus* (pointedtip mariposa lily)
- *Calochortus bruneaunis* (Bruneau mariposa lily)
- *Calystegia sepium* (hedge bindweed)
- *Capsella bursa-pastoris* (shepherd's purse)
- *Cardamine hirsuta* (hairy bittercress)
- *Cardamine oligosperma* (spring cress)
- *Cardamine pensylvanica* (Pennsylvania bittercress)
- *Cardaria draba* (whitetop, hoary cress)
- *Carum carvi* (common caraway)
- *Claytonia perfoliata* (miner's lettuce, winter purslane)
- *Convolvulus arvensis* (field bindweed)
- *Conyza canadensis* (horseweed)
- *Cornus canadensis* (creeping dogwood)
- *Cornus sericea* (western dogwood)
- *Cornus unalaschkensis* (bunchberry)
- *Crataegus chrysocarpa* (red haw tree)
- *Crataegus douglasii* (black hawthorn)
- *Crataegus erythropoda* (cerro hawthorn)
- *Crataegus monogyna* (hawthorn)
- *Crataegus rivularis* (river hawthorn)
- *Crataegus saligna* (willow hawthorn)
- *Crataegus succulenta* (fleshy hawthorn) fruit
- *Cycloloma atriplicifolium* (winged pigweed)
- *Daucus carota* (wild carrot)
- *Digitaria sanguinalis* (hairy crabgrass)
- *Fragaria vesca* (woodland, alpine, or wild strawberry)
- *Fragaria virginiana* (Virginia strawberry)

- *Galium aparine* (cleavers, goosegrass)
  - *Gaultheria hispidula* (creeping snowberry)
  - *Gaultheria humifusa* (alpine spicy wintergreen)
  - *Gaultheria ovatifolia* (western teaberry)
  - *Heracleum sphondylium montanum* (cow parsnip)
  - *Lepidium latifolium* (perennial pepperweed)
  - *Lepidium perfoliatum* (clasping pepperweed)
  - *Lomatium canbyi* (Canby's biscuitroot)
  - *Lomatium gormanii* (Gorman's biscuitroot)
  - *Lomatium macrocarpum* (bigseed biscuitroot)
  - *Malus coronaria* (sweet crab apple)
  - *Malus pumila* (paradise apple)
  - *Malus sylvestris* (European crab apple)
  - *Melilotus albus* (white sweetclover)
  - *Nasturtium officinale* (watercress)
  - *Orogenia linearifolia* (Indian potato)
  - *Pediomelum esculentum* (large Indian breadroot)
  - *Perideridia bolanderi* (Bolander's yampah)
  - *Perideridia gairdneri* (Gardner's yampah)
  - *Perideridia lemmonii* (Lemmon's yampah)
  - *Perideridia parishii* (Parish's yampah)
  - *Plantago lanceolata* (narrowleaf plantain)
  - *Polygonum bistortoides* (American bistort)
  - *Polygonum douglasii* (Douglas's knotweed)
  - *Prunus americana* (American wild plum)
  - *Prunus angustifolia* (Chickasaw plum)
  - *Prunus armeniaca* (apricot)
  - *Prunus avium* (sweet cherry)
  - *Prunus besseyi* (western sandcherry)
  - *Prunus cerasus* (sour cherry)
  - *Prunus domestica* (European plum)
  - *Prunus dulcis* (sweet almond) seed
  - *Prunus emarginata* (bitter cherry)
  - *Prunus fasciculata* (desert almond)
  - *Prunus gracilis* (Oklahoma plum)
  - *Prunus mahaleb* (mahaleb cherry)
  - *Prunus pensylvanica* (pin cherry)
  - *Prunus pumila* (sandcherry)
  - *Prunus rivularis* (creek plum)
  - *Prunus serotina* (black cherry)
  - *Prunus spinosa* (blackthorn)
  - *Prunus tomentosa* (Nanking cherry)
  - *Prunus virginiana* (western chokecherry, black chokecherry)
  - *Pyrus communis* (common pear)
  - *Raphanus raphanistrum* (wild radish)
  - *Raphanus sativus* (garden radish)
  - *Rheum rhabarbarum* (garden rhubarb)
  - *Ribes hudsonianum* (western black currant)
  - *Ribes inerme* (whitestem gooseberry)
  - *Ribes leptanthum* (trumpet gooseberry)
  - *Ribes niveum* (snow currant)
  - *Ribes oxyacanthoides* (Canadian gooseberry)
  - *Ribes viscosissimum* (sticky currant)
  - *Ribes wolfii* (wolf's currant)
  - *Rubus arizonensis* (Arizona dewberry)
  - *Rubus armeniacus* (Himalayan blackberry)
  - *Rubus deliciosus* (delicious raspberry)
  - *Rubus idaeus* (wild raspberries)
  - *Rubus laciniatus* (cutleaf blackberry)
  - *Rubus leucodermis* (whitebark raspberry)
  - *Rubus neomexicanus* (New Mexico raspberry)
  - *Rubus occidentalis* (black raspberry)
  - *Rubus parviflorus* (thimbleberry)
  - *Rubus pedatus* (strawberryleaf raspberry)

- *Rubus pubescens* (dwarf red blackberry)
- *Rubus ursinus* (California blackberry)
- *Sagittaria cuneata* (wapato, arumleaf arrowhead)
- *Sambucus nigra* (blue elderberry)
- *Sambucus racemosa* (red elderberry)
- *Sambucus racemosa* var. *melanocarpa* (black elderberry)
- *Stellaria media* (chickweed)
- *Streptopus amplexifolius* (wild cucumber, claspleaf twistedstalk)
- *Streptopus streptopoides* (small twistedstalk)
- *Symphoricarpos albus* (snowberry, waxberry)
- *Symphoricarpos occidentalis* (western snowberry)
- *Thlaspi arvense* (field pennycress)
- *Trifolium cyathiferum* (cup clover)
- *Trifolium repens* (white clover, Dutch clover)
- *Vaccinium membranaceum* (thinleaf huckleberry)
- *Vaccinium myrtillus* (whortleberry)
- *Ziziphus obtusifolia* (lotebush)
- *Ziziphus zizyphus* (common jujube)

FLOWERS: YELLOW

- *Abutilon theophrasti* (velvetleaf)
- *Amsinckia tesselata* (bristly fiddleneck)
- *Argentina anserina* (silverweed cinquefoil)
- *Artemisia frigida* (fringed sagebrush)
- *Artemisia tridentata* (big sagebrush)
- *Balsamorhiza hookeri* (Hooker's balsamroot)
- *Balsamorhiza incana* (hoary balsamroot)
- *Balsamorhiza sagittata* (arrowleaf balsamroot)
- *Barbarea orthoceras* (American yellowrocket)
- *Barbarea verna* (land cress)
- *Barbarea vulgaris* (garden yellowrocket)
- *Berberis fendleri* (Colorado barberry)
- *Brassica juncea* (brown mustard)
- *Brassica napus* (rape mustard)
- *Brassica nigra* (black mustard)
- *Brassica rapa* (field mustard)
- *Bromus breviaristatus* (mountain brome)
- *Bromus carinatus* (California brome)
- *Bromus diandrus* (ripgut brome)
- *Bromus japonicus* (Japanese brome, field brome)
- *Bromus marginatus* (mountain brome)
- *Bromus secalinus* (cheat, rye brome)
- *Bromus tectorum* (downy brome, cheat grass)
- *Calochortus aureus* (golden mariposa lily)
- *Camelina microcarpa* (lesser gold of pleasure)
- *Camelina sativa* (gold of pleasure)
- *Chrysothamnus nauseosus* (rubber rabbitbrush)
- *Chrysothamnus viscidiflorus* (douglas rabbitbrush)
- *Corylus cornuta* (beaked hazelnut)
- *Crepis acuminata* (tapertip hawksbeard)
- *Crepis atribarba* (slender hawksbeard)
- *Crepis capillaris* (smooth hawksbeard)
- *Crepis intermedia* (limestone hawksbeard)
- *Crepis modocensis* (Modoc hawksbeard)
- *Crepis nana* (dwarf alpine hawksbeard)
- *Crepis occidentalis* (largeflower hawksbeard)
- *Crepis runcinata* (fiddleleaf hawksbeard)
- *Cucurbita foetidissima* (buffalo gourd)

- *Descurainia incana* (mountain tansy mustard)
- *Descurainia obtusa* (blunt tansy mustard)
- *Descurainia pinnata* (western tansy mustard)
- *Descurainia sophia* (flixweed, herb sophia)
- *Diospyros virginiana* (American persimmon)
- *Elaeagnus angustifolia* (Russian olive)
- *Elaeagnus commutata* (silverberry)
- *Helianthus annuus* (common sunflower)
- *Helianthus anomalus* (western sunflower)
- *Helianthus arizonensis* (Arizona sunflower)
- *Helianthus ciliaris* (Texas blueweed)
- *Helianthus cusickii* (Cusick's sunflower)
- *Helianthus maximiliani* (maximilian sunflower)
- *Helianthus niveus* (showy sunflower)
- *Helianthus nuttallii* (Nuttall's sunflower)
- *Helianthus pauciflorus* (stiff sunflower)
- *Helianthus petiolaris* (prairie sunflower)
- *Helianthus pumilus* (little sunflower)
- *Helianthus tuberosus* (sunchokes, Jerusalem artichoke)
- *Lomatium ambiguum* (Wyeth biscuitroot)
- *Lomatium cous* (cous biscuitroot)
- *Lomatium foeniculaceum* (desert parsley, desert biscuitroot)
- *Lomatium grayi* (Gray's biscuitroot)
- *Lomatium nudicaule* (pestle parsnip, barestem biscuitroot)
- *Lomatium triternatum* (nineleaf biscuitroot)
- *Lonicera involucrata* (twinberry honeysuckle)
- *Lonicera utahensis* (Utah honeysuckle)
- *Mahonia aquifolium* (Oregon grape)
- *Mahonia fremontii* (Fremont's mahonia)
- *Mahonia repens* (creeping Oregon grape)
- *Matricaria discoidea* (pineapple weed)
- *Medicago lupulina* (black medic)
- *Medicago polymorpha* (California burclover)
- *Melilotus indicas* (Indian sweetclover)
- *Melilotus officinalis* (yellow sweetclover)
- *Nuphar polysepala* (spatterdock, Rocky Mountain pond lily)
- *Oxalis corniculata* (creeping woodsorrel)
- *Oxalis stricta* (yellow woodsorrel)
- *Portulaca oleracea* (common purslane)
- *Prosopis glandulosa* (western honey mesquite)
- *Ribes aureum* (golden currant)
- *Ribes velutinum* (desert gooseberry)
- *Rosa × harisonii* (Harison's yellow)
- *Shepherdia argentea* (silver buffaloberry)
- *Shepherdia canadensis* (russet buffaloberry)
- *Sisymbrium irio* (London rocket)
- *Sonchus arvensis* (sowthistle)
- *Sonchus asper* (spiny sowthistle)
- *Sonchus oleraceus* (common sowthistle)
- *Taraxacum officinale* (common dandelion)
- *Tragopogon dubius* (yellow salsify)
- *Tragopogon pratensis* (goat's beard, meadow salsify)

QUESTIONS & ANSWERS

Q: I notice that, for the most part, you avoid technical botanical terms when describing plants. For example, what you call "berries," others might technically term "drupes" or "fruits" or other terms. Why?

A: I specifically avoided botanical jargon when writing this book (in most cases) because I wanted the book to be easily useful to everyone, which starts with using common, not technical, terms. If you are looking for technical botanical information on the plants found in this book, you can search the scientific names listed here at the US Department of Agriculture plant database, found online at plants.usda.gov, or at Plants for a Future, at pfaf.org. For really technical details for some plants in this book, visit the Consortium of Midwest Hebaria at midwestherbaria.org or other university herbaria websites.

Q: You say you want this book to focus on usefulness and common language, but you have listed all the plants by their Latin names rather than their common names.

A: When practicing plant identification, it is critical to use Latin names rather than common names because Latin names are the only way to be accurate. For example, there are dozens of plants in the United States that are called "pigweed," including several species in this book. There is no safe way to teach people about edible "pigweed" because that word refers to different plants depending on where you live and who taught you the lingo. I grew up in a very small town that used pioneer and regional names for many plants that, I discovered later, were commonly known by different names in more densely populated areas of my state.

Today, people use the internet to search for information about edible plants, and if you search by common name instead of scientific names, you get a dangerously unreliable Wild West of information—info that ranges from completely false to dangerously misguided to correct. The most important consideration when scouting for wild edibles is safety, and there is no way to be safe when using common names because they change sometimes from county to county, let alone state by state. I can't tell you how many times I've had people in my classes say, "That's what pigweed looks like? I always thought pigweed looked like something else." And they are right: "pigweed" means many things to many people, and some versions are edible and some are possibly poisonous, so Latin names are crucial for safety. If you are not familiar with using Latin names, take the time to get comfortable with them before attempting to research or scout wild edibles.

Q: You discuss the importance of Latin names, but some plants in this book have one or more Latin synonyms. In addition, some of the online resources and print books don't seem to match the Latin names that you use in this book. Help!

A: You have stumbled upon one of the great frustrations of botany—changing scientific names. I have strong opinions about this: it needs to stop. Once upon a time, scientific names were changed rarely and only if there were strong reasons to do so. Today, thousands if not tens of thousands of plants have been renamed, and it seems that each year more names are changed.

Why? Here's my opinion: University botany professors and doctoral researchers used to discover plants. Today, they seem to focus on renaming them in a fight for relevance. Discovering new plants has become difficult, and many of the new species to be discovered are in places that are either dangerous because of war or hostility to outsiders or because they are in extreme locales. I think it's safe to say the easy botanical discoveries have been made. In addition, there are now far more botany professionals, each of them fighting for funding, resources, and attention in a world where university herbariums are being tossed out instead of expanded. Tenure and teaching positions depend on botanists making a name for themselves, presenting papers at endless conferences.

In short, they struggle for relevance and try to make a name for themselves in any way they can, including making arguments to their fellow scholars to convince them to change scientific names that have been long established.

The practical impact of all this has been seismic. Books published only a century ago now sometimes spread confusion because some of the scientific names have been changed. Many websites and printed books list different Latin names for the same plants. Anyone who wants to learn about plants finds themselves trapped in an ever-changing miasma of names. All of this is compounded by the endless arguments over what are genuine species and what are subspecies. How many species of elderberries are there in nature, really? Decades have been spent arguing, and the arguing will probably only continue, at least until botanists come to their senses and take responsibility for the damage they are doing to the common understanding of plants.

Meanwhile, the people who have to deal with such nonsense have sort of given up. The US Department of Agriculture plant database, instead of trying to weigh in on the nonsense, simply lists them all (or so it seems to me). The same plants are listed multiple times under different species names and different subspecies names. I do not blame the USDA—what other choice do they have? They cannot arbitrate the ridiculousness. The International Association of Botanical and Mycological Societies has not shown the willpower to put an end to the damage that unnecessary name changes strew in their wake. Changing names should be rare. Each time a name is changed, it damages the efforts of the rest of us to participate in botany. The mess left behind, both in print and online, will never be cleaned up. Shame on those who vote in favor of these changes unless absolutely necessary.

I recognize that these are strong words. I think they are warranted. No more botanical name changes unless there is a reason compelling enough to warrant the eternal confusion the changes leave behind!

Q: Why have you not listed the subspecies for the species in this book? Why have you not listed all the Latin synonyms?

A: There is simply not room to address all the thousands of subspecies and even commercial cultivars that exist—not to mention the years of work it would take to catalog them all. And there is considerable debate among experts over whether many subspecies are valid or not, and that is not a debate I want to wade into. As far as synonyms go, it is beyond the scope of this book to try and catalog all the historic and current and debated Latin synonyms. I have tried my best to use the most common Latin names for the plants in this book, which may not have always been the most recent Latin name. I have tried to mention some synonyms that are common for some species, if they were at my fingertips. It would be nice for some person with a lot of time on their hand to compile a catalog of the original Latin names of all US species and the history of the scientific names changes over time. Many have changed, and it makes it very frustrating for someone like me who loves to read the old books, only to be forced to spend time researching what the modern equivalent of the old name is so that I can know which plants the old books are talking about.

Q: Have you listed every poisonous look-alike in this book? If a poisonous look-alike is not listed in this book, should I assume there is no poisonous look-alike?

A: I have not even attempted to catalog look-alikes for this book. I certainly don't know every plant in the West, and I'm certain there are poisonous look-alikes for some edible plants in this book that I'm not even aware of. I have also learned, by taking students on many walks and canyon tours to find wild edibles, that there is absolutely no way to define what a look-alike is. Some students confuse species that I think look absolutely nothing alike. No one will ever be able to say they have compiled a list of wild edibles and all their look-alikes because so much of the definition relies on opinion and experience. **No one should ever, ever ingest any part of any wild plant unless they are certain that they know for themselves what they are eating.** Online searches and books are not enough. Come to a class by me, find a class near you, or find a local expert.

Q: I have tasted a plant that you list in this book, and I disagree with the flavor you have listed. For example, I tasted X berry that you said was sweet, and it was tart. I tasted X green that you said was mild, and it was bitter! Why?

A: Peak flavor exists only for a short time. If you harvest a berry even hours before it is fully ripe, it will be tart or bitter instead of sweet. All plants can be bitter if exposed to drought, or if picked after the flower stalk appears, because this changes the plant. Most plants taste best when tender. For greens, this means early. For berries, this mean when soft. For roots, it means at peak storage instead of when the plant is using the energy stored in the root or tuber for growth. You may have to return to a wild plant several times before you find it at peak harvest time.

ABOUT THE AUTHOR

Caleb Warnock is the popular author of *Forgotten Skills of Self-Sufficiency*, *The Art of Baking with Natural Yeast*, *Backyard Winter Gardening*, *More Forgotten Skills of Self-Sufficiency*, *Trouble's on the Menu*, and the Backyard Renaissance Collection. He is the owner of SeedRenaissance.com and blogs at CalebWarnock.blogspot.com, where you will find a link to join his email list to learn more about forgotten skills. He resides in Provo, Utah.

ALSO BY CALEB WARNOCK:

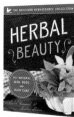

FAMILIUS

ABOUT FAMILIUS

Welcome to Familius! We publish beautiful books that help families live our 9 Habits of Happy Family Life:

1 Love Together
2 Play Together
3 Learn Together
4 Work Together
5 Talk Together
6 Heal Together
7 Read Together
8 Eat Together
9 Laugh Together

Learn more about us at our website:

www.familius.com

JOIN OUR FAMILY

There are lots of ways to connect with us!

Subscribe to our newsletters at www.familius.com to receive uplifting daily inspiration, essays from our Pater Familius, a free ebook every month, and the first word on special discounts and Familius news.

GET BULK DISCOUNTS

If you feel a few friends and family might benefit from what you've read, let us know and we'll be happy to provide you with quantity discounts. Simply email us at orders@familius.com.

CONNECT

Facebook: www.facebook.com/paterfamilius

Twitter: @familiustalk, @paterfamilius1

Pinterest: www.pinterest.com/familius

Instagram: @familiustalk

> **The most important work you ever do will be within the walls of your own home.**

PHOTO CREDITS

- *Acer glabrum.* All: Walter Siegmund.
- *Aegilops cylindrica.* Top & Side 1: Matt Lavin. Side 2 & 3: Stefan.lefnaer.
- *Agastache urticifolia.* Top: By Katja Schulz. Side 1: Jane Shelby Richardson. Side 2: Drew Avery.
- *Allium bispectrum.* Top and Side 2: Andrey Zharkikh.
- *Allium brevistyium.* Side 1: Sherel Goodric.
- *Allium macropetalum.* Top: Andrey Zharkikh.
- *Allium textile.* All: Matt Lavin
- *Amaranthus blitoides.* Top: Stefan.lefnaer. Side 1: Krzysztof Ziarnek Kenraiz. Side 1 & 2: SB Johnny.
- *Amaranthus blitum.* All: Stefan.lefnaer.
- *Amaranthus palmeri.* Side 1: Pompilid.
- *Amelanchier pumila.* Top: Salicyna. Side 1 & 2: Krzysztof Ziarnek Kenraiz.
- *Amelanchier utahensis.* All: Stan Shebs.
- *Anthriscus caucalis.* Top: Curtis Clark. Side 1: Olivier Pichard. Side 2: TeunSpaans.
- *Aquilegia formosa.* Side 1: Walter Siegmund. Side 2: Christophermluna.
- *Artemisia frigida.* All: Franz Xaver.
- *Asclepias cordifolia.* Top: peganum. Side 1: First Light.
- *Asclepias erosa.* All: Stan Shebs.
- *Asclepias involucrata.* Side 1: Western New Mexico University Department of Natural Sciences and the Dale A. Zimmerman Herbarium.
- *Asclepias verticillate.* Top: Joshua Mayer. Side 1: George F Mayfield. Side 2 & 3: Fritz Flohr Reynolds.
- *Asclepias viridiflora.* Top, Side 1 & Side 2: Matt Lavin. Side 3: Fritz Flohr Reynolds.
- *Balsamorhiza hookeri.* Sides 1, 2 & 3: Walter Siegmund.
- *Barbarea orthoceras.* Top, Side 1 & Side 2: Walter Siegmund.
- *Barbarea verna.* Top, Sides 2–4: H Brisse.
- *Bromus breviaristatus.* Side 1: Howard F. Schwartz.
- *Bromus carinatus.* All: Matt Lavin.
- *Bromus diandrus.* Top & Side 2: Harry Rose. Side 1: Andrey Zharkikh.
- *Bromus japonicus.* All: Matt Lavin.
- *Bromus marginatus.* Top: Howard F. Schwartz.
- *Bromus secalinus.* Side 1: Kurt Stüber.
- *Bromus tectorum.* Side 1, Side 3 & Side 4: Stefan.lefnaer. Side 2: Petr Filippov.
- *Calandrina ciliate.* Top: Joe Decruyenaere. Side 1: Franco Folini. Side 3: Kurt Stueber.
- *Calochortus ambiguous.* All: Bill Bouton.
- *Calochortus apiculatus.* Top & Side 1: Bill Bouton.
- *Calochortus aureus.* All: JerryFriedman.
- *Calochortus bruneaunis.* Top & Side 2: Matt Lavin.
- *Calochortus elegans.* Top: Tom Hilton. Side 1: Bill Bouton. Side 2: Walter Siegmund.
- *Calochortus eurycarpus.* Top: Noah Elhardt. Side 1: Miguel Vieira.
- *Calochortus flexuosus.* All: Stan Shebs.
- *Calochortus invenustus.* All: Joe Decruyenaere.
- *Calochortus kennedyi.* Top: Jim Staley. Side 1: Bill Bouton.
- *Calochortus leichtlinii.* Side 1: Bill Bouton. Side 2 & 4: Jane Shelby Richardson. Side 3: Dawn Endico.
- *Calochortus panamintensis.* Top: Justin Ennis.
- *Calochortus striatus.* All: Stan Shebs.
- *Camelina microcarpa.* All: By Matt Lavin.
- *Camelina sativa.* Top: Fornax.
- *Cardamine oligosperma.* All: Walter Siegmund.
- *Castilleja applegatei Fernald.* Sides 1–4: Stan Shebs.
- *Castilleja aquariensis.* Top: Elizabeth Neese.
- *Castilleja sessiliflora.* Top, Side 2 & Side 3: Matt Lavin. Side 1: photogramma1.
- *Celtis laevigata Full Page: Gaberlunzi (Richard Murphy).*
- *Celtis reticulata.* Top, Side 2, Side 3 & Side 4: Stan Shebs.
- *Cenchrus longispinus.* Top: Bubba73.

- *Chenopodium berlandieri.* Top: Bernell MacDonald. Sides: Matt Lavin.
- *Chenopodium murale.* Top & Side 2: Forest & Kim Starr. Side 1: Stefan.lefnaer.
- *Chrysothamnus viscidiflorus.* All: Stan Shebs.
- *Cirsium ochrocentrum.* Top: Jane Shelby Richardson.
- *Crataegus chrysocarpa.* Top & Side 1: Matt Lavin. Side 2: Michael Wolf.
- *Crataegus succulenta.* Top: Lokal_Profil.
- *Crepis acuminate.* Top & Sides 1–4: Matt Lavin.
- *Crepis intermedia.* All: Stan Shebs.
- *Crepis modocensis.* All: Walter Siegmund.
- *Crepis occidentalis.* Top and Side 2: Andrey Zharkikh. Side 1: Jason Hollinger.
- *Crepis runcinate.* Top, Side 1 & Side 3: Andrey Zharkikh.
- *Cucurbita foetidissima.* Top & Side 1: Curtis Clark.
- *Cymopterus purpurascens.* All: Curtis Clark.
- *Cymopterus purpureus.* All: Andrey Zharkikh.
- *Cyperus erythrorhizos.* Top, Side 1 & Side 3: Andrey Zharkikh. Side 4: Fredlyfish4.
- *Cyperus fendlerianus.* All: Western New Mexico University Department of Natural Sciences and the Dale A. Zimmerman Herbarium.
- *Cyperus odoratus.* Sides: Franz Xaver.
- *Cyperus schweinitzii.* All: Vanderhorst, James P; Cooper, Stephen V; Heidel, Bonnie L; United States. Bureau of Land Management; Montana Natural Heritage Program
- *Descurainia obtusa.* All: Western New Mexico University Department of Natural Sciences and the Dale A. Zimmerman Herbarium.
- *Descurainia pinnata.* Top: Curtis Clark.
- *Descurainia Sophia.* Top & Side 1–2 : By Fornax. Side 3: Sanja565658.
- *Equisetum laevigatum.* Top: Matt Lavin. Side 1: Andrey Zharkikh.
- *Equisetum scirpoides.* Top & Side 2: Meneerke bloem. Side 1: H. Zell.
- *Equisetum variegatum.* Top: Jnn.
- *Eriogonum alatum.* Top & Sides 1–2: Andrey Zharkikh. Side 3: Tyler Bourret.
- *Eriogonum baileyi.* Sides: Matt Lavin.
- *Eriogonum cernuum.* Top & Sides 1–2: Matt Lavin. Sides 3–5: Andrey Zharkikh.
- *Eriogonum corymbosum.* Sides 2–3: Dean Wm. Taylor.
- *Eriogonum davidsonii.* Top: Joe Decruyenaere.
- *Eriogonum fasciculatum.* Sides 2–5: Stan Shebs.
- *Eriogonum flavum.* Top & Sides 1–3: Matt Lavin. Side 5: Katja Schulz.
- *Eriogonum hookeri.* All: Krzysztof Ziarnek Kenraiz.
- *Eriogonum inflatum.* All: Stan Shebs.
- *Eriogonum longifolium.* Side 1: Trilobitealive. Side 2: Steve Shirah.
- *Eriogomum microthecum.* All: Stan Shebs.
- *Eriogonum nudum.* Top & Side 2: John Rusk. Side 1 & 3: Jane Shelby Richardson.
- *Eriogonum plumatella.* All: Jules Jardinier.
- *Eriogonum pusillum.* Side 1: Arizona State University Herbarium.
- *Eriogonum racemosum.* All: Andrey Zharkikh.
- *Eriogonum rotundifolium.* Top and Side 1: Patrick Alexander.
- *Eriogonum umbellatum.* Top: Stan Shebs. Sides 1–4: Walter Siegmund.
- *Gaillardia pinnatifida.* Top & Sides 1–3: Andrey Zharkikh. Sides 4–5: Nadiatalent.
- *Gaultheria hispidula.* Top: Jomegat. Sides: Colocho.
- *Geranium bicknellii.* Side 1: Superior National Forest.
- *Geranium caespitosum.* Top: U.S. Forest Service, Southwestern Region, Kaibab National Forest. Side 1: Hectonichus. Side 2: Antony Jauregui.
- *Geranium richardsonii.* Side 1: Stan Shebs. Side 2: JohnIngraham.

- *Hedysarum alpinum*. Top: Daniel Case.
- *Hedysarum boreale*. Top: Matt Lavin. Side 1, Side 3, Side 4: Andrey Zharkikh.
- *Helianthus annuus*. Side 1: Michael J. Plagens. Side 2: Ekabhishek. Side 3: 3268zauber.
- *Helianthus anomalus*. All: Max Licher.
- *Helianthus ciliaris*. All: Western New Mexico University Department of Natural Sciences and the Dale A. Zimmerman Herbarium.
- *Helianthus niveus*. Side 1: Frankie Coburn.
- *Helianthus pauciflorus*. Sides 1–3: Matt Lavin.
- *Heracleum spondylium montanum*. All: Benjamin Zwittnig.
- *Iliamna rivularis*. Sides 2–3: Dave Powell.
- *Juglans major*. Top & Sides 2–3: Whitney Cranshaw.
- *Juglans microcarpa*. Top: Alexander Savin. Sides: Jerry Friedman.
- *Kochia scoparia*. Top: Matt Lavin. Side: Stefan.lefnaer.
- *Lomatium ambiguum*. All: Matt Lavin.
- *Lomatium canbyi*. All: Walter Siegmund.
- *Lomatium cous*. All: Matt Lavin.
- *Lomatium dissectum*. Sides 2–3: Walter Siegmund
- *Lomatium foeniculaceum*. Top & Side 1: Matt Lavin. Sides 2–4: Andrey Zharkikh.
- *Lomatium gormanii*. Top: Gustav Svensson (http://averater.se).
- *Lomatium grayi*. All: Walter Siegmund.
- *Lomatium macrocarpum*. All: Walter Siegmund.
- *Lomatium nudicaule*. All: Walter Siegmund.
- *Lomatium triternatum*. All: Walter Siegmund.
- *Lonicera involucrata*. Side 1: Jerry Friedman. Sides 2–3: Walter Siegmund.
- *Lonicera utahensis*. Top & Side 2: Walter Siegmund. Side 1: Robert Flogaus-Faust.
- *Mahonia fremontii*. All: Stan Shebs.
- *Malus coronaria*. Sides: Rob Duval.
- *Medicago polymorpha*. Top: Christian Hummert. Sides 1, 2 & 4: Forest & Kim Starr.
- *Melilotus indicus*. All: Forest & Kim Starr.
- *Nuphar polysepala*. Top: Marshal Hedin. Sides 1 & 3: John Rusk.
- *Panicum capillare*. Top: Harry Rose. Sides 1–3: Matt Lavin.
- *Panicum dichotomiflorum*. Top: Andrey Zharkikh. Side 1: F. D. Richards.
- *Panicum miliaceum*. Top: Isidre blanc. Side 1: Dalgial. Side 2: Stefan.lefnaer.
- *Pediomelum esculentum*. Matt Lavin.
- *Perideridia gairdneri*. Side 1: Matt Lavin.
- *Perideridia parishii*. All: Jane Shelby Richardson.
- *Phlox austromontana*. Top & Sides 1–2: Andrey Zharkikh.
- *Phlox diffusa*. Side 1: Jane Shelby Richardson. Sides 2–4: Walter Siegmund.
- *Phlox hoodia*. Top: Walter Siegmund. Sides: Matt Lavin.
- *Phlox longifolia*. Top & Sides 1–2: Matt Lavin.
- *Phlox multiflora*. Top: Malcolm Manners.
- *Phlox stansburyi*. All: Stan Shebs.
- *Physalis crassifolia*. Sides: Stan Shebs.
- *Physalis hederifolia*. All: Stan Shebs.
- *Physalis heterophylla*. Top & Side 2: Matthieu Godbout.
- *Physalis longifolia*. Top: Bruce Ackley. Side: Fritz Flohr Reynolds.
- *Physalis virginiana*. Top: Dave Powell.
- *Pinus lambertiana*. Side 1: Mitch Barrie.
- *Pinus monticola*. Side: Jane Shelby Richardson.
- *Polygonum arenastrum*. Top: Christian Fischer. Side 2: Harry Rose.
- *Polygonum douglasii*. Top & Side 2: Matt Lavin. Side 1: Andrey Zharkikh.
- *Polygonum persicaria*. Top: Penarc. Side 2: Bogdan Giuşcă.
- *Prunus andersonii*. Top & Sides 5–6: Matt Lavin. Sides 1–2: Jane Shelby Richardson. Side 3: David~O. Side 4: Nadiatalent.
- *Prunus angustifolia*. Top & Side 1: Aberham Nuñez. Sides 2–3: Homer Edward Price.
- *Prunus emarginata*. Sides 1–2 & 4–5: Walter Siegmund. Side 3: Stan Shebs.
- *Prunus fasciculata*. All: Stan Shebs.
- *Prunus mahaleb*. Sides 1–2: Stefan.lefnaer. Side 3: Jean Tosti. Side 4: Athenchen. Side 5: Kurt Stüber.
- *Prunus pensylvanica*. Sides 1 & 4: Halava.
- *Prunus persica*. Top: Fastily. Side 1: Fir0002.
- *Prunus pumila*. Top: Rob Routledge. Sides 2–4: Superior National Forest.
- *Prunus rivularis*. Sides 1–2: Amirza360. Side 3: Homer Edward Price.
- *Quercus gambelii*. Side 1: Cory Maylett. Sides 2–3: Stan Shebs.
- *Rhus trilobata*. Side 3: Stan Shebs.
- *Ribes cereum*. Top & Sides 3–5: Stan Shebs. Sides 1–2: Walter Siegmund.
- *Ribes inerme*. Top: Dave Powell.
- *Ribes lacustre*. All: Walter Siegmund.
- *Ribes laxiflorum*. Top: Christian Hummert.
- *Ribes leptanthum*. Top: Christian Hummert. Sides 1–2: Jerry Friedman.
- *Ribes montigenum*. Top and Side 1: Stan Shebs.
- *Ribes velutinum*. All: Stan Shebs.
- *Ribes viscosissimum*. All: Walter Siegmund.
- *Ribes wolfii*. All: Krzysztof Golik.
- *Rosa × harisonii*. Top: A. Barra. Side 1: Kevmin. Side 3: Helena Borg.
- *Rosa nutkana*. Side 1: brewbooks. Side 2: Walter Siegmund. Side 3: Jerzy Opioła.
- *Rosa woodsia*. Side 3: Acroterion.
- *Rubus deliciosus*. Side 2: Ulf Eliasson.
- *Rubus laciniatus*. Top & Side 4: Severus. Sides 1–2: Michael Wolf. Side 3: Kurt Stüber.
- *Rubus leucodermis*. Top & Sides 1–2: Stan Shebs.
- *Rubus neomexicanus*. All: Western New Mexico University Department of Natural Sciences and the Dale A. Zimmerman Herbarium.
- *Rubus nivalis*. Top: Walter Siegmund.
- *Rubus pedatus*. Top & Side 1: Alpsdake. Side 2: Franz Xaver. Side 3: Walter Siegmund.
- *Rubus pubescens*. Top: Notjake13. Side 1–2: Superior National Forest.
- *Rumex occidentalis*. Top: Walter Siegmund.
- *Sagittaria cuneate*. Top: Andrey Zharkikh. Side 1: Yu Ito. Side 3: Julia Adamson.
- *Sambucus racemosa variety melanocarpa*. Top: B.gliwa. Side: Opioła Jerzy.
- *Sarcocornia utahensis*. Top: Robert Sivinski.
- *Shepherdia canadensis*. Side 1–3: Walter Siegmund. Side 4: Robert Flogaus-Faust.
- *Sisymbrium irio*. Top: ZooFari. Side 3: Krzysztof Ziarnek Kenraiz.
- *Sporobolus flexuosus*. All: Andrey Zharkikh.
- *Streptopus amplexifolius*. Top & Sides 1–2: Walter Siegmund. Side 3: Roger Culos.
- *Streptopus streptopoides*. Top: Σ64 (Shigeru Rokujuu).
- *Symphoricarpos occidentalis*. All: Andrey Zharkikh.
- *Trifolium cyathiferum*. Top: Mary Winter.
- *Trifolium wormskioldii*. Top: Eric in SF.
- *Typha glauca*. Side 1: Wisconsin State Herbarium, UW-Madison, photo by Robert W. Freckmann.
- *Vaccinium cespitosum*. Top: Dave Powell. Side 1: Jane Shelby Richardson. Side 2–5: Superior National Forest.
- *Vaccinium geminiflorum*. Top: Rutgers University.
- *Vaccinium membranaceum*. Top: Christine Majul. Sides 1–3: Katja Schulz. Side 4: Jason Hollinger.
- *Vaccinium scoparium*. Sides: Walter Siegmund.
- *Veronica biloba*. All: Matt Lavin.
- *Viola adunca*. All: Walter Siegmund.
- *Vitis arizonica*. All: Stan Shebs.
- *Vitis labrusca*. Top: Sten Porse.
- *Vitis monticola*. Top: Texas Native Plants Database.
- *Ziziphus obtusifolia*. All: Stan Shebs.